Highland]

Also available from Mercat Press:
Life in the Highlands and Islands, combining Colin MacDonald's
Echoes of the Glen (1936) and *Highland Journey* (1943)

The croft house on the Heights of Inchvannie
(Fiona J Newton)

Highland Life & Lore

COLIN MACDONALD

Part One
CROFT AND CEILIDH

Part Two
HIGHLAND MEMORIES

MERCAT PRESS
EDINBURGH

Croft and Ceilidh first published 1947
Highland Memories first published 1949
This edition published 1997 by Mercat Press
James Thin, 53 South Bridge, Edinburgh EH1 1YS

ISBN 1873644 728

Printed and bound in Finland by WSOY

PREFACE

The year after the demise of Aberdeen University Press in 1992 Mercat Press reprinted the first two of my father's books, *Echoes of the Glen* and *Highland Journey*, under the title *Life in the Highlands and Islands of Scotland*. Now Mercat Press, to my great pleasure, has decided to reprint the second two books written by my father, *Croft and Ceilidh* and *Highland Memories*, under the title *Highland Life & Lore*.

Because the Introduction to the previous volume describes much of the MacDonald family's long association with 'The Heights' it has been decided to print it again in this publication.

A pen and ink sketch of the croft house drawn by my daughter, Fiona, is reproduced as the frontispiece to the book. It shows the original south-facing house built between 1894-96 with the 1979-80 extension on the left (west) side. When it was first built there was no porch and the upper rooms were lit by skylights. As money became available a porch and dormer windows were added in the early 1900s. After my father retired in the mid 1940s large windows were installed in the downstairs rooms.

It may be of interest to readers to learn that in the middle of the last century a typical croft house was single-storey and thatched, often with byre and barn attached. Following the Crofters' Act of 1886 which granted fair rents, security of tenure and compensation for permanent improvements (buildings, fences, drains etc) to crofters it was considered worthwhile for better houses to be built. Consequently between the passing of the Act and the turn of the century a great many houses with upstairs rooms were built throughout the Highlands. Many of these houses are, like my own, still lived in today though few of the original crofters still inhabit them.

Margaret MacDonald Newton
Heights of Inchvannie
Strathpeffer, Ross

INTRODUCTION

The suggestion that the books written by my father between 1936 and 1949 should be reprinted brought great pleasure to my only surviving brother Bill, William MacDonald of Dornoch, and to me. I am delighted to have been asked to write an introduction to this re-issue of the first pair of his four books.

So here I am, sitting and writing by the fire in the house built by my grandfather nearly a hundred years ago, on the croft on the Cromartie estates where our ancestors have been tenants since the eighteenth century, and possibly for longer. The house is on the high south-facing slope, the Heights, between Dingwall and Strathpeffer. It commands a spectacular view. To the south lies the valley of the Peffrey river backed by the long range of Knock Farrel, the Cat's Back and Cnoc n'Eglais, with glimpses of the Monadhliath mountains and the Grampians beyond. East lies Dingwall with the Black Isle behind it. Westward is sheer beauty: Castle Leod nestling in trees, where the present Earl of Cromartie still lives, the charming Victorian spa village of Strathpeffer, and the peaks of the western hills.

My brothers and I had always admired father's books with their fund of information, humour and tales of the past, so many of which we had heard told and retold in our childhood. We knew, however, that there was more to his writing than mere entertainment. As the *Inverness Courier* put it in 1943 after publication of *Highland Journey*:

> When Colin MacDonald published his first book *Echoes of the Glen* we considered it to be such an important contribution to the story of social life in the Highlands with its vivid and faithful portrayal of the characteristics and daily living of the Highland people that, in a leading article on Highland matters, we recommended everybody interested in Highland problems to read it and take it to heart. The same may be said of *Highland Journey*, for nobody who wants to understand the Highlands and the Highland people can afford to neglect it.

Offspring of generations of Ross-shire crofters, Colin MacDonald left school at a little over thirteen, and worked his father's croft until at the age of twenty-six he matriculated at Marischal College, Aberdeen. He was then on the staff of the Aberdeen and North of Scotland College of Agriculture: he worked for the Board, later the Department, of Agriculture for Scotland and finally became Gaelic-speaking member of the Scottish Land Court. He was a man large in stature and mind, generous by nature and with a delightful sense of fun. His upbringing and the many jobs he had undertaken as a boy and young man—herd boy, shepherd, drainer, fencer, roadmaker, lumberman and many more besides—had made him a very practical and down-to-earth man, but deep in his soul there was something of the poet. He savoured words and was deeply moved by the beauties and miracles of nature. He had perhaps a slight eccentricity in the matter of dress because, except at funerals, weddings and such serious occasions, he invariably wore a plus-four suit, usually of a crotal colour beloved of the Hebrides and tailored by the Fifty Shilling Tailors of happy memory. The plus-fours were worn at Head Office in Edinburgh as well as on his many field trips to the Highlands and Islands. Accompanying this somewhat conspicuous outfit were stout hand-made shoes with welt and soles which projected like a gutter round the uppers. A 'fore-and-aft bonnet' of the same tweed as his suit completed the outfit. In the days of tram-cars he had a method of crossing roads—even Princes Street in Edinburgh—which brought heart flutters to relatives, and to drivers, but nevertheless worked for him. Glancing briefly to ensure that no vehicle was within striking distance he would set out with long deliberate strides and cross unflinchingly to the other side, confident in his assumption that any on-coming traffic would slow down for him.

In 1913 his eldest sister, a schoolteacher, brought to the croft for the summer holidays a friend who taught in the same school. She was Margaret Stewart Young from Crieff in Perthshire. The following year she and my father were married and spent over six years in Thurso, where my two elder brothers, Colin and Bill, and

I (christened Margaret but known as Paddy) were born. It was after my father's transfer to the Head Office of the Board of Agriculture for Scotland in Edinburgh that my youngest brother was born. At that time my father was trying to wean an alcoholic friend from his weakness and by way of encouragement he said that if his friend would keep sober the expected baby, if a boy, would be called after him. The bribe must have worked because this squirming new life was given the names Lewis Gordon Grant MacDonald—but at home he was always Sandy.

My mother was gentle and self-effacing, very supportive and with great inner reserves of strength. My father was the first to admit that it was her influence and encouragement that allowed him to develop in the way he did. He was a wonderful story-teller and could hold an audience enthralled. To his credit he could take a story against himself with the greatest good humour. Colin MacDonald was a tolerant man but pomposity, hypocrisy and 'man's inhumanity to man' could rouse his impatience or rare anger. Education in its widest sense ranked high with him and he and my mother made considerable sacrifices—for in those days there were no university grants—to fit the four of us for careers in medicine, dentistry and veterinary sciences. But it was the informal education which remains in my memory. Long weekend walks over Edinburgh's Braid Hills, and the Blackfords and the Pentlands, where birds, flowers, trees and animals were studied and such things as the rules of golf, the rotation of crops and the chances of fishing and the like were touched on. There was that Sunday when he and I, in the interest of an article he was writing, walked miles round central Edinburgh, both old and new towns, to discover which streets were paved with Caithness flagstones. Research for another article involved a hunt through the telephone directory for surnames which were also the names of colours. A fascinating tapestry emerged of Greens, Blacks, Silvers and Scarlets, Whites, Golds, Browns, Blues and Pinks. Museums were visited and my mother was encouraged to take us at half-terms to the Border Abbeys, or to Stirling Castle and Cambuskenneth Abbey.

My father's thirst for knowledge was insatiable and the house was full of books of all kinds—dictionaries, quotation books, atlases, bird books, wild flower books, collections of poetry, history, mythology; the works of Burns, Scott, Dickens, Shakespeare and John Buchan and—my father's inseparable companion—*Para Handy* by Neil Munro. I well remember the excitement when we took delivery of the new 1929 edition of the *Encyclopaedia Britannica*, all 24 volumes of it, in its exceedingly shiny, 'mahogany' bookcase. This was something he could ill afford but which he longed to acquire. There were few days when he did not look up something in one or other of its volumes. I still have this set of books, battered, dog-eared and patched: much loved and still in frequent use.

Life in Edinburgh in no way lessened my father's love of, or interest in, the family croft on the Heights of Inchvannie. He continued as tenant and arranged with neighbouring crofters to have the use of the seventeen acres of land. The house was lent rent-free to anyone in need of a temporary home on condition that they kept it wind and weather-tight and that they moved out for the six weeks of our school summer holidays. He wanted to ensure that we were familiar with country as well as town ways. To my brothers and to me the Heights has always been a very special place. When school closed for the summer holidays, uniforms were tossed aside; large trunks were filled with blankets, sheets, pots and pans; a compartment was reserved on the morning train from Waverley station and into this, northward bound, piled two adults, four children and 'Sporran' the family Cairn terrier. Excitement rose as familiar landmarks brought us nearer and nearer to Achterneed station. There a neighbour, Jock, would meet us with horse and cart to take the luggage up the hill, but not for us youngsters the sedate pace of such transport. After a day of sitting in the train the steep open road called and we scampered this way and that, renewing acquaintance with familiar places and covering two or three times the distance plodded by the shaggy-footed shire horse. As the boys grew older they cycled north, taking with them a small tent and camping a night *en route*. These holidays were spent in primitive but blissful conditions and, barefoot, we roamed the hills, helped with hay-making and learned how to hoe turnips and to make ourselves useful at harvest time. From quite an early age an annual pilgrimage to the summit of The Ben was one of the highlights of the holiday. (Ben Wyvis is always The Ben to those in its shadow. It is over 3,400 feet high.) We chose a good day—there seemed to be so much sunshine in the 1920s and 1930s—each took a knapsack with food, drink and reference books and possibly a fishing rod. We would set out about 9 a.m. and return about 6 p.m., weary but happy, rejoicing in the weather, the wonderful views and the many interesting things we had seen. Sometimes we were rewarded by a sprig of white heather, more rarely white bell-heather. On one particularly hot day about half way up the Ben my father, clad in ancient plus-fours, produced a pair of tiny folding scissors and begged a family friend who was with us to hack off the lower parts of the plus-fours to produce instant shorts. Thus attired and with a knotted handkerchief to cover his bald head he was able to enjoy the expedition to the full.

We got to know our crofting neighbours and great characters many of them were. Two of my favourites were Mairi à claidheamh (Mary of the Sword) and Dannie Phadraic: both were MacDonalds but unrelated to each other or to our family. Mairi was a tiny bent person, in her eighties when I was a girl, with bright eyes, no teeth and plentiful conversation. She took snuff and Sandy and I used to love asking what her favourite brand was, in order to hear her invariable reply: 'Ach, *m'eudail* [my darling] the black snuff with the white dottacks.' Once every week she would cover her long dark skirts with a large snow-white starched apron and walk the two miles to Strathpeffer for bread and other 'messages' and trudge back up the long steep road weighed down by her purchases. She showed us the kist in which she kept her 'Claes against the daith'— the garments in which she was to be buried. She never referred to toes, they were 'the fingers on my feet'. Dannie was a stone mason, and a wit. He was a great gardener and no lady (including myself at the age of 8 or 9) ever left his house without a 'bookay' of flowers:

roses, maidenhair fern, and other blooms. One of his many sayings was 'Never turn your back on a lady or a ladder'. Dannie was looked after by his sister Mary, a gentle creature, one of the most beautiful women I have known.

Bob Aird, tall, lean and eagle-eyed, and his diminutive wife Mary (a cousin of my father) were great friends of ours. It was on their croft that we learned to turn our hands to any task, and to feel at ease among the cattle and with the huge shire horse. Many were the feasts of home-made scones and pancakes with raspberry jam, washed down by scalding tea from a milk-pitcher, after helping at hay-making or harvest. My poor mother! During the holidays she had to feed a hungrier than ever brood with the inconvenience of an old black range and a few iron pots. Never a word of complaint did we hear from her. The boys kept the family pot boiling by snaring or shooting rabbits, with which the countryside was grossly over-populated. Sandy and I collected the milk daily from the only farm on the Heights.

These Highland holidays were magical and must have had a profound influence on us because when war service was over and circumstances permitted, Colin became a general practitioner in Skye, Bill took over the dental practice in Dornoch and I joined the Strathpeffer medical practice. Sandy's heart was in the Highlands but he did not come home from the war—the Anzio beach-head claimed his young life.

When working days were over it was back to the croft for my mother and father. My mother viewed the move away from Edinburgh and a large circle of friends with some trepidation, but for my father's sake she went north. It was not long before the glorious views, the tranquil pace of life, the charm and fascination of the changing seasons cast their spell upon her. She became devoted to the place and the people. Alterations were made to the house to ensure comfort and convenience as they grew older. Electricity was installed, water from the well was pumped to the house, larger windows made and a bathroom and a new kitchen were fitted up. The old range disappeared from the living room to be replaced by a fine open fireplace with back-boiler. (Oh, the luxury of running water, and hot at that!)

There followed a period of great contentment filled with writing, gardening, walking and enjoying the endless streams of visitors who came from far and near. Neighbours always found an open door and a welcome. The floor of the living-room was deliberately covered with a washable rubberoid material, so that father's crofter friends would not be frightened off by fear of dirtying a fine carpet with their muddy boots.

Ill health, pain and several operations marred the last few years of Colin MacDonald's life, but his articles continued to appear in various national and local newspapers. The pleasure he took in family and friends was undiminished. In spite of the pain I think his verdict would have been 'It's been a grand life and never a dull moment.'

Now read on and, if you will, take pleasure in his writings.

Part One

CROFT AND CEILIDH

OR

CORRA-CHAGAILTE

CONTENTS

CHAPTER XV

CHAPTER XVI

CHAPTER XVII

CHAPTER XVIII

CHAPTER XIX

CHAPTER XX

CHAPTER XXI

CHAPTER XXII

Foreword

HERE I am again with more yarns of bygone days in the North! The remarkable success of the *Echoes* and the *Journey* (at the moment the demand for both is far greater than any hope of its early satisfaction) all but made me lose my head. I began to fancy myself as a " Writer " or a " Man of Letters "—though with a deep-down doubt that the little books didn't warrant so imposing a title for their author. But spurred by a species of vanity I determined to write a book more worthy of the fellow I was beginning to fancy myself to be. It must be an imaginative effort, built to a proper plan; it must have a dignified theme, characters of some social standing, dramatic treatment of incidents and human actions and reactions. So I sketched a skeleton story designed to provide full scope of the " well-known writer's " abilities.

In the leisure hours of nearly three years I laboriously wrote screeds and screeds in an effort to build round the skeleton a book which the professional critics might regard as real literature. It proved a heavy-handed task which gave no pleasure in the doing and brought but little satisfaction in the result.

Loth to accept my own unflattering judgment in the matter, I resorted to the ruse of trying it on the dog—to wit my wife; and her agonised reactions, despite some conjugal bias, drowned out the last smouldering ember of conceit.

" This formal plan of setting out to write a book doesn't seem to suit you," said she; " but why don't you just sit down and write some more of your recollections and experiences of real life and real people?—just ' tell ' one story, and then another and another as they come to your mind? and when you have enough you can arrange them in sequence suitable for a book?—and there you are! If they are something like the others you have written people will want to read them all right."

So, in the spare hours of the next six months I had much joy in writing out the yarns which appear in this book. Be they literature or not, they represent the only sort of stuff that I can write to my own satisfaction. At least they truly portray some of the ways and daily doings of those largely unlettered but highly-intelligent and independent-minded men and women who lived in the Highlands of Scotland towards the end of the nineteenth century; and I venture to hope that, in respect of such men and women my tales may to some extent answer the questions so poetically propounded in the *Scotsman* by my late Chief, Sir Patrick Laird :—

THE GREAT UNKNOWN

What great men do, and what the poets sing,
The thoughts of the philosophers, the tales
That story-tellers weave—all these are veils
And trappings to that shapeless, unseen thing,
The varied life of man the underling.
How fares he? Where succeeds he, or where fails?
What air of hope or discontent inhales
From those dull duties that the long day brings?
All but a fraction of this life of man
Goes untold to the grave. Year after year
Men, women, children for themselves alone
Fulfil, scarce memoried, their allotted span,
Leaving behind a word, a sigh or jeer—
While History proudly mounts her baseless throne.

Now a brief note explanatory of the Gaelic title of the book :—

It is a night in winter. Outside the moon is riding clear in a star-studded sky. Frost flowers are forming on the window-panes. But inside, all is cosy. Your day's darg is over. You relax luxuriously in your favourite chair. No lamp has been lit; you prefer the faint and flickering light that comes from the lowing fire into which you gaze reflectively. And as you continue to look into the fire you see in its glowing heart, in its leaping, fuffing flames, figures of fancy and delight. Softly the spirit of Peace comes to you. Your thoughts get purged of worry and fear and anger and envy and all those other wretched emotions that so poison human relationships. Finally a feeling of exaltation comes over you. You are under the magic influence of the emanations from the fire—or as we have it in the Gaelic, *you are under the spell of the corra-chagailte!*

C. M. D.

CHAPTER I

Who, What and Where are They?

BEFORE starting off with more yarns about croft and ceilidh it might not be out of place to say a few words about the country which—so to speak—is the home of my heroes : that is, about the Highlands of Scotland. Readers who are familiar with the Highlands may skip this chapter, but some idea of the nature of the country and of the people may help others to a better understanding.

Well, for official purposes the Highlands are regarded as that part of Scotland which comprises the seven counties of Argyll, Inverness, Ross, Sutherland, Caithness, Orkney and Shetland. By the way, Shetland is now officially " Zetland," but as nobody thinks or speaks of it that way I shall continue to refer to it as Shetland.

Perthshire, which to a considerable extent is still a Gaelic-speaking county may—or may not !—resent its exclusion; and Caithness, Orkney and Shetland which, topographically and racially, are not Highland may—or may not !—feel complimented on their inclusion in the official Highlands. But anyway, there we are with our " Seven Highland Counties."

It was the Crofters' Act of 1886 that brought all these counties into political unity, for, while in many respects they differed greatly from each other they were alike in that each contained a large number of the small type of agricultural holdings known as crofts. These crofts, in the days before Prince Charlie tried and failed to capture the British crown, were occupied by the Clansmen of the

13

respective Chiefs. The rents were mainly paid in kind, in the form of military service, when the Chief was at variance with his neighbour or wanted to be in the good graces of his Sovereign who might be requiring a regiment of Highlanders to deal with *his* enemies. The unsuccessful rebellion changed all that, and a system of cash rents was substituted. The friendship which, under the old Order had characterised the relationship between Chief and Clansmen soon deteriorated under the new regime of Landlord and Tenant and—but I am not to scratch open old sores that are best forgotten—by early in the 19th century was so dead that bitter opposition had taken its place.

Organised political pressure by the crofters ultimately led to the appointment of a Royal Commission to enquire into their grievances; and that in turn led to the passing— 1886— of the Crofters' Act—which for the first time conferred on crofters the much-prized protection of the Law.

From then on, their rents were fixed by a judicial tribunal—The Crofters' Commission. If a man wanted to give up the croft he could do so by giving the landlord a year's notice, and on quitting he was entitled to receive from his landlord as compensation for permanent improvements effected by himself or his predecessors in the same family, such sum as the judicial tribunal reckoned their value to be to an incoming tenant.

On the other hand, if a man does not wish to leave his croft practically no power on earth can put him out so long as he pays his rent and behaves like any decent citizen. This is a very remarkable form of tenure which enables generation after generation of the same family to continue in the holding till the end of time if they so desire. The Crofters' Act applied only to holdings not exceeding £30 rental and in the Seven Crofting Counties, but the Small Landholders' Act of 1911 extended similar rights to practically all holdings not exceeding £50 anywhere in Scotland. And now the old term " croft " is largely submerged in, or synonymous with, the more comprehensive title of

" Small Holder "—and the Scottish Land Court is the tribunal instead of the old Crofters' Commission.

Although, as has been explained, there are now crofts or small holdings in every county in Scotland, the crofts with which I am here concerned are those situated in the Highlands : the real original crofterdom. Of the 19 million acres of land surface in Scotland, the Seven Highland Counties account for no less than 9 million acres, or nearly half of the whole. But that is not to say that nearly half of the agricultural wealth of Scotland is in the Highlands; far from that ! for, as the name implies, there is indeed in the Highlands a high proportion of " high " land. This will perhaps be best grasped from the fact that of the 9 million acres in the Highlands there are less than half a million acres of arable land. The remaining $8\frac{1}{2}$ million acres are mainly heather-clad moors and mountains, of which as much as ten acres may be insufficient to give sustenance to one sheep.

Nor must it be assumed that crofters occupy the whole of the Highlands. By far the best lands in these counties are taken up with large farms on which the standard of agriculture compares favourably with that of any area in Britain. Indeed, on the large farms in the Highlands are reared some of the best sheep and cattle in Britain, if not in the world. In certain parts of the Highlands too, potato growing and dairying of a high order are to be found.

With regard to the standard of agriculture on crofts it is too often forgotten that quite the general rule is that crofts occupy only the inferior land. Always the more fertile soil in the straths and glens is included in the big farms, while the crofts are pushed up on either side or to the top of the valley to the limit of cultivable soil. Given equally good land to work with, the standard of achievement by crofters will compare favourably with that of the best big farmers—as witness what took place in Caithness and Easter Ross. There, following on the 1914-18 war,

many of the large farms were broken up into small holdings. " Disaster " was the general prophecy at the time.
But within a few years of their establishment the small
holders—mainly drawn from the crofting population—were
beating the big farmers at their own game in the sale ring
and romping off with more than their share of cups and
medals at the agricultural shows.

Many people I have met seem to think that a croft is
something quite definite and that all crofts are alike; they
are sure that, agriculturally, it is something very insignifi-
cant on which the crofter and his family are ever on the
brink of starvation. I have met certain government officials,
too, of a more suspicious nature, who were anxious to know
just what the value of the croft's contribution is to the
livelihood of the family. Well, that is far too big a question to be gone into fully here, but here are few facts that
should give some idea of the depth and breadth and
intricacies of the subject.

1. The upper limit of a croft—or small holding if you
   prefer that name—is 50 acres and £50 rent; but so
   long as it does not exceed both limits it qualifies.
   For instance, I know a small holding of over 3000
   acres, but, as its rent is only £25 (i.e. does not exceed
   £50) it still ranks as a small holding. That is a hill-
   sheep small holding in Sutherlandshire with a rent of
   about 2d. per acre. Conversely, there are small holdings of 50 acres (but not exceeding) with rents well
   over £100—such small holdings, for instance, as you
   may find in a good dairying district.
2. There is practically no lower limit. One holding I
   can think of in Lewis consists of the site of house and
   byre and the right to graze a cow on a common hill
   pasture, and the rent is 10s.

In between these extremes there is a tremendous variety
of type and size of holding. There are the " full-time "
arable holdings of Caithness and Ross worked on much the
same lines as the large arable farm.

There are the arable-cum-grazing holdings typical of Sutherland, Ross and Skye. Here the inby or arable land is held in individual occupancy, and the relatively large area of hill grazing is held in common, sometimes with a common or " club " stock and in other cases with stocks individually owned; and in either case there is a properly elected committee of management to ensure equity and efficiency.

In Lewis and Shetland there are thousands of holdings of only three or four acres of arable land and a limited right of hill grazing. The rent may be anything from a few shillings to a very few pounds. Obviously in such cases much of the family subsistence must come from sources outwith the croft—as it usually does, from fishing, seafaring, tweed-making and the like. But in Lewis and Shetland and similar communities the emphasis on the croft as a home and a contributor to the family maintenance and well-being is very great. Then there are the small-holding specialists—the market gardener, the tomato grower, the poultry expert, and combinations of these—whose capital may run to many thousands of pounds and whose wage bill may exceed that of a large farmer; so that all over the income from a croft may range from £5 or less to £1000 and more.

These are but a few examples of the many types of holdings and holders that go to form the crofting communities of the Highlands.

And what do they amount to in numbers, these crofts and crofters? The war has put our available census figures rather out of date, but taking such figures as we have and adjusting them as well as I can guess to conform to the trends of the past fifteen years, here is what I make of it :—

County.			No. of Crofts.	Population on Crofts.
Argyll -	-	-	2,400	8,400
Inverness	-	-	6,800	25,500
Ross -	-	-	6,400	26,000
Sutherland -	-	-	2,250	7,900

Caithness	-	-	2,100	7,300
Orkney	-	-	2,650	10,600
Shetland	-	-	3,150	11,500
			25,750	97,200

So there you are : In the Highlands of Scotland not more than 100,000 of them altogether, in their less than 26,000 homes! Not much to make a song about! Yet during the course of the past century it is from these homes that are the very shrine and cradle of the ceilidh that unnumbered thousands of men and women went out to settle in the cities of Scotland and England; to the Prairies of Canada; to Australia, New Zealand and South Africa; to the United States of America—in short, to every utmost corner of the Empire and of the world—where they and their children and their children's children appear ever to have exercised an influence out of all proportion to their numbers.

I doubt if it is generally realised how much of the character of the people from the crofts is a direct outcome of that Charter of Liberty, the Crofters' Act. Indeed it is almost impossible to compute the effect on character of the solid security of tenure and continuing independence which that Act conferred on them, but it is certainly great, for, be the livelihood afforded by the croft meagre or ample, no shadow of " fear of the boss " ever crosses the crofter's mind. He has no boss and is free to plan his own life and way of living.

Further, he acquires skill and efficiency in a wide variety of crafts in having to do and make so many things for himself. From merest boyhood the son of the croft becomes familiar with all ordinary farming operations. He knows how to care for animals and handle horses, and in every department has prominently in mind the need for economy and thrift. By the time he succeeds his father—and often long before—he is well able to buy, to sell, to make his own decisions in regard to everything about the place. No wonder that the lads and lassies who went out into the world from the crofts were so often selected to fill positions of responsibility and trust! for they took with them those cardinal virtues of decency, honesty and a capacity for hard work which soon proved invaluable in the land of their adoption. They also, more than any other race, brought with them their language and their customs. Scarcely a sizable town in the Empire but has its Gaelic-speaking coterie—and a larger coterie of would-bes!

Caledonian Societies—mainly Celtic in origin—have spread like an infection all over the world. Perhaps at their annual Gatherings—those orgies of patriotism and sentiment—a stranger might be excused if he concluded they were somewhat prone to indulge in the soothing practice of scratching each others' backs and inclined to a blatant blowing of their own trumpets: as if, indeed, they considered themselves the salt of the earth. Well, I'm not saying but they *have* a fairly good conceit of themselves; and I'm not saying but they have a right to! But anyway, at the risk of being accused of having a tendency in that unseemly way myself, I do advance it as a self-evident proposition that to be reared on a croft is the luckiest start in life that a young man or woman could have; and we here in the Old Country are mighty lucky to have so many of them in exile who are bound to us by ties of patriotism and sentiment that are stronger than bands of steel.

CHAPTER II

I HAVE a suspicion that those of us who write about the old *ceilidh* nights in the north are prone to recall only the pleasanter aspects of them! Mostly, indeed, they were delightfully friendly gatherings where gossip and story and song and good-neighbourliness prevailed. But that is not to say that they were at all times free of uncharitable talk and criticism: indeed no! If someone was indiscreet enough to violate the local canons or conventions, that was sure to be a sappy item for the next *ceilidh*; and it was surprising the amount of pleasure we derived from animadverting on his or her peccadilloes! Naturally, of course, some were more given to such censorious talk than others. At the other extreme in our circle was Sandy. Sandy was our philosopher: a quiet kindly man, given more to deep thinking than loud talking: and scarcely ever would he say uncharitable things of others. Indeed when the talk went too much that way—as it sometimes did—Sandy, hitherto quiet, would make his gentle plea for tolerance—so nicely and so eloquently that he achieved his purpose without giving offence.

I remember one New Year's Night when the question of making good resolutions was under debate. In that discussion the case of Geordie Frocan had, of course, to be cited as an outstanding example of the futility of making good resolutions at all. Now, apart from his one failing, Geordie was a grand worker, a nice fellow and a good neighbour; but he was afflicted with a thirst which fairly frequently got the better of him. Indeed on this same New Year's Night it had proved so impelling that he was at the moment *hors de combat*—and would in all probability remain so for several days. But the point is, that when Geordie sobered up he would be full of remorse, and would sign the pledge and wear a blue ribbon in his buttonhole till the next time. That had happened so often that it had become one of our best jokes. On this night it was used with effect in the debate on good resolutions—until Sandy joined in in his gentle philosophic way. What he said was something to this effect, but ever so much more eloquent as spoken by him :

"Mind you!" began Sandy, "I am not sure that we are quite fair to Geordie. Geordie himself is in dead earnest every time he joins the Templars; and isn't it the sincerity of the intention that lies at the back of an action that is the great thing? Besides, the signing of the pledge does help to keep him sober for weeks on end; and doesn't it say a lot for his courage that, in spite of getting so badly knocked out by his adversary, times without number, he is always game to put on the gloves again for another round?

"And isn't courage," Sandy proceeded, warming up to his theme, "the finest thing a man can have? I am not thinking of a courage that is cheap and false. It is all very well for one who has never been cursed with a first-class thirst to condemn the Geordies of the world for insobriety; to chuck out their chests and brag how they can keep to the rails; and so they can, but it is easy for them : that is not evidence of courage but of good fortune. Are we sure that good resolutions are not good things even if we don't always manage to stick to them? But any way," Sandy concluded on a whimsical note, "all I am saying is that I hope I may be blessed with the courage that Geordie has—the courage to continue to make them."

Speaking of Geordie brings Maolan to mind. Maolan was one of our few chronics. He was a feuar in the village and didn't have a croft. He was the despair of our leading light in the Templars—who was himself a weakly wizened worm of a *creutair*, and thus at heavy disadvantage when arguing with Maolan on the evil of his ways—for, despite his dissipations, Maolan was as strong as a railway horse. He had two vulnerable spots though; one was a strong aversion to work and the other an inordinate concern for his own carcass. He used to read every advertisement for patent medicines that he could lay his hands on. In that way he had acquired an intimate knowledge of the many things that might be wrong with him. Between that, and his fear, and a lively imagination, he had some terribly anxious times. Every time he had a headache—and heaven knows he might easily have traced its cause!—he put it down to beginnings of brain fever; a pain in the stomach was certainly the start of the equivalent of our appendicitis (an apple-seed sprouting in his small gut); a sore throat meant nothing less than incipient cancer, and so on.

His wife was getting fed up with these frequent alarums—especially as, after the pain was gone, Maolan was quite ready for another spree. But one time yonder—it was at the Old New Year—he got the fright of his life. He had been on the spree, off and on, since New Year's Day. After going to bed this night he got awfully sick. The wife had to bring a basin, and Maolan, blind with sickness, had to pay the usual humiliating toll.

Suddenly the wife let out a shriek and began to wail "Ochanee! Ochanee! It has come to this at last!" says she, and her pointing to the basin.

Maolan half-opened his eyes to see what was the matter—and there, to his horror, in the basin was about half a gallon of his life-blood! His face went as white as chalk, and with a moan he lay back in his bed, certain that his last hour had come. The wife was twisting her apron and wailing her fear that indeed it must be so : but she had the presence of mind to shout to the boy Johnnie to run for the minister and the doctor.

Soon the minister arrived. Maolan was still breathing, but that was all. The minister made intercession as best he could for so depraved a soul, and Maolan nearly passed out. Just then the doctor was heard at the outer door, and the wife went to meet him and explain the nature of the case.

The medicine man rose nobly to the occasion. For a fortnight the wretched Maolan was made to suck ice and swallow the vilest concoction of " pheesick " in the druggist's shop. By this time he was reduced to such a state of physical weakness and abject terror that he was ready to believe and do anything. He even swallowed the doctor's tall tale about the extraordinary and dangerous type of hæmorrhage with which he was afflicted. It seemed that physical activity in the form of steady work was the only cure for it—steady work and, of course, nothing stronger to drink that water from the well. Even one glass of whisky would lay him dead on the spot!

Our old neighbour lived for years after that, a pattern of diligence and sobriety. No doubt his wife had a less worrying time with him, but I am bound to say he was less interesting to the rest of us than in his reprobate days.

It was some time after Maolan left this vale of tears that the story leaked out. It seems that, when he got sick that night, his wife had in the house the materials for making a *marag dhubh* (black-pudding), including a pitcher of sheep's blood. When Maolan called for the basin it came to her of a sudden that here was a chance of giving him a fright; so she poured a couple of pints of the blood into the basin, covered it over with a bit of muslin and rushed to the bedroom with it, chancing that her man would be too blind to notice; and it worked!

CHAPTER III

LIKE most rural communities we had our Wandering
Willies: odd types of humanity who for one reason or
another preferred life on the open road and in shady woods,
and a precarious larder, to the humdrum certainties that
were the result of an existence tethered to the conventions.

Some were definitely "m.d.," or would be so classified
by our present-day educational standards—not but what
some of the daftest of them sometimes said something that
made those of us who thought we were so much wiser
wonder if we were! Others, despite their rags and revel-
ries, bore some of the unmistakable hall-marks of education
and culture and "better days." One such was "The
Artist," who would stay for months in the smiddy woodie
painting local features—and also a self-portrait from his
reflection in a pool of the river—which he sold for a living.
The Artist never begged, and was not a man that the boys
could make fun of, or who readily made intimate friends.
One or two who were so favoured spoke of him as a man
of profound learning and philosophy; which, of course,
was sufficient foundation for the local conviction that he
had at one time been an Oxford Don.

Some of our wandering visitors did not stay at all—
except when overtaken by a cold winter's night. Then they
would look for supper and a doss in the straw in the barn.
More often than not they didn't wait for breakfast, but at
streak of day would be off on the tramp again.

There was the usual merry-making when my eldest sister got married. A few days in advance I went to Dingwall, with the horse and cart, to bring home various items that had been purchased in preparation for the feast. Amongst these was the whole carcass of a black-faced wether weighing 64 lb. It cost 4½d. per lb or 24s. for the lot. There was also a nine-gallon *pigeadh* (jar) of whisky, which both for " decency " and safety was wrapped round with layers of empty corn-sacks.

It was a terribly cold night of keen frost, and late by the time I got home, so I just backed into the cart shed, lowsed the mare, suppered her, and then made for my own supper, leaving the cart and its contents to be dealt with in the morning. On going to the cart shed to sort things out, next morning, what should I find but an Irish tramp (who used to give us an occasional call) huddled up in the cart, sound asleep under an empty bag and with his head resting on the sack-swathed whisky-jar as a pillow !

Even as I looked at him he stirred into consciousness, sat up, and made profuse apologies for having made himself at home without the usual permission. " But, sor," says Moike, " it was lhaite before Oi kame an' Oi wasn't for throublin' ye. An' be the holy Jasus," says he, " it's the divil av a hard pillow Oi had annyway! "—and him trying to twist his head to ease the pain in his neck and his teeth chattering with the cold.

I absolved him from fault, sympathised with the pain in the neck, and suggested something must be done about it. So he got up and slapped his arms and danced about the cart shed to restore the circulation, while I went to bring a cup of tea. I also brought a tumbler. To see the growing astonishment in his eyes as I unwrapped the *pigeadh*, took out the cork, and poured out a gurgle for him, was well worth the half-tumblerful.

" Moike," says he, " is it aloive or dead an' in hiven ye are? Or are ye just dhraiming? "

As if to test the possibility of illusion he swallowed the

best part of a gill of Ferintosh without a breath; then, gasping, says he:

"Sure, that's no dhraim! And begob! Moike," says he, "for siven hours ye wis schlaipin' on it!"

Wullie Doolie was one of our local characters. Wullie used for years to frequent the auction mart, giving such hand with the moving of the cattle as his decidedly limited mental capacity, aided by a long hazel stick, made possible. One day I brought to the mart a cow belonging to *Bantrach Uistean* (Hugh's widow). She had been a handsome horned heifer in her day—but that wasn't yesterday! The *Bantrach* was so attached to this her "puir earth-born companion and fellow-mortal" that she couldn't make up her mind to part with her till "Sineag" grew to un-numbered years of age that finally transformed her into a gaunt, uncomely old runt, of which hat-hanger hook-bones, a large head and long crinkled horns were the prominent features. I was heartily ashamed of having to lead so derelict a specimen through the town, and was mightily glad when at last I got her into a pen at the mart and moved off from her immediate vicinity. But this base desertion was too much for Sineag, who had never before been off the croft (except on her annual visit of an amor-ous nature to the neighbouring farm), and who had been distracted and terrorised by the yappings and shoutings and traffic of the town. She was in a sweat of fear by the time we arrived at the mart, and there was a wild glare in her eye. Now, on seeing her last contact with sanity moving stealthily away from her, it was the last straw. She circled the pen and bellowed like a lost soul and tried to shove her head between the pen rails—and all so frantic-ally that I had to run back to speak her words of comfort. But before I got there she had somehow managed to get her monstrous head, horns and all, shoved through between two of the rails—which soon proved to be like one of those Chinese wire-puzzles that refuse to become unstuck. Nothing I could do, even with her help, would get that big head and horns of hers back between the rails. While I was still pondering the problem who should come along but Wullie Doolie! Wullie at first glance merely saw that there was a cow's head in the wrong place and, to rectify the position, applied his usual remedy for such incongruities: a none-too-gentle rap on the nose with the hazel stick. Sineag emitted a roar of protest against this last indignity and tried to rug her head back. But it was no use. Wullie, evidently sensing that the case was not so simple as he had thought, looked at Sineag, turned his comical bearded face this way and that, like a terrier trying to look into the dark depths of a rabbit-hole, and tersely summed up the problem thus: "O ye ugly owld bitch! Hoo yi git yir hade un dere?"

That was exactly what had been puzzling Sineag and myself; nor did we ever find the answer, for it was only after I had hammered one of the rails loose that Sineag was enabled to withdraw her head, and assume an air of gloomy dignity which seemed to reflect unfavourably on the terrors of the town as compared with the peace and bliss of chewing her cud amongst the broom bushes on the *Bantrach's* back parkie.

Heather Harry, or Harry the Besom as we called him, was a nice gentle old man who came round every August and stayed for a month or six weeks. Where he came from or where he went to we knew not, but while in our district he lived in a little canvas tent, which he set up inside the circular walls of an old sheep fank out on the moor, and where the rabbit-eaten green grass was as smooth as velvet. Sometimes we would be unaware of his arrival until he came round selling his heather *squaibean* (besoms) and *bruiseagan* (pot-scrubbing brushes), but usually the gamekeeper or the shepherd brought news of his arrival. In either case, no sooner did we learn that Heather Harry had come than up we would go to *ceilidh* on him in his tent at the fank, and to watch him (and help him) sorting the heather into bunches appropriate for the particular purpose in view, then binding them, separately and together, with wire and fitting them to a birch handle to form a *sguab* that would sweep the floor of the house or barn, or into the little *bruiseag* with which to scrub clean the inside of pots and pans.

Harry's working tools were a strong-bladed jack-knife and a pair of pliers; his raw materials were pieces of birch, heather and wire. With these and his pair of skilful hands he would make brushes so neat and firm and well-tied that they would last the year round till he came again. The *bruiseagan* he sold at from threepence each to sixpence, and for his best and biggest *sguab* he seldom asked more than a shilling.

Sometimes we would help in the pulling of good heather and in selecting birches suitable for handles; and for such services we would be presented with a *sguab* or a *bruiseag*, in accordance with the value of services rendered.

Near the old fank where Heather Harry made his temporary home was a favourite haunt of the *gabhar adhair* (air goat or snipe), that in the darkness of the autumn evenings would make our flesh creep with its eerie bleating cry.

While it is generally true that boys brought up in the country may not be *consciously* sensitive to the manifold beauties of colour and form and sounds which daily surround them, there is no doubt that when they forsake the country for the city they are keenly conscious of the loss of such! And in the case of some country boys not even familiarity can dull the thrill of joyous appreciation that comes from the contemplation of a starry night in the hills, a moon that scuds behind white clouds and across blue windows in the sky, the song of a burn as its waters dash from rocky ledge to ledge to swirl and rest in the pool below; or the shrill complaint in the peesweep's cry, the tremulous call of the curlew high above the heather, the

"Go back! Go back!" of the cock grouse as he flaunts his scarlet lobes; of the tender green of spring, the blue riot of wild hyacinth and harebell, the purple of the heather, the golden brown of the bracken, the glory of autumn colours on the trees; even the swirling drifting snow that makes men gasp for breath but makes men tough and strong, the——But *Ar chall!* That anyone could be insensitive to such, be he town or country bred!

CHAPTER IV

The Royal Family—Witchery of Spring—Pots and Pans—
The Curse on the Cattle.

THERE used to be swarms of tinker tribes wandering about
the Highlands in summer and autumn. Where they lived
in winter we never quite knew; presumably it was in one of
the less aristocratic quarters of the town. But, come a
week of April sunshine and they would sure be on the road
again; perhaps three spring-cart loads in a gang, the men
and the stronger of the family trotting alongside the cuddy,
while the very old and the very young were enthroned on
top of rags and bags in the carts, surrounded by an assortment of pots and pails, pans and poles and poultry. The
lurcher, tied to the axle, trotted below the cart.

One might suppose that an illiterate class of people so
sordid in outlook and squalid in habits would be impervious
to the annual stirrings of nature, yet—whether they were
conscious of it or not—surely yon jaunty sprightly step,
yon debonair swagger (despite the tattered trousers) so
characteristic of the tinker as he headed for the woods and
the glens could have been no other than a physical and
spiritual reaction to the witchery of spring.

Our chief tinker tribe were of the Stewart clan: the
" Royal Family " of course to us. *Ali-Beag-an-ceard* was
their king. Ali was but a little wizened mannie with a
wispy beard, but he ruled his numerous brood with an
absolutism which Hitler might have envied. Only his wife
dared question his authority—and then only when she was
spirituously inspired to truly eloquent flights of vitupera-

tion. Our tinkers still had amongst them a smattering of the Romany tongue but to us they spoke in a whining Gaelic.

The " Royal Family " would reach us in late April or early May and stay for perhaps a fortnight. By then, if the weather was still good, their feet would be itching to be on the move again, further west into the hinterland of hills. It might be autumn before they again bivouacked near us; then they might stay till the October gales would drive them—with reluctant, heavy step!—to their hovels in the town till spring came round again.

They had recognised camping sites. A favourite one for many years was by the side of the Allt mhòr, not far from the *Fidhleir's* house. I remember several tinker weddings at this place—memorable occasions at which Ali's sons played appropriate tunes on the bagpipes with which several of them had some skill. But bad luck fell on the Allt mhòr site when a daughter and a grandson of the tribe died there. Not for many years after that did they pitch their tents by the side of the Allt mhòr.

Donald *Uistean's* gravel-hole and a clearing in the *Grayach's* broom were other camping grounds, but the most favoured of all was at the *Clachan Gòrach*—a small circle of Druidical stones right out on the moor close to the march between the Cromartie and Tulloch estates. It was said that one reason for favouring this site was this proximity to the two estates : that the tinkers, when poaching, could on the approach of a gamekeeper easily slip over to the other side of the march ! Personally I doubt if the tinkers of that day poached to any serious extent : indeed they were rather scrupulous in the matter of poaching or peat or sheaf-stealing which might earn for them the ill-will of the community or the attention of the police—two contingencies they were most anxious to avoid.

In those days tinkers still worked at their trade as tin-smiths. Many an evening would we sit in the tent watching Ali or one of his sons shaping his ware. Sometimes they used brand new tin from the factory but often they made do with old tins and canisters of any description, and it was fascinating to watch the metamorphosis of your syrup or biscuit tin into a milk basin or a skillet. They could make almost anything to order in tin, but their usual items for sale were pails, milk-basins, milk sieves and skimmers, skillets and mugs, all in a wide variety of sizes. A bargaining bout in the kitchen between *bean-tighe* and *ban'-cheard* over the price of a pail was a perfect demonstration of the now nearly forgotten art of buying and selling.

When engaged in their favourite pastime of begging (and you were only immune from that when you visited them in their tents—they never begged there) they were difficult to resist—especially the women. They had an adroitness in attack and a whining appeal that would get through to all but the hardest of hearts. Yet they had another side too. One day an old neighbour and myself were walking towards Dingwall. We met a tinker woman who immediately turned on the famous whine for a fill of tobacco—*pìos tombaca!*

" Indeed," said my friend, " I haven't that for myself. I haven't had a smoke to-day and I can't get one till I reach the town."

" Oh, helpless man! you should never let your tobacco run so low as that," says she, handing him a couple of fills!

But some of the tinkers were wicked old wretches, who, if their begging efforts failed, did not hesitate to invoke demonic aid to bring calamity and confusion on the obdurate one's family, crops and bestial : one of those comprehensive blood-curdling curses that not infrequently resulted in an immediate change of heart—and the appropriate lifting of the ban. In one case we knew of, though, the cursed man just laughed in the *ban'cheard's* face and challenged her to do her worst. She went off, muttering more, and more awful curses. Nothing happened. Then one day about three months later a fine in-calf heifer became ill and died in a day or two. A few days later one of his best cows died. Within a fortnight four cattle beasts were dead. A veterinary surgeon was called in. His verdict was " died of lead poisoning." Search was made; on the pasture field lead was found in various places. There was no shadow of doubt in our minds as to how it had got there—but despite every effort, nothing was *proved*.

CHAPTER V

The Suist—Saga of the Flail.

ONE day last winter I was up the Glen again. The threshing mill which the Agricultural Executive Committee had promised so long ago had come at last. Half a dozen neighbours armed with field forks had rallied round on short notice. After much snorting and slithering the mill was satisfactorily set for dealing with Robbie's two stacks of corn. Two hours later there were thirty-eight half-quarter sacks of oats under a tarpaulin all winnowed and weighed and ready for the Agricultural Company's lorry to take it away. The straw, all tied up in bunches, had been built into a big stack. All hands had a good meal, and then the mill pulled out from the debris of chaff and straw-stumps to move on to do a similar job at the next croft! *Treoraich mise!* The same sort of two stacks that it took Robbie's grandfather with his *suist* (flail) the equal of one hour of every day from October to May to thresh! The development in threshing and winnowing technique in the past seventy-five years is so remarkable that it is worth a chapter to itself. Before 1870 there wasn't on one of our fifty or so crofts any means of threshing other than by beating the sheaf with the flail or of winnowing the grain than by taking advantage of the wind. For many years after that—well into my time—those primitive methods were still common. Even after the hand threshing mills came in, every croft still had its flail waiting in some corner of the barn against a possible break-down in these new contraptions. In 1897 when the pinion wheel of our hand thresher broke, and during the fortnight we had to wait for a new one from the "foondry" at Inverness, the old flail had to come into action to keep the beasts in fodder. Everyone of my generation could use the flail like an expert and often on a Saturday did we youngsters thresh a stook or two to help out some *cailleach* with her Sunday straw.

The first hand-mill came to us in 1872. Soon several others came. There were three main types, two of wood and one all-iron. Of the former, one had treddles whereby the feeder could supplement the efforts of the man turning the handle. The other had two handles but no treddles. Both had one big pinioned wheel articulating with the small wheel at the end of the drum axle. Neither of the wooden mills "cleared the straw" properly, so that constantly the straw had to be removed with a fork. Also, unless you kept up a high speed, they choked readily, and it nearly burst your heart to start them up again.

The all-iron mill ("Tiny") was the favourite. It had multiple gearing so that by giving one turn to the handle you got twelve turns of the drum—which meant about 720 revolutions per minute and a grand "kick" to the straw that would send some of it a distance of fifteen feet.

The "millies" were such an improvement on the flail that for quite a number of years they were much in favour. Often, crofters who hadn't got one of their own got one on loan for a big night's threshing. On such a night as many as a score of lads and lassies would foregather and there would be some sweet compensations to lighten the intervals between the very hard spells of turning the mill handle! In four hours of a winter's night we would thresh a four-quarter stack—and sometimes danced a few reels to finish up with! What between the terrific heat and sweat and dust inside the barn and the arctic cold of the outside night I still wonder how half of us didn't die of pneumonia.

But in course of time we came to loathe the hand-mill!

It was such a tyrant in its demands on our time. Every night from October till May (Sundays excepted, but there was a double shift on Saturdays) we must thresh the quota of straw for the following day : that cursèd threshing must always be done !

When Billy got his water-driven mill its use was freely granted to all and sundry, and for years he could hardly call his barn his own.

Then one year an enterprising neighbour got a gearing unit that could be attached to the hand-mill from outside the barn and pulled round by a horse ! Within a few years every substantial croft in the place had one of these most blessed gears. It was grand being birled round and round on the wooden lever and letting the horse do the work ! In an hour we would thresh enough to do the week.

Soon small oil engines and a brand new type of mill that separated the grain from the chaff began to make their appearance. The horse-mill became old-fashioned.

For the past few years most of the threshing—even on very small crofts—has been done by portable mills supplied by the Agricultural Executive Committee. They have been a blessing to the district in a difficult time—but they have their disadvantages : (a) you can never depend on getting in the mill on the promised day—thus involving the house-wife in much trouble and expense in getting food ready to no purpose, and (b) your cattle don't thrive nearly so well on long-threshed straw as they do on straw that is newly threshed—but I want to look back at the flail !

What is a flail like anyway ? (Readers who know should skip this bit.) Well you take two pieces of any tough hard-wood, preferably in its natural round (i.e. not sāwn to be rounded later like the handle of a hoe), straight and free of knots. One piece should be about $4\frac{1}{2}$ feet long, 2 inches in diameter at one end and tapering (naturally) to about an inch and a half at the other. The second piece should be $2\frac{1}{2}$ to 3 feet long and about $2\frac{1}{2}$ inches in diameter. Both pieces should be peeled and made as smooth as possible.

The first piece is to form the handle of the flail (*" cas,"* as we called it) and the other the striking end (*"buailtean"*). They have now got to be connected. This is best done by burning a hole with a hot poker through each piece—about 2 inches from the stouter end of the handle and the same distance from the end of the striking piece. Then round-off these two ends with a knife or spoke-shave and lay the two pieces in a line on the floor with the holed ends a couple of inches from touching each other. Next get a strong and supple leather thong, thread it through both holes and make it fast by knotting or whipping with a piece of string— and there is your flail: the implement that has threshed much of the cereal crops of the world for ten thousand years.

In the hands of a novice a flail is as dangerous as a scorpion: he never knows where it is going to bite him. Instead of hitting the sheaf as per intention the *buailtean* has a nasty habit of landing him one in the eye—and a nasty skelp it gives! But by practice and perseverance the demon is soon exorcised; and before long you will swing with confidence and efficiency and be on the way to emulating Geordie Frocan who was a master *suistear* that would thresh his eight bushels per day of eleven hours, and nearly half as much again if the crop was heavy headed and thoroughly ripe.

Even some of the big farmers in the valley depended entirely on the flail up till the eighteen-sixties. It was their custom to bargain with some young men from the crofts to give them so many days or weeks with the flail throughout the winter. My father used to be so employed at Inchvannie Farm. His wages were one shilling per day of eleven hours—6 a.m. till 6 p.m, with an hour off for the "piece" of oatcake and a bottle of milk. An alternative arrangement was one shilling per quarter of grain threshed. He usually preferred this piece-work rate as it left him free in the matter of hours. Sometimes he made as high as nine shillings in a full week.

The barns on the big farms had strong wooden floors. Croft barns had only earth floors—so that most crofters had a wooden "threshing-board" on which the sheaf was laid to ensure cleaner threshing.

Often in a big barn two or more *suistearan* would be flailing at the same time; usually every man on his own sheaf, but sometimes two men—one right-handed and the other left—worked as a pair on the same sheaf, facing each other; and bonny work it was to watch this *buail 's buail mun seach*—strike and strike about!

If you are a right-handed *suistear*—i.e. swing your flail up by your left front and round and down by your right to strike the sheaf—you will stand with the sheaves piled up on your right-hand side. You take a sheaf, lowse it, and lay it on the floor in front of you, with the grain end pointing to the left. You then swing and bring the flail down so as to strike the grain at the extreme point of the sheaf. Each successive strike should be a fraction further back than the previous one till after a dozen to a score of strokes you have reached half-way along the sheaf. Now stop swinging and, with the handle of the flail you pull the flattened sheaf towards your feet. With a knack which cannot be described you flick the sheaf between foot and flail so that it is turned under-side-up on the board—just as the wife does with a fish in the frying-pan. This over-turn takes only about two seconds, and then you resume your whack, whack, whacking till you have worked back to mid-sheaf again. By this time there are very few heads still unthreshed and what there are you get in the next half-dozen whacks directed towards the bottom of the sheaf and to which you give a peculiar twist to break up the sheaf into the amorphous shape of a bundle of straw—which, with the handle of the flail you clear away to your left rear, then down with the next sheaf! With average stuff 18 to 20 sheaves, yielding off and on about a bushel of grain per hour, is quite good going.

As day after day passed, the heap of sheaves grew

smaller and the heaps of straw and grain grew bigger
around you, but always you kept your sheaf-board clear for
action.

Winnowing was the next concern.   In preparation for
this the ordinary farm hands would shake the grain through
hand-riddles to remove bits of straw and other roughage.
Then the grain—with which most of the chaff was still
mixed—was taken for winnowing in the draught between
the opposite outer doors that were a feature of the old-time
barn.   At this stage you were of course at the mercy of the
Weather Clerk.   Waiting for a wind was for us as anxious a
time as it was for the crew of a sailing ship becalmed in the
tropics.   When it did come, be it day-time or in the middle of
the night, no time was lost : it was a case of all hands to the
winnowing by candle light and right through the night if
need be; never a thought of hours or overtime : it was just
a job that had to be done.

In times of protracted calm the minister's intercession
was sometimes sought—but some of the *bodaich* seemed to
have more faith in the efficacy of a fire of withered broom
or whin just outside one of the barn doors.   Certainly such
a stratagem did create somewhat of a draught, but it was a
wearisome business compared with a good natural breeze.
With a well-established draught the winnowing was simple
—if considerably less complete than the work of the fan-
ners.   The mixture of grain and chaff would be riddled
breast-high near the draught-entrance door.   The good
heavy grain dropped straight to the floor.   The " seconds "
blew along a bit and the chaff carried well away—sometimes to outside the draught-exit door.   It usually took
quite a while to get the separation into first and second
quality grain up to the desired standard, but finally the best
grain was bagged for seed or milling and (at any rate on
the croft) the " seconds " or " lights " were retained for
horse and hen feed.   The heavier end of the chaff end,
which had in it a lot of very light or green corn, would keep
the poultry scraping for weeks.   The real good chaff was

much in demand in those days of board-bottomed beds. In the best circles the huge sack that we knew as the "chaff-bed" was filled with fresh chaff once every year. As the year went on the bed grew flatter and harder, and by the end of the twelvemonth it made but a middling couch. But oh, the ecstasy of sinking into the luxurious depths of a newly filled chaff-bed!

CHAPTER VI

I somehow had it in my head that Trade Unions were of
comparatively recent origin, and was surprised to be informed by the *Encyclopædia Britannica* that the first Trade
Union was formed as long ago as 1868! Anyhow, for
many years their expansion was slow and their influence
limited. In our northern parishes they were practically unknown in the eighties and nineties of last century. At that
time our masons and joiners or men of other trades had
their local " Society " or " Lodge " or " Guild " into the
funds of which they paid a small weekly contribution.
The main purpose of the fund was to provide help to any
of their fellow-craftsmen unfortunate enough to experience
prolonged unemployment or ill-health; and many a good
turn did such Societies do in their day and in their own
quiet way. Occasionally the fund was called on to help
them with the expenses of an annual outing or a dance.
The Society, too, supervised the then important function of
" brothering " the time-expired apprentices to their trade.
If this custom of brothering still survives at all, it is certainly not the feature it used to be in our rural local news;
for, in those days, after a lad had served his years of
apprenticeship he had still, before being regarded as a fully
fledged journeyman, to be formally initiated into the full
fellowship or brotherhood of his particular craft : a ceremony in its significance something akin to what the
" capping " ceremony is to the University graduate—with
the difference though, that while the capping is usualy done

in the light of day and in the presence of interested "outsiders" the rites of the brothering were a jealously guarded secret, usually performed in the dead of night and confined to fellow-craftsmen only.

Originally the ritual was no doubt a serious function at which the initiates were solemnly adjured by their elders ever to uphold the reputation of the Brotherhood for good and honest work. They were also, I have heard, let into some of the deeper secrets of the trade and the use of special tools and formulæ known only to comparatively few master craftsmen; indeed even in my time, while the brothering had shed much of its former solemnity, I understood that there was still observed a considerable remnant of its more serious aspects.

It was considered a great honour to be elected "High Priest" of the brothering ritual. For many years an alert old mannie known as The "Oighre" ("Heir"—an old aunt once left him a legacy of £10 which he "blew" in record time) was unanimously voted to this high office by our local joiners; sometimes, too, his services would be requested by some of the neighbouring groups. At such functions the Oighre was in great demand; but I suspect that the old rogue's reputation rested more on his entertainment value than on mere technical qualifications!

For weeks before the great occasion it was the main topic in the workshop and out on the job. The old hands sought to invest the ceremony with an awesome atmosphere of mystery of demonic origin that would work the youngsters into a goose-flesh feeling of excitement mingled with apprehension as they set off in their best clothes for the ordeal-by-fire that by this time they conceived the brothering to be. But they also took with them their dungarees and an extra clean collar—for there was no knowing what might be the latest mad ploy to evolve from the inventive imagination of the Oighre!

Amongst farm servants too, particularly in the case of ploughmen, the cult of the brotherhood was strong. Certain men in the parish had a reputation for a mysterious mastery over horses. Even the most vicious of "kickers" or otherwise intractable beasts (mostly mares, by the way!) after a week of "private schooling" by one of these experts would be transformed into a well-behaved working slave, as docile as you please. Whether it was that such men were quite unafraid of vicious horses (a circumstance which a horse is quick to sense) or whether they had some method of disciplinary treatment which soon taught the refractory one that docility was its wisest course, I don't know; but certainly the schooling, in most of the cases I remember, was efficacious.

The female progenitor of generation after generation of the Balnaird horses was Sally: a sturdy brown mare with one white fetlock and a star on her forehead. In the twenty five years of her mature life Sally reared twenty foals—some of them growing into beasts nearly twice the size of herself, but all of them kindly and friendly and ridiculously easy to break to plough or cart—*all bar one,* and that one, "Doll" seemed to have gathered up into her own explosive character all the vice and devilment that the rest of her kind had missed. As a foal she was as frolic-some and friendly as you like; and so it continued till the day that Balnaird decided that Doll, as a three-year-old, should have her first spell in the harrows. At the very first touch of the chains of slavery Doll squealed and kicked and squirted gallons of ill-natured urine over her astounded owner's person.

This one black sheep in his equine flock was a sore point with Balnaird: that he should have to admit that one of Sally's brood was a renegade hurt him like a personal disgrace. For a time he kept the disgraceful secret to himself, but a thing like that can't hide long in the country, so, ultimately he had to admit the trouble. It is interesting to recall, though, that he brazenly tried to extract some merit from misfortune: since he had to admit having got a "bad one" from Sally at all, he seemed to derive some satisfaction from the boast that he was now owner of the wickedest horse that was ever in the parish!

With such a reputation as she soon acquired for herself Doll was, of course, a non-marketable commodity. For the whole of that summer she lived in luxurious leisure on Balnaird's good grass, growing fatter and wickeder— if that was possible.

Then early one autumn morning, what should I see passing along the road in front of our house but Doll with Murdo on her back! He evaded my best efforts to have my curiosity satisfied: all I got was a wave of the hand as he and Doll passed on and took the peat road to the hills and soon vanished into the blue. That night I took a turn down to Balnaird in search of news. It was little I got. Balnaird had called in Murdo—who had a reputation for mysterious skill with refractory horses—; Murdo had slept the previous night in the empty stall next to Doll's; they had gone off together that morning—to where, and for how long, Balnaird could not say!

Actually they were away for nearly a week, and I never learned of anyone who had seen them during that time. I did not see them coming back, but one morning I saw in the distance that ploughing was going on at my neighbour's, that there were two men at the job, and that it wasn't the usual pair of horses. When I got down, there in the plough was old Sally, and alongside her, Doll, as steady and tractable and well-behaved as a veteran! Balnaird himself, while duly gratified at the exorcising of the devil that had been in Doll, had some lively conscience-scruples as to the unchancy Powers whose aid must have been invoked to effect so remarkable a transformation!

As will be readily understood, it was the great ambition of most young ploughmen to graduate into their brotherhood as soon as possible; such were athirst to learn those mysterious secrets which would give them skill with and domination over horses—particularly over "wicked" horses—and for the prestige and deference which such skill would bring them from their fellows. Several ploughmen with whom I was on friendly terms were held in high respect—not unmixed with awe!—on account of the undoubtedly remarkable " way " they had with horses, and the process of being "brothered to the horses" was usually quite seriously regarded, and very secret. On the other hand there was sometimes the case of an *ablaoich*—blockhead—of a ploughman who, though daft to get brothered, was not considered a fit and proper person or a safe repository for the sacred rites. Merely to refuse such was but to increase their importunities to get brothered, and in order to put them quiet a ploy would be arranged in that hot centre of rural roguery and rough play, the smiddy!

Pàruig Mòr was the victim on this occasion. Pàruig was a tall, gaunt bewhiskered creature who had come to the farm about two years before. In his first week in the new place he had sounded the prospects for getting himself brothered, and ever since, he had been pestering all and sundry to help him to achieve his ambition. It was clearly a case for the smith and some of his confederates. In secrecy one winter's night the smiddy was prepared for the occasion. Every ploughman in the valley (and others too!) got wind of the ploy.

As directed, Pàruig came to the smith's house after the " eight o'clock," dressed in his funeral suit—including a tall lum hat. He duly paid the " brothering fee " of twenty-five shillings—on the credit of which the smith had already procured ten bottles of good whisky from Nicol the grocer —and was solemnly warned in preparation for the perils which might beset him in the process of initiation to the brotherhood. He was to carry in his hand, held high above his head a white flag bearing a brown horse rampant (at least it represented the best joint-effort of the smith and the "vreight" in that direction) and under no circumstances must he lower the flag once the ceremony was under way. Pàruig was then securely blindfolded and led to the smiddy. Here the anvil and the hundred other things that usually littered the floor had been moved aside. On the cleared floor was a " carpet " of loose sheets of old corrugated iron. A two-year-old Highland bullock was quietly munching hay in a corner, while Robbie Ruadh's Billy-goat—a whiskered fierce-butting brute—was securely tied to the anvil in another corner. The audience had disposed themselves safely (they hoped!) on benches round the walls, and there was a hanging oil lamp shedding a smoke-bedimmed light over all. But not a peep of all this could Pàruig see through the three-fold blinding on his eyes.

In sepulchral tones the vreight (who had his face blackened and was enthroned on a stool on the forge) commanded Pàruig to advance—which he did under guidance of two assistant officials till he stood near the middle of the floor. Here the Highland bullock was led towards him and in a jiffy Pàruig was hoisted on to its back, his feet securely tied together beneath its belly and a hand gripping each horn. No sooner had the assistants jumped clear than a sharp jet of cold water from a nozzled hose-pipe was directed to the bullock's ear. The shock was so sudden and he wheeled so quickly that Pàruig all but forgot about his flag with the horse rampant. Next the jet would squirt a blow on the other ear or on the beast's posterior so that it began to barge this way and that, making the most infernal din on the loose corrugated iron sheets. Sometimes, by accident or design, the jet aim was bad and it would be Pàruig himself who got it full in the face; but ever he held the flag aloft. Suddenly his feet were untied; he was removed from the back of the bullock (which was put outside to grass) and made to sit on the floor. His hat, which had been repeatedly knocked off his head but as often replaced, was showing signs of battle but was still in position. At this point the officiating assistants made hastily for the side benches and safety—for the next Act was the unleashing of the Billy-goat who was at once the terror and delight of the boys of the place. No sooner did this monarch of a goat get his freedom than he pranced with proud step and flashing eye towards the sitting Pàruig. But soon it appeared that a goat can have niceties of etiquette in attack. This one was like a good sportsman who refuses to hit a sitter. The vreight, quickly grasping the nature of this contretemps, commanded Pàruig to stand up, which he did—for a fraction of a second. Then a well-directed butt, charged with all the pent-up fury of frustration, got him square behind and landed him flat on his face on the floor. Observers disputed for years over this point, some maintaining that, for a moment at least, the flag with the horse-rampant went down; others stoutly maintaining that not even in that desparate emergency did Pàruig falter in his trust.

But the prostrate Pàruig contributed little to the fun, so to his feet he was ordered again and again, only to be butted fore and aft with an efficiency that seemed to be as satisfactory to the goat as it was hilariously delightful to the audience. But soon the goat was removed, the corrugated iron made quickly to disappear into a shed. The vreight went to his house to wash his face. Many willing hands quickly restored the smiddy to its usual everyday appearance and Pàruig had the blinders removed from his eyes in a silence that seemed eerie in contrast to the dreadful din of what seemed but a moment ago.

The more convivial side of the evening then began. It was well past midnight ere the last of the " fee " was liquidated. By then Pàruig had attained to heights of bliss, and ever after he was inordinately proud of having, throughout all the trials and terrors of the initiation, held the horse-rampant aloft and so entered into full brotherhood.

CHAPTER VII

Good Neighbouring—The Ploughing Match

In our modest circle ploughing-matches did not rise to the grand scale; mostly they took the form of giving a leg-along to a neighbour who, on account of illness or some such misfortune had fallen so far behind with his work as to be in danger of violating local canons relating to dates on or by which certain jobs of work must be completed; for instance, you dared not sow your ley oats before April 9th, but you had better sow that day—and certainly not more than a week later if you were to escape public obloquy. The last week in May and the first week in June were specially consecrated to the sowing of swedes: if you didn't sow them within that period you had better not sow them at all. Then the yellow turnips must all be down by 15th June. Later sowing might mean having to single them in August; and that was very bad: you should have all your turnips singled before July was out! Hallowe'en (1st November) must see your potatoes snugly happed in the pit. The reason for this last was fairly obvious: severe frosts seldom came our way during October, but once November came in you never knew when you would get a frost that would ruin your crop if still in the ground. With the harvesting of cereals you were conceded to be in the hands of Providence (though that conferred no licence to slack your own efforts!), but with most other important functions you had better have regard to time-honoured dates if you were to merit local esteem. Otherwise, only sickness or dire misfortune excused you; and then it was that we would club together to give a hand. That was what happened yon spring Hector was down with pneumonia and his wife expecting. One night a batch of the lads and lassies threshed out one of his stacks of corn; next night another batch winnowed the grain for seed. On the following day eight pairs of horses happened to congregate at Hector's place, and the ensuing "ploughing-match" made short work of his ley ploughing. A week later—*on the ninth of April*—Johnnie Ruadh sowed the seed and somebody else did the harrowing—and that was that.

It was much the same when Mary's only cow died of milk fever. There was no "meeting" or "subscription list" or formalities of any kind. Donald and Sandy and Jimmie were just having a taste in the bar. They happened to belong respectively to the east and the west and the middle of the Strath.

"If you take the East side, Donald, and you the West side, Sandy, I'll take the middle myself," Jimmie remarked casually and apropos of nothing that had gone before.

"Just that," agreed Donald, and

"Right enough, the poor *creutair*," concurred Sandy, and him finishing his nip.

And so it was: each knew exactly where to call and where not to (and there was gossamer delicacy in this!) and met with the expected:

"It will be about a cow for Mairi of course?"

"Just that."

"Just that, of course, of course."

And all the crowns and half-crowns and shillings and sixpences went into the left-hand trouser pockets of Donald and Sandy and Jimmie. And the first that Mairi knew about the whole affair was when she wakened early on the Thursday morning by the *ranail* of a cattle beast and went to the byre and there, to her astonishment, saw a beautiful red-roan cow demanding to be milked. Nor was there a prying press to give unseemly publicity to what was merely the right thing to do.

As a display of rural art and craft and pulsating human interest is there anything on earth that quite equals a ploughing-match on a sunny day in Spring? Those powerful horses, proudly stepping as if all-conscious of perfect coats, of black shining harness with silver buckles, of gleaming hames and glittering chains, of colourful and artistic display of rosettes and ribbons in manes and tails!

The unploughed surface of the field—which has lain in grass for years—is covered as by a green carpet of a texture that delights the heart of a ploughman. Disc and coulter, cutting ahead into the green, are followed by sock and board which " tweel " the furrow over so that the grass goes down and the brown earth comes up to be well and truly packed against the neighbouring furrow. Screaming sea-gulls dart daringly at the ploughman's heels to gobble up rudely awakened red fat worms before they have time to gather their wits. There is a multitude of critics, in whose judgment a streak of partisanship is sometimes discernible; but only the merit of the " job " counts in the decision of the stern all-seeing judges; that is, so far as prizes for ploughing go. Fortunately, though, there are other prizes : prizes for best-kept harness, for best-matched pair, for best-groomed pair, for steadiest-going pair, and after that an ingenious range of prizes based on more fortuitous circumstances—the youngest ploughman, the oldest, the tallest, the shortest, the best-looking, the latest-married, the longest-married, the one with the largest family—so that nearly every competitor gets some sort of prize.

Yes : the ploughing-match is certainly a great event. It is a grand display of art and craftsmanship that has for weeks—till well on into the wee small hours of the morning —kept the lads intensely interested in preparing for it; will be the main topic amongst them for weeks to come, and will in due course send them to their secret and sacred hoard of treasures in the way of rosettes and ribbons, shining bits and silver buckles, which must be so sedulously burnished up again for the next great day.

CHAPTER VIII

Cupboard Lore—Hotel Menu—Oat-Meal Bannocks, Porridge
and Brose—Pitting Potatoes

In these times of rationed ounces of this and that necessity,
and the nearly complete absence of all luxuries from our
diet, the profusion and variety of foods and fruits on which
we guzzled in the years between the wars is something which,
to the twelve-year-olds and under, must seem incredible.
In those days the management of a restaurant with any pretensions to popularity would be letting themselves down if
they didn't offer their patrons a selection of appetising
foods and tit-bits running not into dozens but scores : actually the normal menu-card on the tables of most Edinburgh
and Glasgow restaurants offered a choice of between fifty
and sixty dishes—and at that, I have heard a customer
grumble because her favourite *bonne bouche* wasn't on the
list !

An old doctor friend from the islands put that sort of
thing in its proper perspective for me one day. While his
wife was away for a fortnight's holiday on the Mainland,
the doctor was staying in the hotel. In the middle of our
talk in came the servant lassie to ascertain the doctor's pre-
ference in the matter of the dinner which the cook should
prepare for him. As it was still not near dinner-time and
as the doctor was very deaf he quite mistook the purport
of Chirsty's visit.

"Eh? What? Whose wife?" he enquired, with hand
to ear.

"Och ! " said Chirsty. " It's not that at all doctor ! I'm

only wanting to know what you would like for your dinner
—will it be roast beef, boiled beef, stewed beef, cold beef
or mutton? and would you like a bittie fried haddock or
boiled cod?"

"But bless me! She should be all right yet," protested
the doctor; "she shouldn't bother me for a month yet.
Is it Rory himself that's here? Tell him to come in."

"Och! but doctor, it's not Rory's wife at all! I'm only
asking you about the denner," yelled Chirsty at him—and
she bawled the list at him again.

"I can't make out half of what you're saying, Chirsty,"
said the doctor testily, "but tell Rory to come in."

There was another frantic effort by Chirsty to get the
information desired by the cook—but with no better result
than a repetition of the demand for Rory to come in. While
this last tussle was going on I had scribbled on a piece of
paper the precise nature of Chirsty's errand and now
handed it to the man of medicine.

"Ach! Wumman!" said he in high disdain, "is that
what all the bother is about? Bring me anything you like
for dinner. I have always thought that these menu-cards
were meant to show a man how much he could do *without*";
and then he chuckled to himself: "but I'm glad I was right
about Rory's wife!"

Well, we of the Glen weren't so much concerned to have
a *variety* of food as to *have* food, and plenty of it. Not
that we didn't appreciate a savoury tit-bit when it chanced
along: we did, and all the more so because of their in-
frequency: but throughout the year our great stand-bys
were:—

Oat-Meal.—This we got in the form of porridge, brose,
gruel (special cure for colds), sowens (from the "suds"),
and oat-cakes.

Porridge and/or brose was our daily portion—New
Year's Day excepted—and there was not even that exception in the case of oat-cakes. As to what constituted good
porridge or good oat-cakes, tastes differed. Dònull swore

by the thick, stiff porridge that his spoon would stand upright in, and he wouldn't thank you for the watery boneless stuff that was creeping into fashion even in his day—and is the all-too-common form of porridge now. Personally I favour the happy mean—and *no lumps or singeing,* PLEASE!

Then Dònull was partial to oat-cakes of nearly half an inch thickness and almost green with baking soda, while I detested these and was all out for the thin, crisp, hard, nutty-flavoured variety—than which I know no other bread more palatable.

On a croft like ours the amount of oats sent for milling each year would be about twenty quarters (sixty cwts.), yielding around twenty-five bolls of meal; our boll was one of 140 lbs. Of this, about half would be sold to merchants or villagers; the other half—say twelve bolls—were used at home. But, of course, hens, pigs, horses, cows and calves had some of their food "laced" with a handful of oatmeal; so that there were heavy demands on the meal-kist. Assuming a family of two adults and five bairns, these would eat rather more than half of the twelve bolls in the year.

Potatoes.—As in the case of the oat-meal, the live stock —particularly the pigs and poultry—were competitors with the family for the contents of the potato pit. The combined requirement may be put at a stone per day, or say 45 cwts. in the year.

We favoured potatoes boiled in their skins—lovely, laughing, mealy tubers of which, as a complement to salt herrings, you ate a prodigious quantity.

Then there was the "chappit" form, flavoured with chopped onions and washed down with an amplitude of milk that was nearly cream.

As a special treat we occasionally had the scrumptious "stovies" or the equally delightful brown-fried *sliseagan.*

The varieties of potatoes then commonly grown were Dalmahoy Regents (Earlies), Brown Rocks, Cups, and the famous Champion, whose quality and flavour have never quite been equalled, but whose deeply indented surface rendered it unpopular with the advent of the fish-and-chip shop and the mechanical peeler.

As might be expected in the case of so vital an item of diet, meticulous care was taken with the cultivation and handling of potatoes at every stage. Never a diseased or bruised tuber was allowed into the pit. The pit itself would be on slightly rising ground so that any surface water could be easily drained away to the lower end. A few days before the lifting we would go to the moor with a *caibe* (special type of spade) and cut divots of about two feet long by a foot broad and about two inches thick. These were carted home and stacked near the pit in readiness for the lifting. Immediately the potatoes were neatly heaped in the pit they were covered with overlapping divots from ground level to near the apex, but the ridge was covered only with shaws or bracken for about a week, so that the potatoes could " sweat " (thus improving their " keeping " prospects) and still be safe from frost. After a week the straw would be removed, the ridge happed over with divots and then the whole pit covered with earth to a thickness calculated to defy the keenest of winter frosts. Usually we erred on the safe side by putting on not less than twelve inches of earth. In a winter of exceptional frost I have seen all the earth frozen solid, but never have I seen the frost get through the divots to the potatoes; and when a few of the divots were removed so that the *culaiste* (inside store) could be replenished there were the potatoes as safe and fresh and bonnie as the day they were put in the pit!

CHAPTER IX

HERRING.—What on earth we would have done without
the herring it is impossible to imagine. In summer and
autumn we had it mostly fresh, and in winter and spring in
salted form from the barrel laid in the previous back-end.
How often and how eagerly on the hay or harvest field did
we listen for the *Baob's* cry of "*Sgadan Ur*" that would
reach us from over the valley two miles away! For it
might mean for us the difference between potatoes-and-milk
and potatoes-and-fresh herrings at dinner-time. What his
right name was (if he had one) I never knew—nor did any
of those I asked. To us he was just the "Baob" who at
uncertain intervals came along with his ragged horse and
smelly spring-cart selling herring. Twenty for sixpence
was the normal rate of exchange; at ninepence a score we
thought them dear; only dire necessity would move us to
give the extortionate price of one shilling.

Usually the Baob got his supplies off the Skye train at
Dingwall. Other days he met them at Garve station where
they arrived by mail coach from Ullapool, fresh out of
Lochbroom that morning. In either case the question that
concerned us was: would he come up our road?—for on
days of short supply he would keep to the main road and
give us the go-by. When therefore the Baob approached
the end of our road—we easily kept track of him by his
lusty bellowing and his large white gravat—there would be
many anxious eyes turned in that direction. If he took

the right turning, someone would run off to each house to get a pail for the herrings that would be along within the next half-hour—and the sun would shine more brightly. If he passed on, the day darkened and depression took possession of our spirits : it would be potatoes-and-milk after all !

One year yonder—if I remember right just fifty-two years ago—hardly a herring came in to Lochbroom; that is a habit of this fish of mysterious migrations. Never once that season did we hear the bellow of the Baob coming our way. That was bad enough, but the possibility of being without salt herring for the winter was a matter of grave concern. Then one day came the great news !—*via* Wullack who got it from the stationmaster who got it from the guard who had got it from the stationmaster at Garve who had got it from the Ullapool maildriver—that Lochbroom was swarming with herring and that for want of buyers (who had gone away disgusted) the fishermen were dumping good catches in the sea !

That was a dispensation of Providence which it would be unwise to disregard. A conclave was hastily summoned. It was decided that those who were fit for the journey and had suitable horses and carts should start at six o'clock next morning on the forty-three mile trek to Ullapool. Johnnie Ruadh, Sim Macathail, Uilleam Mòr and my father formed the final team, but as Uilleam, for some unforeseen reason was unable to go, there was a lucky lad of twelve who got the thrill of his life when he learned that he was to have two days off school to join the herring team, and to take charge of Uilleam's horse and cart !

We were to start so early next morning and there were so many preparatory things to be done that we hardly got to bed that night at all. Harness had to get a rub-up; horse tails and manes got an extra combing; cart axles were well-greased; back-chains and sliders had a drop of oil; a bushel of oats in a bag had to be lashed firmly underneath each axle and a large bag of hay put into each cart. Most troublesome of all, fore and aft boards had to be fitted to the box of the cart at a height nicely calculated to prevent the herrings (which in bulk are nearly as fluid as water) from spilling on to the horse's back when going down a steep brae, or over the tail-board when going up a steep one. The alternative to having such boards was to three-quarters fill your cart only with herrings—but, as the herrings would be bought *per cart-load* that alternative was not to be thought of!

Prompt at six in the morning the convoy of carts met at the road-end while it was still barely daylight: and, believe me, there was one supremely happy driver sitting on his hay-bag as we set off. We rattled through the Strath while the folks were still abed. It was a lovely morning. By eight o'clock we were passing through the birches near the Falls of Rogie—a veritable fairyland of light and shade on the yellow-green carpet of moss—and on to Garve where for an hour the horses munched corn and hay in the hotel stable while the drivers had a second breakfast and a drop of refreshment in the hotel kitchen. By the way, at this and every other lowsing on the way, the horses' shoulders and backs were meticulously bathed with a strong brine as a precaution against collar and saddle sores; also, as a reviver after a long tramp and as a fortifier against fatigue on the next section of the journey, the men imbibed a quota of their version of Atholl brose—a jumbled-up mixture of oat-meal, raw egg and whisky added to about a pint of milk. As far as Garve, the road was familiar to me, but from there westwards by the *Diridh Mhòr* I was breaking new country and felt like an explorer in high adventure. On our right was the bulky western shoulder of Ben Wyvis; to the left the heathery waste of Lochluichart deer-forest— and always by our side the *Amhuinn Dhubh* that, from quiet pool to quiet pool ran fast and broken over jagged rocks, while far ahead the hazy blue of Ben Dearg rose to meet the clouds.

Scarcer and scarcer grew the houses as we approached

the old Inn at Altguish; it and the roadman's house were
the only human habitation in sight for miles and miles.
Lame Davy of the Inn was some sort of forty-second cousin
to Johnnie Ruadh, but however remote the degree of
cairdeas, it was sufficient to secure for all of us a warm
welcome and a high degree of Highland hospitality. After
a two hours' rest for the horses and of eating and drinking
for the men—and a solid hour's sleep in the hay-loft for
the boy—we were off again.

The keeper's house at Loch Drom—some half a dozen
miles on, and right on the water-shed between east and
west—was our next objective. Here it was only a cup of
tea and a dram while the horses had a rub and a bite, for
we must reach Inverlael that night. But we hadn't gone far
on the now down-hill road till for me all interest ceased!
—Sleep? . . . Only when the wheels rattled on the rough
cobblestones at Inverlael steading at half-past nine did I
come to—and that only temporarily, for, while the men,
with a marvellous toughness, after attending to the horses,
went off to feed and gossip in the manager's house, I made
straight for the barn to bury myself in a huge heap of
straw. It seemed but the next moment that I was being
painfully wakened by Johnnie Ruadh rubbing my ear.
Actually it was five o'clock in the morning. I had been
dead for seven hours!

Within an hour we were on the road again and arrived
at Ullapool about eight. That first sight of this white-
washed fishing port strung along the silvery shore, the
cobalt-blue of the loch, the boats gliding in under sail and
all gleaming in the morning sun was well worth the travail
of our forty-three-mile trek. A glorious morning—and, as
we soon learned, plenty of herring and no buyers! Instead
of being beggars of favours we were in the advantageous
position of being begged for our custom. Each cart was
filled till the herrings spilled over at the wheels—and the
price was £1 per cart-load of about four barrels of the
fattest and freshest herrings I had ever seen.

It would be wearisome to detail the homeward journey. Enough that at all the stops on our outward journey there was a halt in the passing, and soon we and our hospitable friends were feasting on fried herrings, and that we arrived home at six o'clock next morning. A dozen of the women and girls of the Glen were waiting ready with barrels, tubs, cogs and pails and a mountain of salt. By night the job was finished and everyone got a fair share—from Murcha with his large family, who got a whole barrel to Iseabal Bhan living all alone, who got a good pailful.

The all-in cost of the herring, including "travelling expenses" of the carters (but not including anything for their time) worked out at 8s. 3d. per barrel and it was at that rate the neighbours had to pay. There was no thought of profit-making, and some old folks like Iseabal got their quota "without money and without price."

CHAPTER X

MILK.—Here was another vital item on our bill of fare.
Even on a very small croft nearly everyone kept one cow.
Two-cow crofts were more common and some ran to
three or four. Shorthorns, or Shorthorn crosses with
Aberdeen-Angus were the favoured type. We never went
much in for forced milk-production methods. This of
course meant lower yields of milk, but I think this was more
than compensated for by the health and longevity of our
cows. In a modern dairy herd with milk-forcing methods
the majority of cows are broken-down wrecks of creatures
after five or six lactations. The average croft cow fed
simply on turnip and straw in winter and field-grazed in
summer and autumn would milk well for ten to twelve years
and still be a healthy comely animal—and that despite the
fact that not in cubic space, ventilation or lighting did its
byre remotely approach the minimum standard now officially laid down. Besides, except for about eight weeks after
the New Year, when most cows were dry, we had ample
milk for our needs, including butter and some cheese.
Here is a fair picture of the matter, *taking one cow only*
and assuming calving early in March.

1st March to Mid May, say 75 days at aver-
      age of 2 gals. .... 150 gals.
  Mid May to end of August, say 96 days at
      average of 3 gals. .... 288 gals.

September-October, say 60 days at average of
    2 gals. ....   120 gals.
November to end of lactation, say 60 to 70
    days, giving ....   50 gals.

                      Total ......   608 gals.

Of that the cog-fed calf would get, say ......   150 gals.

            Leaving for family use ......   458 gals.

$458 \times 8 = 3664$ Pints in the 300 days the cow is milking.

Take an ordinary working man's family of father, mother and four bairns in the city; how many of such, even in unrationed times, could afford to buy more than two pints of milk per day? that, in 300 days would be 600 pints for the family. Compare that with 3664 pints in the same period for the family on a one-cow croft! If the bairns on the croft drink even three times as much milk as the bairns in the town (and they do!) there would still be available for butter-making 1864 pints or, say, 233 gallons, and as every three gallons of milk or so should yield a pound of butter you have for family use some 78 lbs. of butter—and of course lashings of skim milk for cheese (very tasty but sometimes so hard that a dog can only bark at it!) and to put a kick into the pig and poultry diet. With two cows your benefits are roughly doubled. These are sober facts that crofters are apt to ignore when contrasting their luck in life with that of the wage man in the city.

If some readers challenge 608 gallons as too high a figure for the average croft cow I can only say that in our district it was not. The best cow we ever had—and we had her for fifteen years—seldom came below the 5 gallon-per-day mark for the best three-month grass period—or say 450 gallons— and for the rest of the lactation the equivalent of that again, or a total of 900 gallons. She was admittedly far above the average, and there were many which fell below the 600 level; but there were many well above it, and if you kept a cow that gave less than 600 gallons that was usually your own fault.

I'm not saying that every wife in the Glen made good butter; far from it! In too many cases by the time the butter was four days old it had developed a degree of rancidity that only a trained palate could stand. But every woman cherished the belief that she was the best butter-maker in the Glen, and it would give mortal offence even to hint that her butter was not quite to your liking; so you did your best and told gallant lies about it.

We were usually hard-up for milk in January and February—till the calves came. But nearly always in the neighbourhood was one considerate cow out of step with the others, and in that case we could usually depend on getting a bottle or half a bottle or at least a droppie for the tea; nor must you ever offer to pay for it! It may happen that you will be the one with the lucky cow next year. If there was no milk for the porridge we had to fall back on sugar, treacle, or Lyle's Golden Syrup with its bees feeding on the dead lion.

But there is milk *and* milk! The quality of milk one got depended on the generosity—or lack of it—with which the female head of the house was endowed. Indeed the women of the Glen were by this test mainly divisible into two classes: those who gave you yellow milk and those who gave you blue. The former out of her kindness of heart and love of children always gave to a boy the sort of milk that gladdened his eye: yon stuff she poured slowly off the top of the basin and that burbled and gurgled with blobs of cream! *Mo thàir air bainne am baile-mòr!* while the other gave him yon twice-skimmed blue-green stuff that tasted worse than whey!—By the way, would hotel managers please note? There *are* some hotels in Scotland where cream is a normal item on the table, but in the case of the great majority, despite the seven, eight, nine or ten guineas a week tariff, one might well wonder if there is any cream in the milk of Scottish cows. In two months of hotel life in Canada and the United States I got more cream than I have got in Scottish hotels in twenty-five years; so, *fhear-tighe-osda*, put that in your pipe and smoke it—and may you mend your ways!

Siùsag was our best specimen of the blue-milk breed : she just couldn't make up her mind to part with a drop of cream. Had she converted it into palatable butter there would have been *some* justification; but no! She would hoard the cream so long that it went wrong and in less than a week her butter tasted like a good sample of cart grease. Her family tried to train her to better ways, but Siùsag was untrainable. One Sunday when she was at church I went to see Roddie. Roddie was terribly fond of cream. The milk was set in basins in a large " press " standing in an outhouse. The door of the outhouse was only snecked but the door of the milk-press was securely locked. There were some large augur holes in the sides for ventilation. We could see the basins inside. The contents of one— probably that morning's setting—looked good. Roddie's eye lusted for cream as he squinted through the augur hole. We had a good look at the lock : no use! No knife or wire would move it. Roddie had another look at the cream.

" Come to the barn," says he—to get away from temptation thought I.

Roddie fell to examining a sheaf of corn.

" This might do," says he selecting a stout, long, tough straw and going back to the milk-press. I doubt now if that was the first time he had tried the plan, but at the time I thought it ingenious. Just a little bend on the straw at the right place—and there you were! As Roddie was interested *in cream only* it required delicate handling to adjust the bottom end of the straw to the right level. But Roddie was expert : in a few minutes he had sooked up the last vestige of the yellow top that was to him as nectar is to a *bodach ruadh*.

That creamless state of Morag's milk was a fair puzzle

to Siùsag until, after a few subsequent similar phenomena she hit on the sinister truth—encouraged in that direction by Roddie I'm afraid—*that Peiggi Mhòr was up to mischief with her Evil Eye again!*

CHAPTER XI

IT is curious to note, looking back over the years, the fascination which the hills held for us: yon strong subtle pull that was compounded of longing for spiritual solace and physical well-being. The mere thought of a day up amongst the heather was a tonic that drove dull care to limbo and set our hearts aglee. Little wonder then, that when opportunity offered it was to the hills we turned for real holiday; and if there is a grander anticipatory joy in life than you get on that morning when the hay is all safe and the turnips all singled and there is a promise of early rain and you have decided that *this is a day for the trout* and you have looked over the rod and are now filling a cocoa tin with fat worms; or it may be a day at the deer or grouse or ptarmigan or hares or foxes, or even gathering the sheep—well, I would like to know what it is!

.   .   .   .

It was a bonnie morning in August. Rain had fallen in the night but now the sun was up and a faultless blue showed between piled-up masses of snow-white cloud. Up from the grass sprang a couple of larks to indulge in an ecstasy of competitive song that rose and fell and trilled and thrilled one's very heart.

Yet, just then, to the very heart of me came that premonitory stab of depression which is apt to assail a boy towards the end of the holidays. To-morrow would see the end of the enchanting freedom which holidays confer on a country boy. Once again it would be washed faces and books, and a bell that would ring us into the seats of learning—*mo thruaigh!*

My momentary spiritual gloom was lightened by the voice of Black Sandy who, with customary stealth, materialised from nowhere. Sandy was a lithe, dark, hairy ageless neighbour, held by us in reverential awe on account of his uncanny skill with rod and gun and snare—and some less legitimate but more effective devices for keeping the pot boiling, and a little forbye.

Many a worry did Black Sandy cause to the Laird and to Big John the keeper; and it must have been a relief to the latter a little later that morning to see Sandy—as you may swear he did—start off so innocently equipped with a home-made hazel rod round which was wound tuppence worth of brown fishing-line with worm-hook attached, for a day at the trout at Allt nan Caorach.

" You'll be nearing the end of the holidays," said Sandy to me, voicing the very thought that had caused yon stab.

" Yes," said I, " to-morrow will be the last day."

" Och, Och," said Sandy, " too bad! Too bad!" Then with a friendly advance new in my experience of him, and which, I am now convinced was inspired by a kindly sympathy with which he was not generally credited, Sandy asked : " What about a day at Allt nan caorach with me?" There was no spoken answer : just a rush for a cocoa tin!

The pace up the peat road was fast and conversation limited, but occasionally Sandy, whose eyes missed nothing, would stop and study closely some spoor or mark or droppings that told him as would a written book where a deer or hare or fox or grouse had been.

I was not without some skill at burn trout fishing myself, but Black Sandy was superb. Pools I might think promising and spend fruitless time on Sandy would pass by. Into others—to me seeming less likely places—the artist, with consummate skill would steer his bait—and tug tug! wobble wobble! A perfectly timed swing, and a bonnie speckled trootie was wriggling on the bank!

In two hours, after returning to the water all that proved short of our rough six-inch standard, Black Sandy had twenty-three in his creel and I a round dozen in mine.

At midday, with a dexterity that a multi-badged boy scout might well envy, Sandy lit a fire and cooked a dozen of the best of our catch in its embers—a savoury addition to the " piece."

We fished till well on in the evening; then the breeze died down and out came millions of midges which swarmed my face, sang in my ears, searched more intimate parts of my person and finally put me to complete and precipitous rout. Black Sandy's leather skin seemed not to feel the stings of the accursed hordes, but in sympathy with my plight he agreed to my vote for home.

On the way home I had a unique exhibition of one of Black Sandy's many accomplishments. It happened in the twinkling of an eye and was all over in a matter of seconds. We were walking through a patch of knee-high heather. Whirr! went a grouse from under Sandy's feet. Like a shot he spread-eagled himself on the heather.

" There might be one or two below me " said Sandy, now as alert as a wild cat—and there were—four of them —which we deftly " released "; and bonny and plump they looked too, laid out in a row at the side of the burn.

" I didn't mean it, at all at all," Black Sandy explained; " it just happened. And och! wouldn't Iain Mòr be wild if he knew! You gather up the loose feathers, *laochan,*" said he, " and put them where they won't hurt his eyes; and we will put the birdies here."

He transferred some of his trout to my basket, took out half of what was left, arranged the birds neatly on top of the trout remaining in his creel, covered them carefully over with the removed trout—and there you were!

"He's a sispeeshious man Iain Mòr," said Black Sandy; "we'll better go down his way."

And down his way we went. Big John gave us a hail in the passing.

"Any luck?" said he.

"Och! not so bad; not so bad," said Black Sandy, but not offering to show his basket.

"Are they any size?" said the keeper, coming nearer.

"Och! not so bad; not so bad," said Sandy, now frankly raising the lid.

Iain Mòr came over and looked in. "A good basket of trout," said he, in honest admiration.

"Och! not so bad; not so bad," said Black Sandy, casually closing the creel; and we resumed the homeward road.

Our combined catch—exclusive of "extras"—numbered 90 trout weighing 18 lbs.

．　　．　　．　　．　　．　　．　　．　　．

In these days when the red fox (Gaelic—*Madadh ruadh*) is perhaps the most heartily anathematised agricultural pest in the Highlands it is interesting to reflect that there was a time when Highlanders regarded him with warm affection. That was when the native black cattle—and in many cases the natives themselves—had been cleared from the glens to make room for the *caoraich bhàna* (white sheep), and the *ciobair Gallda* (Border Shepherd). Both were detested and bitterly resented as the forerunners of the ruination of the country. So much so that the bards did not hesitate to invoke in verse the aid of the fox to rid the country of those twin scourges. Duncan Ban Mac-Intyre, the greatest of all the bards, sang :—

> "Mo Bheannachd aig na balgairean
> A chionn bhi sealg nan caorach,"

meaning :—

> "My blessings on the foxes
> Because they kill the sheep."

He then goes on to lament that the sheep . . . "have made a desert of the country . . . put an end to cultivation"; that "now there are no cows rearing calves in the glens which were wont to rear people." Duncan finishes by crying curses on the man who would harm the foxes or their cubs "snug in their rocky nursery."

Happily Duncan's curses proved not altogether potent: from the *caoraich bhàna* we now get a substantial contribution to food and wool; but there was long-range wisdom in his regret at the clearing of the cattle from the glens. Only recently has that wisdom come to our legislators who are now alive to the fact that the switch over from cattle to sheep was too drastic: that in course of time the herbage of the uplands would coarsen under a monopoly of fine-feeding sheep and that for its restoration and improvement, cattle in considerable numbers are a necessity. Now a policy of cattle-on-the-hills is being actively pursued and officially encouraged.

And the fox—now the *bête noir* of hill farmer? His depredations amongst our hill flocks, always lossful, are in these days of food scarcity trebly so. Newly-born lambs disappear as by magic. Later, older sheep will be taken; and while in his implacable hatred the hill farmer is apt to attribute to Reynard more than a fair share of the loss, there is no doubt that, with his remarkable capacity for ranging, his proverbial cunning and the clamant needs of his hungry cubs (which unfortunately for the farmer are coincident with the hill-lambing season), the real score against the fox is pretty steep. Moreover, with the increasing scarcity of gamekeepers—one of whose main functions is the killing of vermin—foxes have greatly increased in number during the past few years; and that too despite the vigilance of Agricultural Executive Committees in dealing with such pests. Some indication of the efficacy of such efforts can be gathered from the fact that in Inverness-shire alone in the past three years some 1000 foxes were killed. That might represent 200 dens. It would be a poor pair that couldn't collect 20 lambs for their family in the season. That would mean 4000 lambs in one county; and the foxes have to live for the other ten months of the year. Truly the annual toll in Scotland as a whole must be heavy, and in this connection there is a smile in the reflection that rabbits (which would normally form the greater part of Reynard's menu) have become so scarce in consequence of the Agricultural Executive Committees' activities that the fox is forced on to a lamb diet as the only alternative. One can imagine an old fox arguing hotly for a square deal in a difficult world!

.   .   .   .

A night and a day of over fifty years ago stands clear in my memory. An unexpected invitation to join a party of three gamekeepers and four cairn terriers all intent on destroying the inmates of a *saobhaidh* (fox's den) put me in a dither of excitement and delight. The den was in a hollow by the side of Alltandubh some ten miles off. There was a road for eight miles of the way and then two miles up a trackless glen. We started off in the afternoon in a dogcart. The terriers, no doubt sensing the occasion and thereby excited, quarrelled most of the way, under the seat, and more than once caused the spirited garron in the shafts nearly to bolt. In good time we got to the keeper's house at the bottom end of the glen. There we had a meal, and at the " mouth of night " set off for the *saobhaidh*.

The guns were posted so as to cover all exits. Then Fraochie was put to one entrance and Speireag to the other. Garry and Suilleag, to their intense disappointment, were held in reserve.

For a few minutes there were muffled rumblings and occasional sharp squeals which left the outside terriers and myself nearly demented with excitement. Soon, out from a bolt showed Fraochie's tail, to be followed by the rest of him dragging an already dead cub. While Fraochie was being complimented on his quick kill the expression of mixed pride and ferocity on his shaggy face was comical in the extreme. Within a minute Speireag was being similarly complimented.

Suileag was now put to work, and within an hour from the start four cubs lay dead on the heather. Expert opinion was to the effect that only one of the parents was at home —probably the vixen. The torn faces and ears of some of the terriers were the evidence.

" We'll better try Garry on her," said Sandy; and to Garry was assigned the principal rôle. He was a brindled nondescript tyke and the hero of a hundred battles—some results of which were evident in his puckered, twisted face in which there was only one good eye. But what an eye! And what a courage! He couldn't have scaled more than ten pounds but he seemed to have the explosive force of a miniature atom bomb. With tail erect into the hole he plunged. Almost immediately came sounds of battle; snarls, yaps, muffled squeals.

Would it be a fight to the death or would he bolt her? Opinion inclined to the latter view—now that the cubs were probably all dead. But Garry had other views. For nearly an hour, off and on the battle raged. At long last Garry's posterior, tail up, began to surface. Inch by inch he tugged and tugged—to an accompaniment of blood-curdling canine curses—till finally the corpse lay with those of the cubs. Garry's one eye was closed, his two ears were shredded. He was an all-over unholy mess of earth and blood, but it was a proud dog that trotted to the burn to drink his fill of clear cold water.

That was about 11 p.m. and nearly dark. It was agreed that the dog fox was not at home, and as nothing could be done till morning we made the best of the four cold hours till dawn. The men were sustained by a dram or two—not then financially barred to common people.

At first light of morning, eyes were scanning the surroundings for a blink of the dog.

" He'll see us long before we see him," said my immediate companion Sandy. " Indeed you may be sure he is looking at us this minute with only his nose above the heather."

The next half-hour was weary waiting, and then Sandy sent a thrill through me by saying quietly: " If that is not his snout above yon *bruach,* you can call me a *sasunnach!* "

I looked where I thought Sandy was looking but could see nothing like a fox. Sandy was careful not to point his arm in the direction of the fox.

" If I did that he would disappear like a wink," was the explanation. " But look at yon whitish stone in the face of that *torran* about 250 yards away. Now take a line from the stone square right for about ten yards. That takes you to a black peaty patch. Now look straight beyond the black spot till you come to that little bank of heather. His nose and ears are showing right in the middle of that."

I duly followed the directions but had to confess doubt.

" Och, but he's there all right," insisted Sandy, " and I only hope he will wait there till I get the rifle."

It was a shot-gun Sandy had, but there was a loaded rifle—an emergency precaution—lying not far away. Sandy strolled towards the rifle in casual fashion, lay down, drew it towards him and gradually—very gradually—got into firing position. Through the red whiskers his brown eye shone unblinking as an eagle's. The muscular brown hand closed steady on the trigger. Bang! Then, looking at the clump of heather I noticed it was slightly changed in outline.

" You have either got him or he is gone," said Jimmie.

" I think I got him all right," ventured Sandy.

And he was right. When we reached the heather clump there lay the fox as dead as a herring—and with a brace of dead grouse lying beside him.

CHAPTER XII

QUEER things dreams! They can be so delightfully in
consequent and so regardless of physical and moral laws
and limits. There are those who profess to be able to
interpret our chimerical experiences in the Land of Nod;
who ingeniously associate certain types of dreams with real
happenings in our waking hours. Presumably they have
gathered evidence to warrant their so doing. Personally I
have tried times without number to establish some connection between my somnambulistic experiences and subsequent
or previous things that befell me—but with little success.
On several occasions I did begin to think I had got hold of
a thread that led from phantasy to reality or vice versa,
but later the theory wouldn't pass the test—and I am left
guessing as before. In dreams our credulity is unbounded :
we accept without question the most astounding phenomena.
You needn't tell me that only parrots and jackdaws can
speak human language. In dreamland a cow or a cat or
any other of our day-dumb fellow-creatures can be as
loquacious as a gossip and can protest and argue like a
lawyer.

There was yon ewe we had on the croft at home,
Maillie. She was a Cheviot from Sutherlandshire and
came to us as a gimmer. We had her for eleven years.
In that time she reared sixteen lambs—six singles and five
pair of twins—all of top quality. She was a heavy milker
and had the maternal instincts so strongly developed that

we had the deuce of a job preventing her from stealing lambs from her companion ewes. For, while one of the latter was not yet sufficiently recovered to begin "dressing" her new-born lamb, the solicitious Maillie would butt in, assume the rôle of mother and be off with the youngster before the real mother knew what was happening.

One Saturday in spring Maillie gave birth to twins. Suspecting that another ewe would lamb before long, and determined to forestall Maillie's thieving tricks I was amongst the ewes at day-break on the Sunday. But I was late! The other ewe had already given birth to twins —and Maillie had stolen them both! There she was with yon foolish fond expression on her motherly face and so comically proud to have a family of four staggering round her, while the lambless mother bleated to her offspring in vain. The situation required expert handling and it took quite a while to get matters righted—but the point in all this is that, nearly every spring since then, Maillie has come to me in dreamland. She is still stealing lambs and I am still trying to dissuade her. But she is now able to plead and argue with me in support of her claims in the best of English. Usually I don't let her off with it, but at least on one occasion I did : I just didn't have the heart to resist her eloquent appeal; so off she went with it, proud and happy as of yore—and I was lucky enough to wake up just in time to escape a heart-moving and equally eloquent appeal for fair play from a bereaved mother.

Then there was Maggie-the-Mare, perhaps the most useful (as well as the most pampered and petted and beloved) of all the beasts on the place. Maggie was born sixty-nine years ago—and is still going strong—in dreamland —and has acquired a very good English vocabulary. She visits me quite frequently—perhaps half a dozen times each year—and we have great yarns together. When she reached her forty-fifth birthday I wondered if we could safely claim for her the equine old-age world record. The idea pleased her, but she informed me of an older companion who was still going about and advised delay. But that was many years ago, and for years now we are in agreement that she is alone in her eminence; and so now and hereby I publicly claim the old-age world record for her.

Maggie-the-Mare was very fond of new-laid eggs. When, therefore, a hen of individualistic tendencies scorned to lay in one of the woman-made nests in the poultry house and made a nest for herself in the straw in a corner of Maggie's manger Maggie scrupulously respected that form of independence: she was most careful not to disturb the hen. As soon as the egg-layer cackled her pride in having accomplished her task Maggie's prehensile lips picked up the egg as delicately as you please. With one crunch and very evident enjoyment she swallowed it. Now, as one taking a pride in his horse's coat—and for putting a shine in a horse's skin nothing beats a course of fresh eggs— I used to aid and abet Maggie in her friendship with the hens—which led to spots of trouble with Mother, who was more concerned to collect eggs than with Maggie's skin, which, she said, was always good enough without her good eggs. Well, Maggie-the-Mare comes to me faithfully and quite often. Some ten years ago it came to me as a shock (even when awake!) to learn in a dream that Maggie had died. But that turned out to be an exaggeration, for she has been to see me many times since then, hale and sleek and talkative as ever; and always we plot together how to outwit Mother in the battle for the eggs!

My first flight in an aeroplane was from Caithness to Orkney about twelve years ago; but I was an expert flier long before that! It must have been about 1898 that I stood on a green mound near our house on a summer's day watching some seagulls soaring gracefully overhead. Their movement seemed so easy and natural that I wondered enviously if I couldn't imitate them. So I leaned forward a bit and flapped my arms in gull-wing fashion. To my rapturous delight (but no surprise, mark you!) my feet soon lost contact with the earth and I floated up and up till I was well above the gulls! The sensation of power and well-being was exquisite. I took a turn over above Dingwall and the Black Isle and then up by Knockfarrel towards the Strath. I planed up and down with the utmost ease and perfect control. It was grand! Circling over our nearest neighbour's house I saw old Chirsty standing in characteristic fashion at the gable-end of the barn, with her hand shading her eyes from the sun as she gazed at me in amazement; and as I got lower I heard her give voice in Gaelic to a favourite exclamation: " God preserve me! what will that boy be up to next! "

Not often does a year pass without my having that same delightful experience again, and though Chirsty's bones have lain in the Churchyard for nearly half a century, never once has she failed to attend my landing from that flight over the valley, or to express her surprise at "that boy's " exploits.

Only a few weeks ago I had quite a confab with a bearded collie that a neighbour had early in the century. Like all Johnnie's dogs it was a very good one. At the hill " gatherings " *Cuiridh* (Hero) had a great " cast " that would sweep in the sheep from the face of Cnoc a Bhuraich over two miles distant from the top of Cnoc na Bainnse where his master stood directing him by shouted orders and shrill finger-whistling—and, when beyond hearing range, by waving a handkerchief tied to a stick. Quite recently I was back in the old home land, Cuiridh was there too. He gave me a warm welcome *in Gaelic*—Johnnie always spoke to his dogs in Gaelic so that they didn't understand a word of English. We could see deep snow well down the side of the Ben and there was every sign of a further fall. A lot of ewes had bunched together near the edge of the snow. Cuiridh and myself agreed that they were in a dangerous position and should be brought lower down without delay. I suggested to Cuiridh that he should go up for them. At first—and to my surprise—he said flatly he would not go. He gave as his reason that he knew there were in the lot a few stubborn old ewes that were " jibbers " and they would make it impossible for him to take the others to safety. I saw the point of his argument but assured him that it would not be held against his reputation as a " clean gatherer " if he did have to leave a few stubborn brutes like that; his job was to get to safety as many as he could. On that condition, and without more argument off he set. I kept the glass on him all the way. Up and up he went, semi-circled above the lot of sheep which started to move downwards. Yes, sure enough! there was one that would not run with the rest. Cuiridh didn't bother much about her and came down after the others. But now and again he looked back, and there she was in her stubborn loneliness. What was that? Cuiridh away back for the jibber! He stood quite close to her, but was careful not to force her. After a few minutes she began to move slowly towards the others. Cuiridh scarcely moved till she had joined in with the lot and her courage revived. Then down they came, and in the twinkling of an eye the whole lot were wheeling in safety beside me. *" B'è thu fhein an Cuiridh! "*—" It is yourself that *is* the hero! " I complimented Cuiridh; at which he was obviously pleased, but hastened to assure me that after all, if a dog had a job of work to do it was as well to do it right.

Here is one in which (in view of subsequent happenings) dream " diviners " may find something to test their twigs on. It was the early morning of New Year's Day 1933 I dreamt it. It was so clear and vivid that on wakening I had no difficulty in recalling it. Indeed I related it to my wife that morning as an example of the ridiculous nonsense one does dream. Moreover, that very day, while it was still fresh in my mind I wrote it down in rough draft with a view to touching it up later for a magazine article. But I never did : in fact, I forgot all about it until I found it amongst some old scribbles the other day.

Again I was back in the old home land. Many friends and relations (dead, mostly, forty, fifty or more years ago) were also there, very much alive. It was a grand summer's day. It was " Games Day " down in the valley. There was a great gathering of people including many soldiers and airmen of our own—and also a good smattering of French, Italian, German, Russians and Poles, all in uniforms.

The King and Queen (George V and Mary) came along and danced a reel with some of the foreigners. In by the gate came Stalin dragging Hitler by the arm. He hurries him towards the middle of the field where there is a high wooden erection and with a hay-fork prods Adolph up some rough steps to a very high platform. Hitler stands there with a very white face and black black hair, the picture of misery. A rope is put round his neck and tied to a wooden beam above. With much vituperation and gesticulation Stalin gives a telling off to Hitler. I couldn't make out a word of what he said, but judging by the scowl on his jowl it was pretty hot stuff. Adolph never said a word; he didn't even look. He seemed dazed. Joseph—evidently enraged by this indifference—suddenly kicked a plank from below Hitler's feet. It was the first time I had witnessed a hanging and I must have nearly wakened with the suddenness of the drop. But then a queer thing happened—not that it seemed queer then—for instead of getting dislocated as any decent neck would have got, Adolph's neck began to stretch and stretch and stretch like India-rubber. It stretched till it looked as if he might soon be saved by his feet reaching the ground. It was going to be a wash-out of a hanging after all! But just in the nick of time Rory of Inchvannie farm—who had ever a quick eye and hand, and whose presence of mind was proverbial—rushed up. He called Hitler a name which even in these impolite days must not be printed, and with one stroke of his turnip clipper (it was not the time for clipping turnips and the field was in grass, but let that pass) chopped the neck right across close to the shoulders. Down flopped Hitler's body; up sprang the rubber neck to ordinary proportion attached to the head—and there you were.

Adolph's head made bitter protest against so unfair a use of the turnip clipper, but the crowd howled him down and started playing a game of football with the head as a ball. It was a gruesome sight, but pleased Joe so much that he stood drinks all round in the refreshment Marquee.

There now! Dream interpreters can get busy on that one.

CHAPTER XIII

Further Dreams—In More Serious Vein

THE foregoing are but a few samples of " old favourites '
that come along from time to time and always give pleasure.
But the two most remarkable of my dreams were of a
very different type.

In 1916 I was domiciled in Thurso. My only brother
was in the Transvaal where he had been for a number of
years. He had always kept in close touch with the home
folks. Usually there was a letter every fortnight or so.
Towards the end of February I received from him a letter
written three weeks earlier. It gave the highly interesting
news that he had decided to cease work on the last day of
February and would be coming home as soon thereafter as
possible. He was in the best of health and spirits.

On the night of 1st March I had a most vivid dream
in which Alick was wounded and bleeding and in great
agony. So distressing was the dream that I awoke—and was
greatly relieved to find that what had seemed so terribly
real was but a dream! Soon I was sound asleep again—
but again that horrid dream came! This time it was even
more vivid and distressing, and I was mightily glad to
waken up again, to laugh at the absurdity of the whole
thing, and soon to go to sleep again. There was no further
recurrence, and in the normal activities of the following
day I forgot all about the nasty experience of the night.

But next night the dream came again; not quite the
same in detail, but very much to the same effect: Alick

was in extreme pain and distress. Twice I wakened up and twice went to sleep again—and both times came that horrible dream that had now assumed the nature of a nightmare. In the morning I told my wife—laughingly—of my disturbed nights and the cause of them. We both blamed a too-generous supper. The next night I rather dreaded going to sleep in case of a repetition; but there was none. But if the confounded thing didn't come again on the following two nights! The 4th and 5th of March. That, however, proved to be the last of it.

About a week later there came from Alick a letter written about mid-February, with further news of his plans and saying how much he looked forward to the home-coming. As it happened I had to go to Edinburgh for about a fortnight and left Thurso on the last day of March. The next day a letter arrived from my sister—who was also in the Transvaal. This letter my wife forwarded to me in Edinburgh. It was one of Teen's usual cheery letters, but there was a postscript saying that Alick wasn't too well and had been taken to hospital for observation—but emphasising that there was nothing to worry about.

When I read the postscript I confess that those wretched dreams rushed to my mind and brought a sickening depression of spirits. I scolded myself as a superstitious old wife and bade myself not to be a silly ass; but neither scolding nor laughing lightened the load of depression. For a day or two I tried to overcome it. Then I decided that the best way of getting confirmation that there was no cause for silly apprehensions was to cable my brother-in-law—which I did.

My cable read: " What news of Alick? " and to end the suspense as soon as possible I made it reply paid.

Next evening the reply came. It read: "Alick died 6th March, letter posted."

Actually by this time my wife had got the letter with news of Alick's death. During the last days of February he had felt so unwell that a doctor had been called in. He had been taken to hospital. Pneumonia had developed.

He had been very ill for a few days and had died on the 6th of March.

. . . .

Another example of a dream seeming to have a relationship or connection with a family happening went this way :—

In November 1917 I was staying in Borgie Lodge, Sutherlandshire. At that time, only my father and mother were living in the old home—the family being well scattered : one in Africa, one in Canada, one in Orkney, and myself wandering all over the north of Scotland.

I knew that my father was far from well. His health hadn't been good for some years; but a recent letter from home had made it all too clear that he was now seriously ill and that the end might come any time. So concerned was I that I pondered whether I should start for home by next morning's mail car. Finally I decided that I would attend to a pressing official matter next forenoon and then travel home by private car.

With that plan settled I retired to bed, but of course thoughts of possible happenings at home were much in my mind before going to sleep. During the night I had a startlingly vivid dream. I was at home (I very often am in my dreams!); my father was lying in his usual bed. He was wearing his red woollen night-cap and muttering incoherently. Aunty Maggie was sitting in a chair by the bedside. Suddenly father sat up in bed and in yon peremptory commanding way so characteristic of him demanded :—

"Where is Colin? Isn't he in the house? Bless me! can you not get him? I want to see him at once!"

Aunty said something soothing—to the effect that I would be there very soon. Father lay back, drew a long quivering breath and died—just as I started up, broad awake.

I lit the candle and looked at my watch. It was half-past two in the morning. Then I turned in and slept soundly till eight o'clock. I confess that I couldn't help having a feeling all that morning that very possibly the dream might prove true, or nearly true.

At ten-thirty I saw a boy coming towards the lodge on a bicycle. I waited. The boy stopped and handed me a telegram. It read :—

" Father died this morning at half-past two."

On arrival home that evening I learned that the reality accorded with the dream in nearly every respect.

I was so interested in this second curious experience of what seemed to be evidence of some connection between dream and reality that I wrote that day to my sister in Orkney telling her the whole story. But that same day (our letters crossed in the post) *she* wrote a letter to me telling that on the night of father's death she had seen him in a dream lying in his bed; and she too had seen him die —and she hadn't been a bit surprised to get the telegram on the morrow.

These are the only two experiences of that kind that I have had. They rather shook my scepticism and for a time I endeavoured to get some light—natural or otherwise— on the matter. But the more I quested, the deeper grew the puzzle. Like Omar I

" .   .   .   .   evermore
    Came out by the same door as in I went."

In short I failed to make head or tail of it, and soon let it lie. And anyhow, how much happier would we be if we did find the solution to the puzzle and meaning of life and death and dreams? For aren't these something like a cross-word puzzle?—only of absorbing interest while still unsolved? After you had filled the blanks and the whole thing clicked, they would be as flat and insipid as cold porridge.

I am never quite sure whether this next dream story is one I heard Dònull tell when I was very young (in which case it must relate to a time and people long before my day) or is one which appeared in the newspapers nearly

sixty years ago and relates to comparatively recent events.
I incline to the belief that it was from Dònull I heard it.
In any case, hear it I did, and it went very much like
this :—

One time yonder there lived on a croft in the Highlands
an old old woman. In youth she had been a bright lassie.
She married a decent man and reared a large family; but
one by one they were taken from her, and she was left all
alone. Yet Bellag was neither lonely nor sad, for she retained a bright outlook and had a happy word for everybody. Kindly neighbours helped her to work the few acres
of land, and her cow, half a dozen sheep and a score of
hens provided between them nearly all her material requirements. Everybody liked Bellag and in the long nights of
winter her cottage was a favourite meeting-place for the
lads and lassies of the neighbourhood.

One day late in autumn Bellag went to gather *bioranan*
(small bits of firewood such as withered stumps of broom
and whin) on the common which lay some distance from
the croft. A neighbour, similarly engaged, was starting
for home with her bundle just as Bellag arrived. The two
women had a short gossip exchanging tit-bits of local news.
Then the neighbour went off home, leaving Bellag to gather
her stickies; and that was the last that anyone ever saw of
Bellag!

A neighbour calling in at the cottage in the darkening
couldn't see a sign of her. However, he concluded she
must be out looking after the sheep and thought no further
about it. Next morning a young lassie called for a jug of
milk. She found the door open as usual but couldn't see
Bellag! And there was the cow moaning to be milked!
The lassie ran back and told her mother. The mother came
along to see for herself. Sure enough, although she
searched and shouted all over the place there was no answer
or trace of the old woman.

Soon the news flew through the township. Practically
every soul in the place went to search for the missing

Bellag; but though they searched near and far not a trace of her could they find. On the common there was an old quarry hole half-filled with water. The quarry was dragged and finally pumped dry, but yielded only a few eels and frogs. Next day there was a thoroughly organised search over a wide area—and the next day and the next for more than a week. Ultimately all hope died: Bellag seemed to have vanished off the face of the earth.

Some thirty years later a young man from the district emigrated to America. He had never seen Bellag, but of course was familiar with the story of her disappearance. Out in America he met a man of his native place. This man had known Bellag well, but had left for America a few years before she so mysteriously disappeared. In fact, as he hadn't kept up a correspondence with the home-folks, it was only when he asked the young fellow if he knew Bellag, and when she had died, that he first learned the story of how she had gone gathering bioranan and never returned. He showed great interest in the story and asked the young man to tell it to him over again. After hearing it for the second time he was silent and thoughtful.

Then—"It's a very strange story you have told me, Duncan" said he, "and I will tell a strange story to you. You may laugh as you like, but this is what happened: About two years after I left home (and from what you tell me that would be about the time that Bellag disappeared) I had a very queer dream. I saw Bellag lying dead at a certain spot. When I wakened I was glad to know it was only a dream and thought no more about it.

Then about ten years later I had the same dream again, and it was so clear that, though I was laughing at myself I nearly wrote to an old home-friend to ask if there was any-thing wrong with Bellag or was she still alive. But it seemed too ridiculous and I never wrote—and I don't suppose there is anything in it anyway?"

The young man agreed that it was a queer story—but of course it was just dream nonsense!

But next morning the older man came to see his young friend again.

"You can laugh as you like " said he, " but I will never be happy till you write home and tell them to search a spot that I will describe to you. I had the dream again last night and it was just the same. I saw Bellag as plain as plain."

Under pressure, the young man did write home to his brother—and to save face he treated the message as a joke; and as a joke the brother took it. But one day when a companion and he were walking near the spot mentioned in the letter he passed the joke on to his companion. The companion, though equally amused, suggested they might have a look, just for fun. The exact place was where a strong and wide-spreading bramble bush grew half-way down the almost precipitous side of the old quarry. With difficulty and at considerable risk of falling into the water one of the young men managed to scramble down to the bramble jungle. With his stick he searched as closely as he dared beneath its jaggy runners—and there, in the form of a human skeleton was the solution of the mystery of the disappearance of old Bellag!

Her bones were given a final resting-place beside those of her husband and family. The man in America was duly informed—and never again did Bellag disturb his sleep.

CHAPTER XIV

DEER-STALKING is the Sport of Kings; so please don't think I want to swagger by pretending that such sport has been a commonplace with me. It has not; indeed my earliest responsible experience of deer-stalking was in the humble capacity of pony-boy—flunky to the gillie whose job it was to lead the sturdy garron with stag strapped on its saddle from the point of kill back over the treacheries of bog and ridge and river to the hard road where the carcass could be transferred to the gig that would convey it to the larder.

But I *have* had my days of the Sport of Kings—legal and otherwise. Frankly, the " otherwise " days stand out. Occasionally I have been the duly sponsored " rifle " at days of deer-stalking with all their attendant paraphernalia of stalker and gillie and pony and conventional hours of operation. It may be an indication of a deep-seated objection to being led by the nose this way and that, and have all my thinking done for me, or it may be merely the result of a plebeian origin, but anyway, I am bound to confess that such formal days left me rather uninspired.

Most of my deer days were at the invitation of some friendly stalker who was glad to get a hand with the job when, for some reason or another his sporting tenant had to hurry back to the south leaving him to shoot the remainder of the quota of stags, and perhaps all the hinds later on. Some such days are memorable; but after all, it is rather a milk-and-water affair to shoot a stag that another person has spied and selected and stalked for you to within a hundred yards or so, compared with the thrill that comes from the test of skill, the pitting of wits, the quick-change plan in a changing wind necessary to win to that advantageous position by your own merit!—and it is marvellous how a spice of illegality adds to that thrill!

It was Uncle Colin who first interested us in the subject of deer-stalking. For many years he was stalker with Lady Ashburton at Lochluichart—where Carlyle in his old age used to resort to sulk in the friendship of his hostess; and it is rather interesting to reflect on the reaction which contact with the great man had on his comparatively illiterate but practical and downright contemporaries.

"*Bodach beag stuirdeach, gun chron no fhèum*" (Huffy little mannie, devoid of harm or use) was how those rugged men summed up the great Sage!

Every back-end after their " toffs " had left in October for London, stalkers and keepers from the remote glens would trek to Dingwall for their annual shopping; nor did they buy in pounds or ounces. Half a dozen bolls (one boll = 140 lbs.) of oatmeal, two bolls of flour, two hundredweight of sugar and the same of salt, a 40-gallon cask of paraffin and a " chest " of tea would be some of the normal household requirements. This annual business invasion of the machairs (low country) by the men of the mountains had also in it an element of holiday gaiety and a recapturing of souls; for they would then visit their parents and friends on the crofts, and there once again would expand as free men and forget their chains of slavery for a week or so—not indeed that the chains were so very fettering; but keepers and stalkers mostly came from the crofts, and it went hard against the sons of the croft to have to raise their caps and say " sir " to any man!

At that time politics with us were a simple matter: you were either a Tory or a Liberal, and that was that; that is to say, you were either in the camp of the Haves or of the Have-nots. Landlords, factors, big farmers, "moderate" ministers and (at that time) school-teachers fell automatically into the former lot; crofters formed the main body of the latter. Gamekeepers, gillies and such-like "parasites," although mostly of croft origin were always under suspicion by their own people as "turncoats"—no doubt with justification in some cases. In this connection I remember a parliamentary election when one of the many Tories who unsuccessfully tried to oust Galloway Weir from his safe Liberal seat in Ross-shire was being strongly canvassed by his party. The Lochluichart contingent of stalkers, gardeners, gillies and stablemen were driven in state by their employer in a spanking coach-and-pair all the way to Dingwall to vote for the Tory candidate. Uncle Colin came to see us that evening. My father was bitterly scathing and sarcastic about the "dozen slaves who had sold their birthright for a mess of pottage." For a time the tormentor had it all his own way, but at last the victim could stand it no longer.

"Donald," said he—in Gaelic, and with the added emphasis that language gives—"how many of the dozen voted for the Tory do you think?"

"Every mother's son of them, of course," was the reply.

"And that's the devil the mother's son of them, Donald, and I know it," retorted Colin, thumping the table so that the paraffin lamp nearly went out, "but it will be as well to keep your thumb on that"—whereupon they shook hands and solemnly drank *slainte a mhaith* to each other in a drop of Ferintosh.

There followed for four hours—till well after midnight —story after story of "toffs" and stalking and stags they had got, and stags they had missed; of a stag that had been wounded and gone over to the Fannich forest—only to be tracked for miles by the faithful infallible "Help" who finally brought him to bay and held him to it for hours— till the stalker who had followed the difficult trail of faint blood marks (sometimes lost in the dark and only recovered by the aid of lighted matches cupped in the hand)—at long last arrived and " put the beast out of pain."

This Uncle was a vivid story-teller, and every second beast they got (or didn't get!) seemed to have attached to it a story of cunning, of skill (or the lack of it!), of risk, of tragic failure or brilliant triumph; of physical endurance, of canine sagacity—in short of most of the elements that go to the making of a thrilling tale. No wonder if we youngsters looked forward to the coming of this red-whiskered uncle with his store of tales that thrilled us to the marrow; and no wonder if the height of our ambition was to get for a fortnight's holiday to that land of romance that to us was Lochluichart. Such indeed were practically the only " from home " holidays we ever had or could afford; and the all-in cost was the 7½d. " half return " railway fare. There we lived in an atmosphere of flies and fishing and guns and rifles, and rowing boats and deer and grouse—and midges! Of course we were much too young to participate to any but a minor extent in the activities which such things suggest, but with boyish aptitude we " took in " a lot. It was at Lochluichart at the age of eight that I fired my first shot from a real man's gun—under the supervision of the kindly Sandy. He had been out that day on the hill after the hoodies and was expected back any time. I walked out the path a bit in the hope of meeting him. Soon he appeared with the gun on his shoulder. As we were crossing the hollow of a burn near the house he remarked that he might as well empty the gun now—and opened the breech to take out the cartridges. What impelled him to do what he did next who can say? Perhaps it was a case of vibrating waves of wishful thoughts emanating from me; or perhaps it was just a recollection of his own boyhood. Anyway, instead of taking out the two cartridges he took out only one and closed the breech with a snap.

" Would you like a shot? " said he quite casually.

WOULD I LIKE A SHOT! Just like that! My heart nearly

burst. I couldn't say a word!—which condition Sandy correctly interpreted.

"Here," said he, " put the stock to your shoulder like that—And Don't Touch the Trigger Till I Tell You."

The stock was on the long side but we did the best we could.

" Now," said Sandy, " shut your left eye and look between the dog-heads along the barrel till you get it pointing at that white bit of bark on that birch tree."

The tree was on the opposite bank of the burn and about ten yards away. I did my trembling best to obey instructions.

" Be sure," cautioned Sandy, " that before pulling the trigger you will have the stock pressing firmly against your shoulder and that you will lean forward a little. If you do that it won't give you a kick at all—Now! All ready! —Pull! "

But alas and alack! The occasion was too much for me. I had forgotten all about pressing the stock to my shoulder and I suspect I must have been leaning backwards instead of forward! Anyway the gun " kicked " so good and hard that the next thing I knew was that I was sitting with my stern in a pool of water that lay behind the gravel strand on which I had been standing. The hurt to my dignity in addition to the hurt to my arm made the instant suppression of tears a thing of sheer heroism.

" Toot toot! I doot you forgot about the shoulder," Sandy commented with just that degree of sympathy which left you with a remnant of self-respect, " and look! " he added quickly, " by Jove! You fairly got the tree! "— which indeed I had, and there was a wondrous balm in that knowledge. The black-and-blue shoulder was never reported; nor did Sandy ever let dab about the more unfortunate detail of the incident.

CHAPTER XV

For three seasons the grassing of the Big Royal had been the most desired event in the neighbouring and rival camps of the two manufacturing magnates who annually resorted to their Highland Lodges for a respite from the concern incidental to the care and conservation of their millions. Other beasts and plans might and did get a place in the after-dinner talk, but rarely did an evening pass without someone bringing the Big Royal into the discussion.

But the Big Royal wasn't a Royal for nothing; for one thing—apart from love-inspired adventures in the rutting season and turnip-raiding in hungry weather—he spent most of his life in the vicinity of the high march between the two forests. Of course both sides claimed him as *their* beast (" Mostly feeds on *our* ground the beggar, don't you know ! "); but in this respect the Big Royal showed a judgment and impartiality worthy of a skilled poacher : he seemed always to be on the other side of the march when any one party went after him. So exasperating was this habit of his that there is no saying but there might have been a grain of truth in the indignant allegation of Red Angus, the stalker on the Carnbuie side that " Yon young pup of the duvil (his pet name for the Hon. son of the tenant of Lag-an-Eilean) had a shot at the Big Royal when he was clearly in on the Carnbuie ground ! Didn't I have the glass on him from the side of Ben Beg? "—nor did the remark of Sandy the gillie, to the effect that the same pup couldn't hit a haystack at a hundred yards anyway, do much to soothe the stalker's rage at the recollection of the incident.

It should have been comparatively easy to out-wit the Big Royal had the rivals been prepared to act co-operatively, but that is the sort of suggestion you would expect from one innocent of knowledge of the depths and heights of jealousy that normally distinguish such " gentlemen " in such matters. Who could say what the result of joint action might be? It might be the *other* side that would get him. Not on your life! So the Big Royal lived on.

Now it is sometimes given to otherwise simple humble people to be very wise in certain matters; and that is what happened to Big Dan and another fellow I knew—whom we will call Callum. Big Dan had no particular occupation and he abhorred anything in the nature of regular working hours, but there wasn't many things he couldn't do if the way was on him. His particular interest though, was in guns and rods and rifles and " otters " and things like that—and the things you could do with them! Callum had a steady job in the city but sometimes hungered for a spot of something less monotonous.

" It's a pity about the Big Royal," said Big Dan to his friend over a quick one in a quiet place one evening when the news at the Lodge was that the stag had again eluded them by going over to the Lag-an-Eilean side; " some day one side will get him, and it will be the wrong side," Big Dan added, somewhat ambiguously.

" It is that—and very likely," Callum agreed.

" You may be sure the Lag-an-Eilean people will be after him to-morrow," cogitated Big Dan, " and if only Red Angus would take his man out to near the march tomorrow he might have a chance—but of course he won't because he is mortally afraid that, instead of getting him, he might keep him to the Lag-an-Eilean side and *they* would get him!—and then wouldn't Duncan crow!"— Duncan being the Lag-an-Eilean *vis-a-vis* of Red Angus.

" Just that," agreed Callum, with a ticklish feeling within him that Big Dan was working up to something.

" And when are you thinking of leaving us?" inquired Big Dan, apparently off the subject of the Big Royal.

" By the late train to-morrow," said his friend, rather relieved.

" Fine man! Fine! That will be plenty of time. We should work it before then and you will get your train all right."

" Work it ? Work what?"

" Ach! Fine you know what! And it will be a great day, man!—but we better separate now. I'll be at the *leac ruadh* by seven o'clock in the morning—and you will be there too! I'll have everything that is needed with me. You tell Donal the Boots to put your bag in the mail-coach in the morning—you are going on in advance for a bit of a walk. Of course *you are going by the morning train*," and Big Dan laughed the wicked laugh that is born of cunning.

Well, his friend was maybe weak, but that is how things worked out. They met at the *leac ruadh* at the break of day. Big Dan had gathered the reassuring news that the Carnbuie party were going to the opposite side of the forest that day—*and he himself had left by the morning train* for Dingwall. Actually he *had* gone down by mail coach to the station, taken charge of Callum's bag from the Boots, bought a ticket for the next station down the line—and walked through the empty carriage and out at the other side and waited behind some empty waggons till the porter, who was the only official on duty at that early hour, had gone off for his breakfast. The regulation Service .303 had been conveniently " planted " in the small hours of the morning. Big Dan's sleep that night must have been next to nil, but there he was at the *leac ruadh* with a light in his eye that would have done credit to a general who had worked out every detail of his scheme of battle and was now to put it to the test.

Keeping mostly to the burn-sides and crossing from one

burn to another as inconspicuously as possible, in just over two hours the pair were approaching the high march. This called for a halt and much careful spying of the ground with binoculars that Big Dan had taken from a German—and thereby, too, hangs a tale! But anyway, that German, had he still lived, might well have marvelled at the tapsalterie fate which brought it to pass that his good Zeiss lenses should be used by his quondam enemy for searching for a Royal stag on the High marches between Lag-an-Eilean and Carnbuie!

Near the haunt of the Big Royal the march ran roughly east and west; Lag-an-Eilean forest lying to the south and Carnbuie to the north. But there was a triangle of the Lag-an-Eilean ground that bit northwards into the Carnbuie ground—another cause of considerable annoyance to the millionaires: Carnbuie thought it should be part of their ground, while Lag-an-Eilean complained that, no sooner did they move a beast in the triangle than it crossed over to safety on the Carnbuie side. Anyway the triangle was flat and open ground and was a favourite wallowing-spot for stags when pestered with clegs and other torturing insects for the existence of which not even the most ardent of humanitarians has yet been able to suggest an excuse.

Perhaps it was because of this opportunity of getting his own back on the clegs that the Big Royal so favoured the triangle as a resting-place: but perhaps, too, he had an inkling of an idea that by keeping near to the centre of the triangle he was fairly safe from any Sasunnach shot that might come from the surrounding ridges that were quite 400 yards distant. Not for a moment would he have trusted either Duncan or Red Augus even at that range, but he knew from experience that they would not fire at him: the trigger that fired shots at him must be pulled by more opulent fingers. More than one such shot had indeed come his way—but were merely sufficient to let him know where the enemy lay, and cause him to amble gracefully off in another direction.

Well, after searching the hillside and seeing not a sign of a beast Big Dan and his pal climbed cannily towards the ridge. There, without exposing themselves, they had a glance over towards the Lag-an-Eilean ground—and there, clearly visible to the naked eye and in the middle of the triangle, were a dozen beasts, one of which was almost certainly the Big Royal!

"It's him right enough," confirmed Big Dan after a brief look through the glass.

But the stags were every foot of four hundred yards away and even with the most favourable wind (and the west wind was all right for them this morning) no man could get nearer to them across that open flat.

If only the brutes would move to the north a bit! But they had already breakfasted, and already some of them had lain down. The Big Royal was still afoot and Big Dan was sorely tempted to have a go at him. He had got his beast at longer range than that—but his better judgment cautioned him not to take so risky a shot for such a prize so long as there was any better alternative possible . While the pair were still puzling it out the Big Royal settled the issue by lying down.

"*Mhic an diabhoil!*" said Big Dan, "and he will lie there for hours."

It was then that Callum, knowing well what the suggestion involved, put it into words.

"You wait here Dan, and I'll back well out round the shoulder of Torrandubh, and give them a whiff of my wind; with a bit of luck that should start them moving over in your direction."

That was the very ruse that was in Big Dan's own mind though he did not care to voice it. But as one sportsman to another all he said was:

"*Shin thu fhein, a laochan! 's gun teid maith leat!*"

(That's yourself, my hero! and may good go with you.)

CHAPTER XVI

Big Dan Plays a Hand

It would be all of an hour before Callum could get back round the Torrandubh to give the stags that whiff from which so much was hoped for, so Big Dan snuggled down in the heather to wait and watch as only a deer-stalker can. A change of wind might upset everything. In such an eventuality even Big Dan could rely only on a favourable Providence; but against any avoidable calamity he was determined to take direct precaution. So he kept the most watchful of eyes roving round for the slightest indication of unwanted developments. A pair of hoodies away to his left seemed unduly disturbed—but Big Dan's apprehensions vanished when he spotted below them a fox slinking across the flow. The Big Royal and his companions were still snug in their beds. An hour would soon pass. Just then—and not more than ten minutes after Callum had gone—Big Dan saw something that fairly caught his breath! Two stooping figures on the Lag-an-Eilean ground making for the ridge which flanked the triangle on the south-east! In an instant he had them in the circle of the glass; Duncan, of course—with that pup of the duvil along with him! Screened by the ridge they would get rather nearer to the stags than Big Dan had got on his side—and the Big Royal was on *their* ground! But what the better would they be for that? Even Duncan wouldn't care to risk that long-range shot. Soon the intruders disappeared from Big Dan's sight behind the flank of the ridge. By now no doubt they would have the glass on the Royal!

But the stags were still undisturbed. Confound it! If only the beasts got to their feet that impulsive pup might be fool enough to have a crack at the Big Royal—which he would most certainly miss! and—? *A chruithfhear bheannaichte!* but wouldn't that be the very thing to put the stags up this way!

But the Big Royal was not going to oblige: for ten minutes more he lay there as if asleep. Then Big Dan decided to take a hand in the shaping of events. The plan might go agee, but it was worth trying. With two fingers in his mouth and pitching the tone as best he could to reach the stags, but *not* the enemy (he hoped!), he gave a short sharp whistle. It was like pressing an electric switch: up sprang every stag, quiveringly alert!

"Capital!" chuckled Big Dan, "Duncan will think it was themselves that bungled somehow and startled the beasts!"

But before he got further along this wishful line of thought the next surprise was on him: came the sharp crack of a rifle—and down went the Big Royal like a stone! and the others were off like the wind! This page would go up in spontaneous combustion were I to write on it what Big Dan said in the next half-minute. Nor did he exactly enjoy the sight of Duncan and yon pup making across to their prize—but why the duvil was Duncan *running* like that? Eh?—" I wonder—?—I wonder—?" thought Big Dan to himself, and there came a queer look on his face as he grasped his rifle. Then in an instant he *knew!* When Duncan was still only half-way to the dead stag, the dead stag sprang to his feet and was making up in Big Dan's direction at full gallop. Duncan fired two shots after him, but the stern of a galloping stag doesn't present an easy target and the Big Royal came on unscathed. Over the top of the ridge he came within forty yards of Big Dan—AND BROADSIDE ON. Crack! went the .303 and the Big Royal never heard it; he just turned a perfect somersault and lay dead as a tacket.

Up to this stage not a glint of himself did Big Dan show to the Lag-an-Eilean men. The report of the shot was the first indication they had that there was anybody on the Carnbuie side. Now, to complete their exasperation and humiliation a man partially appeared on the skyline and gave them the wave that signified a kill. Red Angus himself! in his shirt sleeves as usual. (It was the well-known habit of the Cairnbuie stalker to take off his jacket immediately he had killed his beast)—but of course on this occasion the man on the skyline was just a good impersonation of Red Angus by Big Dan.

It would be tedious—and perhaps indiscreet—to follow our heroes further in detail. It must suffice to say that Callum and Big Dan soon foregathered and that there are other ways of transporting a dead stag than by carrying it conspicuously on the back of a pony—and that Callum got his train all right and can vouch that the collops were worthy of their Royal origin.

CHAPTER XVII

Aftermath—Red Angus and Duncan—The Dawn of Truth—
Buried Hatchets

It is only fair to innocent readers, though, to explain that, what happened when the Big Royal went down so suddenly at the first shot was that the bullet had merely grazed his wither where there is located a nerve which, when "shocked" by a passing bullet, produces immediate and complete paralysis; usually this continues for a few minutes and then the beast suddenly "comes to" and is as alive and alert as ever. Duncan suspected this when he saw the Royal go down like yon; that is why he *ran* towards it—in the hope of being in time to slit its throat before it recovered; and that was what Big Dan "wondered" and suspected and finally knew to be the case. It also explains why the Lag-an-Eilean party did not follow up a wounded beast on to the Carnbuie ground (as they would normally be entitled to do); Duncan knew well it was *not* a wounded beast.

Unfortunately the death of the Big Royal led to an aftermath of misunderstanding and distrust between Duncan and Red Angus—in this way:—Angus had happened to be in luck that day at the other end of the forest. Actually his party shot a Royal as well as two smaller beasts; and of course the story went round. But he still lusted for the Big Royal near the high march with Lag-an-Eilean. So, the following day he took a turn up that way all by himself to see what he could see. He spied and further spied and saw several beasts—but not a hair of the big fellow. Puzzled, he turned homewards—and as luck or fate or the devil would have it, didn't he walk right over the spot where Big Dan had put in his good work the day before! Now, while Dan had been careful to cover up the cruder signs of his bloody work he was more concerned with his transport problem than with that; and to Red Angus it was obvious at first glance that a beast had been grassed on that spot within the past twenty-four hours . . . ?

And the Big Royal wasn't on his usual ground! . . . And the Lag-an-Eilean people had the high march to themselves all day yesterday. . . . !

. . . And hadn't yon pup of the duvil already . . . ?

Oh Angus, Angus! How unchristian are the thoughts that feed on suspicion.

But Angus was convinced he had the truth of it : Oh : the indescribable skunks! and there was hot anger in the heart of him as he walked homewards; nor did it help that he couldn't say a word about it to a living soul. But some day—some day!—Duncan would have the sharp side of his tongue about this!

Meantime Duncan was working up a similar heat against his old neighbour Angus. The sneaking thief that he was!—waiting there out of sight to spoil their good chance! Duncan *had* heard the whistle that put the beasts on their feet. The whole thing planned in cold blood!— and then the final insult by Angus waving the hankie at them in pride of his trick! Pagh! It left a nasty taste in the mouth; and wouldn't he let Red Angus know what he thought of him some day!

So it was that these two worthies—who, barring some healthy spots of professional jealousy had rather a liking for each other and were very good neighbours—were anything but friendly when they met some weeks later at the annual shopping visit in Dingwall. There were several mutual friends and fellow-stalkers there, all in jovial mood, and in the pubs there was a great swapping of stories of the " season " and of the " toffs " and their queer Sasunnach servants. But never one word passed between Duncan and Red Angus even when they formed part of a very small group.

" What the duvil is up between you two? " demanded Big Kenny from Tornamuic, who was in grand form himself and wanted everyone to be likewise.

" There is nothing the matter with me," said Duncan, rather stiffly, and

" There is nothing the matter with me at all," declared Red Angus; and neither could be drawn further in public. But each was stoking up his wrath for a full expression of opinion of the other, in private, before the night was over! For they happened to be staying at the same hotel and by this time, with each, the deceit of the other in the matter of the Big Royal had grown into an obsession.

And so it was that, when late that night they met in the corridor just outside Duncan's bedroom they glared at each other the hatred that was in their hearts in no uncertain fashion.

" Come in for a minute," invited—or rather commanded —Duncan, leading the way into his room; " I have a word to say to you."

" Just that! " said Red Angus, following him in. " Just that! Mister Campbell (*Mister Campbell!*—to Duncan!), and I have a word to say to you. There was a day when we had good neighbours in the forests."

" So there was, Mister Cameron, so there was! " agreed Duncan, " but they are getting duvilish scarce nowadays."

" They are that, Mister Campbell; they are that," (his eyes blazing in wrath)—" *and it's a bonny turn when your neighbour comes over your march and kills your beast on your own ground.*"

" I don't know whose march and whose ground or whose beast you are speaking about, Mister Cameron," retorted Duncan, " but I call him a sneak and a thief that would bolt a stag that his neighbour has at the point of his rifle, and then shoot it himself! I would put the name of a dirty thief to him, neighbour or no neighbour!"

"And so would I," agreed Angus with professional fair-play, "and that would be the right name for him,"

"Then why the duvil did you do it?" demanded Duncan somewhat puzzled at the other's agreement on nomenclature.

"Why did I do what?" demanded Red Angus, also rather puzzled.

"Tamnation!" spluttered Duncan, "didn't I hear you whistle the Big Royal to his feet, so that I had to fire on him in a hurry before he would bolt? And didn't I hit him on the top line so that he went down for a minute or two? But he was up before I could reach him with the knife, and off over to the Carnbuie ground? and didn't I hear your shot? and didn't I see you in your shirt sleeves waving your bloody hankie at me after you did the dirty work?"

Duncan's rage was so obviously real that Red Angus was rather taken aback—and he began to wonder—?

"Look here *Duncan*," said he, more quiet-like, "is this the truth that you are telling me? Is that what you think happened?"

"It's the God's truth Angus, and well you know it—though you did put it out that you were on the other side that day," retorted Duncan—but more soberly.

"Duncan, my friend," said Angus, on whom a light was breaking, "I doot there is something far wrong somewhere. I am telling you that I *was* on the other side that day, and that I wasn't within three miles of the Big Royal—but I went up your way next day to see if I could see the Big Royal—and the duvil a cabar of him could I see—but I did see where a beast had been grassed the day before—and I was doubting it might be the Big Royal—and I am not saying but I might be thinking in my own mind that it was yourself or yon pup of yours that had something to do with it—especially so as I heard that Big Dan had gone off in the train that morning—but now I'm wondering? Och Duncan! aren't we the *amadans* that didn't think of that before? I am just wondering, Duncan, how far that big blackguard travelled by the train that day?"

"That is just what is in my own mind now, Angus," admitted Duncan.

But anyway it was fine to be good friends again, drinking out of the same bottle; and even if they were not sparing in their condemnation of Big Dan, each found a spot of comfort in the secret reflection that at least Big Dan had made it sure that *the other* wouldn't get the Big Royal.

CHAPTER XVIII

Dònull—Links with the Forty-Five—Ruairidh Mòr an Drobhair—
The Falkirk Tryst—Murder in the Quarry

As a *seanachaidh* (teller of tales) at ceilidh none could quite equal Dònull. True, he had a rich mine to work in. Dònull himself (who died only in 1921) was born in 1836. His mother (who lived with him and retained her memory and mental faculties unimpaired till she died in 1904) was born in 1814. *Her* father was born about 1760 and died in 1845 and *his* father was a lad in his teens in 1745 and lived to such an age that Dònull's mother remembered him as well as I remember her!

But there was more than mere material in Dònull's stories. For one thing he had an amazing memory. Perhaps that was because it was unburdened by any skill in reading and was thus free to develop a marvellous capacity for recollecting the spoken word. Just how closely the tales as told by Dònull resembled the form in which he first heard them, we never could say. Certain it was that in main theme they remained the same, but I haven't a doubt that under his vivid treatment they lost none of their dramatic effect. If you ask where was it that Rory Drover had his home, where was the Clachan or where the Bealach Garbh, and in what year—or century even—Rory was robbed or Mac-Eachainn was murdered, I cannot tell you; for Dònull had a lordly disregard for such finicky exacitude: he was concerned only with incidents and human characteristics and motives. It was in the art of telling that Dònull so excelled.

Yonder he would sit on a hard kitchen chair as happily as
you would on cushions (which he despised!), his eyes alight
in the reflection of the lowe from the blazing peat, hand
slapping knee to emphasise a point; voice rising or falling
with exquisite flexibility to register surprise, fear, scorn,
anger, amusement or any other of the emotions; the whole
of his powerful physical and mental attributes perfectly
attuned to the art of vivid verbal portraiture. It is bordering
on sacrilege to attempt any of Dònull's stories in English,
but I shall venture one or two—and that in the hope that
Gaelic-speaking readers may, by mental translation, be able
to savour them in the original, and that others, less blest,
will not know the difference!

Dònull had an uncanny gift of " remembering " some
old tale to give point to some aspect of a current topic;
when, therefore, with regard to something under discussion
Dònull would say, " *A dhuine! nach eil sin toirt 'nam
chuimhne?* "—(Man! doesn't that bring to my mind—?)
we would tune in our ears, for that was usually the preliminary to one of his tales; and if it happened to be one
we had heard before, that didn't matter, for Dònull never
failed to infuse it with fresh zest.

About fifty years ago the newspapers were giving
prominence to a series of daring burglaries in Glasgow and
London; they commented on the difficulty the police had in
getting their hands on the criminals. Some arrests had
been made on circumstantial evidence pointing in the direction of certain people, but on closer investigation the evidence broke down. Dònull was much intrigued with the
topic. He would ask to have read over to him again and
again the story of the burglaries and the police theories
about the crimes and criminals. He would then propound
some theories of his own so shrewd that they would do
credit to a Sherlock Holmes.

But mind you! (he would say), it's very difficult to be
sure that you have got the thief unless you catch him with
the money in his pocket—and even then you have to be

careful you are not making a mistake! Man! doesn't that bring to my mind the case of *Ruairidh Mòr an Drobhair* (Big Rory the Drover) yon time he was coming home from the Falkirk Tryst? It was in the time of my grandfather and it was him that told the story to my mother.

Rory had a bit of a croft in the Highlands but it's very little he worked on it! He left the work on the croft to the wife and family, for Rory had the droving in his blood and nothing would keep him from it. Every year by the end of September he would have bought up every marketable beast in the parish and start off with the drove to Falkirk. Some years he would make big profit off the cattle. Other years he would lose it; but loss or profit, Rory would be on the market with his drove next year.

Well, one year yonder the luck was on him. For the hundred and fifty beasts he had brought to the market he was getting nearly double his buying-price. That meant that he would have the best part of a thousand English pounds on him when he left the market for the long road home. And that was a thought that gave him much concern, for in those days the law did not run to much effect in the Highlands, and many were the tales of drovers who had been knocked on the head and relieved of their cash at some lonely point on the homeward way.

For the first few days half a dozen drovers went northwards in company with Rory. They were not well known to him—just casual acquaintances met in bargaining bouts on the market—and he was careful to say nothing about his good luck. Indeed, without telling direct lies about it, he rather gave them the impression that it was the other way about and that he was travelling home with a light sporran.

Well, one by one his companions left him as they reached their homes. By the end of the third day he was alone, with still a two days' tramp in front of him. Unfortunately too, the most dreaded point on the whole journey was still to pass. That was the *Bealach Garbh*

(Rough Pass) where the path ran narrow between rough-strewn boulders that had fallen from the face of a precipice. It was the sort of place that a man carrying a lot of money would do well to avoid in the dark! So, with night coming on and a hunger to satisfy, Rory decided to rest till day-break at the Clachan which lay a few miles short of the Bealach Garbh.

At the *Tigh osda* (Inn) after a manly attack on a haunch of venison, and fortified by a *stòp uisge-beatha* (measure of whisky) Rory experienced that resurgence of strength and courage which such fare engenders. But soon to the inn came three " strangers " that Rory didn't like the look of at all! He had already taken the precaution of mis-representing to the landlord the trend of prices at Falkirk : indeed had given of himself the impression of a man of much hard luck and with a flat sporran; and he had no doubt the strangers had already heard this tale, but he wondered how much they had been deceived by it! Not that they appeared unfriendly : on the contrary they seemed eager to be on friendly terms with him. They even invited him to join with them at the bottle—an invitation which he deemed it unwise to refuse. But the more Rory studied them the less he liked them, and (while pretending to be well under the influence of the strong brew—most of which he had surreptitiously decanted on to the earthen floor) he soon pleaded tiredness and stumbled off to bed.

But when the strangers entered his room after they concluded he would be sound asleep (as Rory anticipated they would, to relieve him of his money) there was no Rory there! Nor (though they made as hard as they could for the Bealach Garbh) did they find hide or hair of him! For, instead of going to sleep, a very sober and alert Rory quietly left the inn by a back-door and, to make doubly sure of getting safely home, he took to the higher ground instead of going by the valley path which led through the Bealach Garbh. Right up over the ridge he went and then down the other side to the neighbouring valley.

Rory was now striding along a rough track which more or less followed the course of a river. He was still a good day's tramp from home. It was terribly dark and he was very weary. He knew there was no house within miles. If only he could find a sheltered spot he would pull a bed of bracken, roll himself in his *breacan* and rest till the break of day. Then he remembered the quarry—the quarry from which, some years before, granite blocks had been removed to build the Big House. It was a sort of side-cut in the rock so that it had a dry hard bottom and its steep sides gave shelter from all winds but the south. Never dreaming for a moment that such a lonely spot might already have a tenant for the night, Rory made straight for what he judged to be the most sheltered corner; and then he got the fright of his life! In that corner there were glowing the last embers of a dying fire! In front of the fire was the recumbent figure of a human being! Before Rory could gather his wits to make a bolt for it, the figure sprang up and, pointing a large "*dag*" (pistol) at him commanded the drover to stand still if he didn't want a hole through his belly. You may be sure that Rory was taking no chance of that! Besides, the fright went out of him, for he recognised the voice.

"In the name of the Creator," he cried, "point that dag of yours another way MacEachainn! Can't you see it is your friend Rory the Drover?"

The relief was mutual, for they had been equally scared and were now equally glad to recognise a friend; indeed MacEachainn was by way of being a bit of a local drover himself and sometimes bought beasts for Rory on a commission basis.

Soon the fire was replenished with bog-fir and a second bed was laid down near it. But instead of going to bed the two of them sat by the fire and for nearly an hour yarned away about the market and prices. As became friends and brothers-in-trade the large flask which Rory had replenished at the inn was much in evidence. Now, that potent spirit which it contained produces curiously different effects on different people: in some it develops the kindlier instincts of sentiment and affability. On some it has quite opposite effects. Unfortunately, both Rory and MacEachainn were of the latter class. An incautious remark by one about the virtues and value of a certain horse, gave hot offence to the other. In two minutes they passed from extreme friendship to bitter animosity and quarrel—which would have culminated in physical violence had not Rory, with a last glimmer of sanity, decided to quit the quarry. Off he set with feathers ruffled.

But he didn't go far when he realised that he was much too far through to carry out his virtuous intention. So he wrapped his plaid around him and lay down in the shelter of a handy rock. He was never sure how long he lay there or how long he slept. He only knew that he wakened up while it was still dark and that he was shivering with the cold. He also felt much sobered and decided to go back to the warmth of the fire, knowing well that when MacEachainn wakened up they would be good friends again. So back to the quarry he went and, snuggling near to the sleeping MacEachainn he also was soon sound asleep.

The sun was shining in on them by the time Rory wakened. MacEachainn lay still, covered with his *breacan*. Rory, sore of head and stiff of body, stretched his arms up to the sunlight and yawned.

Mother of Mary! What was that on his hands? Blood? There was something wrong with his sight!

He rubbed one hand against the other. It *was* blood! Hastily he got to his feet. He had been lying in a pool of blood!

Cautiously he removed the *breacan* from MacEachainn's face.

Merciful God! MacEachainn's head was smashed in and horribly bloody and he was very obviously dead!—Dead!

.   .   .   .

Just as Dònull reached this hair-raising point in his tale we heard a loud whistling from outside. It was the " laad " whom Dònull had helping him on the place, come to report that a bit of turnip had stuck in the throat of a stirk which was in danger of choking. Off went Dònull to deal with the emergency, leaving us in a fever of curiosity as to the sequel. It was just like a serial story in a magazine— stopping at the most exciting point. Not for nearly a week after was Dònull free to come to our house to give us the rest of the story.

CHAPTER XIX

Rory Arrested—Condemned to Death—A Lucky Elopement—
One Good Turn . . .

As I was telling you (Dònull resumed), there was Rory in
the quarry that morning with the sun shining on his bloody
hands and on MacEachainn lying dead in his own blood.
The whole thing was such a shock to Rory that it clean
drove the wits out of him. Not for his life could he clearly
recall the earlier happenings of the night. He could remember up to a point but he then got hazy—! Och yes!
It was coming to him now : MacEachainn and himself had
a dram of two and were very friendly. Then he said yon
about the black horse—that it was weak in a pastern and
couldn't be trusted on a hill—and MacEachainn didn't take
it well! He called Rory a name that no gentleman could
take in humility! And Rory got hot about it, and so did
MacEachainn! And, Blessèd Creator! Had they struck
each other in anger? Rory could not get it clear at all—
at all! There was lying near MacEachainn a jagged blood-
covered lump of granite which might have made that horrible hole in his skull! Rory might be blamed for this
whether he had done it or not!—and anyway, who else
could be at that lonely place in the hills in the middle of
the night? Then a great fear took possession of him. He
must get out of this—at once! And he would go by a
route that nobody would be likely to see him on!

But everything seemed to be against him that night.
He was less than a hundred yards from the quarry and

turning the shoulder of a hill when his heart came to his throat on seeing a man well known to him, out in search of a bit of venison. Nor was he a friendly fellow! He and Rory had no love for each other. Rory was glad that he didn't obey his first instinct to flap in the heather, for the recognition had been instantaneous and mutual. So with just a hail in the passing Rory pushed on for home where he arrived some hours later—having on the way taken the precaution of washing off in a burn all traces of blood as best he could. In the family-circle he tried to look more cheerful than he felt and told of his good luck on the market; but that didn't seem to deceive his wife who would keep asking if he felt all right and him looking so pale. Rory maintained that he was, but agreed that he was tired after the long tramp from Falkirk and would be better of a rest. So to bed he went but not to sleep! If the poacher didn't chance to look into the quarry everything might be all right, for nobody else might go that way for days and days. But if he *did* happen to——!

That day dragged long for Rory. With night coming on he began to feel more hopeful; but he didn't get far on that road! For what but didn't a neighbour call in, full of the news! The deer-stalker *had* happened to look in at the quarry and there had found the dead MacEachainn! That night the news was on every tongue. Early in the morning a messenger was despatched to carry the news of the murder to the nearest representative of the law. Soon the hue and cry were out.

It wasn't long before suspicions began to point in Rory's direction. Didn't the hunter see him that morning not far from the quarry? And why was Rory in such a hurry to pass on, even if they weren't very friendly?

Wasn't it well known to some that MacEachainn was carrying on him a substantial sum of money when he left home a few hours before? And not a penny had he on him when they searched him!

On the other hand there was evidence from the folks at

H

the Clachan that Rory had a bad market of it—he had told them so himself—and was light in the sporran. Yet his own wife and family knew that he arrived home with a sporran bursting with money—and the wife, in pride of her man, had said as much to a neighbouring woman before the news of the murder came out. True Rory was now eager enough to admit the truth about the market; but the people said amongst themselves that of course that was what he *would* say if he had killed and robbed MacEachainn. And besides, who ever before saw Rory so nervous and with that look of fear on his face? And more than that, was it likely that there would have been anybody else near the quarry that night? Of course it wasn't! The quarry was well off the main track through the hills. Very rarely did anybody go that way. It was strange enough that two people should have been there on the one night. That a third should be there was too strange for belief!

And so the case against Rory grew black and blacker with every day that passed until at last there was nothing for it but he must be arrested. A miserable and broken-down Rory was put in irons and carried off to jail.

On the evidence before him the judge had little hesitation in arriving at the conclusion that everybody else had arrived at. Before pronouncing sentence he gave Rory an opportunity of saying anything he could in his own defence; but it was little poor Rory could say, for by this time he was nearly convinced in his own mind that he must *have* killed MacEachainn in a fit of drunken rage and forgotten all about it!

So Rory was sentenced to be hanged. The day of execution soon arrived. A crowd gathered, some no doubt to get such morbid pleasure as a public hanging afforded, but not a few in sorrow at the sad fate of one who had been a general favourite and a good neighbour. Just as Rory was being led to the scaffold a young man on horse-back galloped towards the crowd waving his arm and yelling at them to go no further. He demanded to speak with

the official in authority. There was animated talk between
that person and the horseman. Soon a rumour flew through
the crowd. The hanging was to be postponed! The
rumour was officially confirmed! Rory was led back to
prison!

Now the explanation of these happenings makes a queer
story and shows how far the strange arm of coincidence
can sometimes stretch.

There lived in the same township as Rory a young man
who was courting the daughter of a man over the way of
the Clachan. But the parents on both sides were unfriendly
and bitterly opposed to the courting. (When will parents
learn that such opposition but adds to the lowe of youthful
love?) Anyway, young Angus and Mary had their own
views about the matter. On the very night of the tragedy
in the quarry (as it happened!) Angus set off over the hill
to his tryst with Mary near the Clachan. From there, as
previously arranged, they set off in the early hours of the
morning for Glasgow and marriage, leaving their protest-
ing parents to whistle.

Now those were not the days of daily mails or frequent
letter-writing, so not a whisper did the young couple in
Glasgow hear of what had happened in the glen to Mac-
Eachainn and Rory, until one day about three months after
the murder. It was then another lad from the home
country came to Glasgow and soon searched them out—and
of course at their very first meeting they heard all the news
of home including the recent tragic happening and that Rory
Drover was to be hanged the following week.

Evidently the man in Glasgow was no laggard—in more
ways than in love. As soon as he realised that the murder
had taken place on the very night that he had crossed the
hill to keep his elopement tryst with Mary, and that Rory
was to be hanged the following week, his mind was made
up.

"*Mairi, a ghraidh*," said he to his wife. "It is me for
the north and this very day! Rory Drover was a good

friend to me. Many a kind turn did he do me—and perhaps now I can do one to him." And this was the man who
arrived just in the nick of time to save Rory from the rope.
The story he had to tell was really very simple, but it just
shows you——!

On his way to his tryst that night and while passing not
far from the quarry he almost collided with someone in the
dark. Both must have got a bit of a scare. The young man
demanded to know who the other was and was surprised
to get no reply. Indeed the other made off hurriedly and
said not a word. Yet even in the dark the young man
thought he recognised in him a drunken tramp of ill-repute
who from time to time came round the district. But Angus
had no time for tramps that night and hastened on to his
tryst.

On getting the news of the murder and of Rory going
to be hanged for it, his meeting with the tramp near the
quarry came to his mind!

With this new clue the authorities had little difficulty
in tracing the tramp to his lair in Glasgow where they found
him still in possession of much more money than he could
explain away. He also had on him a knife and a snuff-
mull which belonged to MacEachainn. With such evidence
against him the tramp soon broke down under examination
and confessed the truth. Shortly before he met Angus that
night, he had decided to go into the quarry for a few hours'
sleep. This must have been just after Rory left it on
quarrelling with MacEachainn. In the quarry, much to his
surprise, he found MacEachainn alone, very drunk and
very quarrelsome. He immediately threatened the tramp
with a " dag," and the tramp swore that it was in self-
defence he had thrown the stone at MacEachainn. He had
no intention (so he said) of killing him, but on realising
that he *had* killed him he thought he might as well be
hanged for a sheep as for a lamb; so he helped himself to
MacEachainn's possessions and hurried away—and got the
worst scare of his life when he almost immediately ran into

a man on the moor. And it must have been shortly after that that Rory returned to sleep in the quarry.

So Rory lived to an honoured old age and to see many another Falkirk Tryst; but believe you me he always gave the granite quarry a very wide berth!

CHAPTER XX

It was one day in the smiddy that I heard Dònull tell this
story of Big Rory the Drover. I had made an early start
that morning and taken a short-cut in the hope of being
first in and getting the sock and coulter sharpened without
delay; for the smiddy was a terrible place for dilly-dallying!
Usually the hour that you allowed yourself for an errand
there turned out to be half a day—and not infrequently a
whole day! Not that one really grudged the time, for,
however one's conscience might give an occasional stab as
hour after hour slipped by there was no denying that the
smiddy was a fascinating place to spend a day in!

There was the snorting roar of the bellows, the white-
hot iron, the melodious ring of hammer on anvil, the
showering sparks as the iron bar, under deft strokes gradually assumed the shape of horse-shoe, harrow-tooth or
plough-point; the sizzling, smoking, pungent-smelling hoof
being shaped for the shoe, and those innumerable skilful
turns and touches which ever distinguish the expert craftsman at his trade. Besides—and despite the strenuous
labours of the smith and his apprentice—there was room
for much talk. Indeed as a school for scandal, gossip and
general news of the district the smiddy ranked high, and
in many instances exercised a stronger check on the conduct and morals of the young men of the place than did
the pulpit. It was certainly unpleasant if, in consequence
of some social delinquency, one provided a text for a

denunciatory sermon by the minister, but that was nothing so bad as to be indiscreet enough to allow oneself to become the butt and joke of the smiddy clientele. After all, one *needn't go* to church to get an unflattering verbal portrait of oneself—but one *had* to go to the smiddy!

Well, anyway my good intentions of that morning didn't work out. As I came in sight of the smiddy door, there was Dònull—ever an early bird!—just arrived with Sally and Tom for shoeing. I knew, of course, that horses got priority over all other customers and that that meant for me a wait of two or three hours; but that did not deter me! And in any case it looked like coming on to rain: an early return home mightn't be of much use anyway! So Dònull sat on the hard wooden seat in front of the horses and I sat on a bench amongst a miscellaneous collection of hammers, bolts and cold chisels while the smith started to remove the worn shoes.

But before things got properly under way we heard a baaing of sheep outside. Now no matter how busy he might be, the smith couldn't bear to let beast or body pass his door unscanned. All work and talk instantly ceased while everybody went to the door to investigate. . . .

It was Jeemsie with a lottie of hoggs on his way to the market. Jeemsie was the son of a neighbouring croft. Twenty years earlier, when he was nineteen, Jeemsie was a raw youth who had never travelled outwith the parish. Like most of his contemporaries he had no trade or profession and his schooling was scanty—the gleanings of some three of four winters' irregular attendance at the local schoolie, and amounting to only a moderate skill in reading and writing and reckoning. But many a youth with even less academic equipment had gone out from the Glen to joust with Dame Fortune in foreign lands—and not always unsuccessfully. So off went Jeemsie to America where for nearly twenty years he turned his hand to many a job and had saved up a few hundred pounds which in our circles meant comparative affluence. Only the previous year Jeemsie had got a letter from home to say that his father was getting very frail; he gave up his job at once and started for home, hoping to be in time to see the old father still in life. He was just in time and his presence greatly cheered old Jeemsie's last days. Jeemsie had waited at home with his mother, and the local speculation now was whether he would go back to America at all. He himself didn't want to wait at home, but also he did not want to leave his mother in her old age. While still undecided he had started as a " trocar "—our local word for a dealer in a small way, as distinct from a " drover " who was a big man in that line. But it seemed that whatever skill he might have in other directions, judging the value of sheep or cattle was not Jeemsie's strong suit. We made it our business to know all about his dealing transactions and already the jokes were going round. For instance there was the lot of lambs he had bought from Sandy. Passing the smiddy on the way to market on that occasion the Smith soon got to know the buying price. Jeemsie gave it as his opinion that they were dirt cheap at 12s. 6d. He was confident of getting 15s. for them, or more, and he was a little concerned at having " done " Sandy to that extent. The Smith had his own opinion about that but didn't go further than to suggest that even if Jeemsie didn't gain *any profit* he might gain *valuable experience!*—an involved comment which Jeemsie did not see the force of until, after a long day on the market he was faced with the alternative of taking the lambs home again or accepting the maximum market offer of 10s.! And there were some other tales of that kind about Jeemsie's ventures in that tricky trade.

This morning the lot passing the smiddy door did not quite please the expert eye, but, as usual, Jeemsie was satisfied he had made a good buy and would get a substantial profit. Dònull let him off lightly though :—

" Well, well ! " was all he said, " see that you'll not get into trouble on your way home with the profits like Big

Rory the Drover did coming from Falkirk!"—which obscure remark disturbed Jeemsie not in the least, for he understood not its drift.

It was his mention of Rory Drover that brought to Dònull's mind the story which he told us in the intervals between the vigorous hammerings, filings and blowings that were the accompaniments to the shoeing of Sally and Tom. I have an idea that it helped to lighten the smith's hard labour. I am sure that for one small boy it drugged a conscience to rest and blotted out all sense of time and responsibility.

The big men on the flat fat farm lands of the Lothians had a great year of it, Dònull began. An early spring put them well ahead with plowing and sowing. A good growing summer brought the crops well forward, and perfect harvest weather enabled them to fill their stackyards as they had seldom been filled before. Luckily for Rory Drover he had heard in advance of his buying for the market a whiff of the news from the south—and you may be sure he had a big lot at Falkirk that October! Nor did he have trouble in selling them. Trade was big, for, in addition to his usual requirements, every farmer in the south wanted an extra half-dozen beasts to help to empty his stackyard and fill his middens.

This time the journey north was giving Rory more concern than ever before. He had put every penny he had in the world into the cattle and now he would be carrying on his person the whole of that, plus the very handsome profits he had made on the market—for he put little faith in the banking facilities of those times.

Before leaving Falkirk he took the precaution of going to a saddler's shop and getting a body-belt, with ample but smoothly disposed pouches in which to put his money. Thus equipped he started for home.

For the first few days it was no use trying the old dodge of a poor mouth with tales of a bad market, for the news of the high prices had travelled north quicker than himself. However, nothing alarming happened, and soon he outstripped the news; and by the time he was nearing his native hills he thought it safe to tone down the market news to the few people he met.

As ever on the journey home his main concern was to get safely through the notorious Bealach Garbh—where the path was so narrow and twisted at the bottom of the precipice, and so strewn with huge boulders fallen from above that a man could be hit on the head and robbed before he knew anything about it. That sort of thing used to happen frequently—and even yet on occasion. Rory himself, some years previously had got a fright in the Bealach Garbh that he would not forget in a hurry! On that occasion he had hoped to get through this pass of ill-repute in broad daylight, but had met with one delay after another so that the night was on him before he reached it. When nearing the most fearsome spot he walked softly as a cat and was all ears for any unusual sound. Just as he was about to enter the narrowest part of the pass where the rock rose high on his left and a huge lump of stone lay close on the right with the burn close by, what should suddenly strike his ear but a sound like a half-smothered sneeze! On the instant, and quick as a wild-cat Rory gave a leap to the shelter of the south side of the big stone and crouched to listen. There he was with his heart thumping and him listening as if to hear the grass growing. Was it a sneeze he had heard? Or was it just the fear that was working in his mind?

After a few minutes of sharp listening without hearing a sound but the swish of the water in the burn he was just about to chance it that there was nobody on the north side of the big stone when the same sound came again, though not quite so loud!

"Oh ho!" thought Rory to himself, "it is your north wind that is a south wind to me! That unlucky *cnatan* (cold) in your nose is my good luck!"

Now what to do? To go through the narrow pass

between the big stone and the rock would be walking into trouble—and there might be more than one *spuinneadair* (plunderer).

There was risk in going back too : walking over loose stones in the dark he could not pick his step—and one sound and they would be after him.

The burn which ran close to the big stone was too wide and deep to let him over without a drooking; and that was a thing to avoid at that place and time!

The moon was now beginning to thin the blackness of the night. In its faint light Rory had a look at the very narrow space between the big stone and the burn. It was but a thread that the goat might manage over by! True, Rory himself was a bit goat-footed, but this was too risky a test. Yet what was he to do? He couldn't wait here all night, and even if he waited for daylight what better off would he be?

He was now nearly sure he had heard whispering voices from the north side of the big stone—which meant that there were at least two men there. It also meant that they had not heard him approach and were still waiting for him—no doubt shrewdly guessing that he must pass through the Bealach Garbh either late that night or early next morning.

Thinking it all out Rory began to believe they might have come to the conclusion that he would not now be likely to come till the mouth of the day. In that case they might be a little slack in their watch for a few hours.

He had another look at the risky footing between the stone and the burn. . . . ? With the help of the Creator and a steady head he would try it!

First he fixed his stout *batá-calltuinn* (hazel hand-stick) inside his waist-belt at his back. Then he sprawled himself, breast and belly under, on the stone which sloped slightly away from the burn, and toes gripping the narrow verge as best they could. Inch by inch and without a sound he slowly wriggled along. It was only a matter of a few yards but it seemed a long road and a slow journey! At long last, though, he was safely over to near the north-east corner of the big stone. His feet got firm ground!

Cautiously Rory raised his head and keeked round to the north side. What he saw made him flatten out again in a hurry! There were *three* burly fellows round there, sitting on a heap of bracken in which their feet were buried, comfortably waiting for the Drover to come through the Bealach Garbh!

Fear and anger chased each other through Rory, but it was the anger which waited with him. Then discretion advised him to bottle his anger and make a dash for home. The chances were that they would get such a fright from the suddenness of such a move that he would reach safety before they could gather their wits. But then the anger came again: that these Sons of Satan, could wait there in cold blood to rob a man of his money!—and maybe of his life!

Carefully Rory stood erect to get the right feeling of his legs. Then he reached round for his faithful bata-calltuinn and getting a firm grip of it by its lower end he swung it with such force and precision at the head of the robber nearest to him that the man slumped in the bracken without knowing that anything had happened. With a yell Rory let out a blow at the next fellow, who also went down like a log.

But before Rory could get in a whack at him the third man ran to the shelter of the big stone and from there blazed a pistol-shot at him. Fortunately the gunman's nerve was too shaken for good shooting; but Rory decided that the bata-calltuinn (good as it was!) was no match for a pistol—and before the man behind the stone could get the pistol loaded again the Drover took his legs for it and didn't stop till he reached home!

CHAPTER XXI

Robbed at the Bealach Garbh—Turned Tables

AFTER that experience, continued Dònull, on his way home from the market you may believe that Rory gave the go-by to the Bealach Garbh! But this had meant hours of extra walking and crossing by a ford of a river which at that time of the year was liable to be in spate. Besides, by this time Rory's new route would be well known to those who made it their business to know the roads the drovers took and there was no saying when trouble might meet him on the new road. That was the way Rory was thinking about it that year of the big market as he tramped to the north with his worldly wealth belted round his body. What would be his safest way? How would he look at it if he was the man that was planning to do the robbing? Long he pondered over that, and, by the time he came to the point where he must make up his mind one way or another, he had decided in favour of the Bealach Garbh—and that on the reasoning that any man who had got such a fright at the Bealach Garbh as he had got was not likely to risk that way again! So, to the Bealach Garbh he set his face.

But the other side were not slack. They too must have puzzled over Rory's problem; but they went a step further, for, knowing the cute customer they had to deal with, they had decided that Rory in an effort to outwit them *would* go by the Bealach Garbh in spite of his fright!

There was no sight or sound of living creature as Rory neared the narrowest part of the pass. By this time he

had grown confident in the wisdom of his choice—and perhaps a little proud of his cunning; so perhaps he entered
the dangerous bit with less caution than usual. He had
made only a few steps between the big stone and the
precipice when down behind him with a loud clatter came
a fall of stones to block the opening. Like a hare Rory
sprinted forward to find safety beyond the big stone—but
mo thruaighe! It wasn't far he got! The other end of the
narrow pass was already solidly blocked with a collection
of stones and birch-tree stumps—and there was Rory
Drover trapped like a mad bull in a pen as neatly as you
like! Nor did the masked men moving in the light of
torches fail to pay off with interest the debt they owed to
Rory and his *bata-calltuinn*. It was a man broken in body
and stripped of every penny he had in the world who
ultimately managed to crawl home to the croft.

.   .   .   .

It was autumn once more. Soon the market would be
on him. But *mo creach!* There would be no market for
Rory this year or in years to come, for, though he had
mended in body there was no mending of his fortune. An
empty sporran wouldn't buy cattle—and there were good
beasts round about too!—and the people would *have* to sell
them. . . . ?

Rory had bought their cattle for so many years that the
people felt it would be strange selling them to a *coigreach*
(stranger), besides, though he could drive a hard bargain
they had to admit he had been fair on the whole; indeed
his generosity to the *caillich* (old women) of the Glen was
well known.

In every ceilidh the topic was the same : how to sell the
cattle? Out of much talk a plan evolved : they would sell
to Rory *air chreideas* (on trust) and get paid when he
returned from Falkirk.

A few of the *bodaich* (old men) went down to see Rory
and tell him of the plan. It was a compliment that caused
the Drover to blow his nose and stroke his whiskers in

embarrassment, but while he thanked them he said the risk for everyone was too great. For one thing, he might get robbed again on the way home—and then where would he and all of them be?

But the *bodaich* said it was the wish of the place—they had no other plan and it would just have to be that way. So Rory, with not a pound to bless him, but with the usual jokes and haggling, bought every beast as usual; and his step was light and his head and hopes high as he drove the lot to the market.

But it was a different tale that met him at Falkirk this year! It seems that the Clerk of the Weather had been applying to farmers a dose of that humour with which he treats them from time to time to keep them from getting uppish. A cold late spring and summer was followed by a late wet harvest that rotted their stooks and broke their hearts. Already the turnip crop was yellow in the leaf. Winter keep would be scarce, and of poor quality. There was no heart in the market at all. Rory had to sell the cattle at a lot less than he had contracted to pay for them! He was in a desperate plight! He had some earnest talk with his son, *Ruairidh Beag* (Little Rory) who was now bigger than himself and had for the first time accompanied him to the market. The result of the talk was that Little Rory set off in a hurry by the shortest route for home, leaving his father to follow at a pace more in keeping with his years.

Now the strange thing was that as old Rory drew near to the north he grew cheerier and cheerier. He dropped hints of a great market at Falkirk; last year's prices were nothing to it! Any amount of money going!—and he would slap his sporran and thump his chest, to show how he was bursting with it. He also seemed to be far gone in drink—for a man who was usually discreet that way. The innkeeper at the Clachan hinted that if he wanted to reach home in safety he would be wiser to drink water and keep a guard on his tongue. He should know there might be long-eared people about who would gladly relieve him of the burden of his money. But Rory wouldn't be advised or frightened or sobered: he had made money and he wasn't ashamed of it. He would go home that night—and he would go home by the Bealach Garbh too—and God help any *spuinneadair* that dared interfere with him again! He would show them! Other friends at the Clachan were sore perturbed and offered to escort him through the pass, but Rory indignantly refused the offer. He would go by himself and he would look after himself.

As he neared the Bealach Garbh the black dark of the night was on and it seemed his courage needed support, for he started to sing at the pitch of his voice. He was still singing when he entered between the precipice and the big stone where only a year ago he had been trapped and nearly murdered—Och Ruairidh! Ruairidh! Isn't it the wit that is out when the drink is in? If ever a man went asking for trouble isn't it you?

And trouble came quick enough! As he neared the spot where the stones and the birch had blocked the pass last year there were two big bearded men, each with a pistol pointing straight at the Drover! At the same moment a voice at his back told him there were other two pistols there.

The swaggering Rory soon changed his tune. He begged of them not to hurt a poor man as they had hurt him last year. He would give them all he had if they would let him go in peace.

There was a difference of opinion about that. One— probably one of those he had laid out with the *bata-calltuinn* a few years ago—was for putting an end to him without more ado; but the others were in favour of taking his money and letting him go—and that is how it was decided.

Poor Rory was so scared and nervous that he had diffi- culty in taking off the new money-belt he had bought in Falkirk, but at last he got clear of it, and when handing it over let out such a wail of grief that a startled owl hooted

a challenge. Next moment the four robbers disappeared
and Rory sat on the ground and laughed like a woman in
hysterics. The whole thing had been too much for him.
However, after a short rest he got to his feet and started
off with a steady step.

But instead of keeping the track for home he cut away
up the valley to the left. Up and up he went by the side
of a burn. By break of day he reached a ridge from which
he could get a distant view of Beinn an Uaimh. Here he
lay in the heather and as the light strengthened kept a sharp
eye on the distant mountain face.

Ah ha! At last he saw what he was looking for : four
dots moving up towards the gully made by the waters of
Allt nan Uaimh. Soon the dots disappeared into the gully
and Rory got quite excited. He looked and listened and
looked again, but nothing happened. This wait, waiting
was. . . . Ho ho! That was it! Sounds of shots from
the far gully! Soon from the gully appeared another dot,
this one waving a white sheet. Rory made straight for it,
and little did he look like the seeming drunken braggart of
yesterday! In less than an hour he was entering the gully.
At the cave were about a dozen of the young men from the
Glen. The four robbers were lying on the heather trussed
like cockerels for the pot—and one of them was still wearing the money-belt he had taken from Rory only a few
hours before. Its pouches were filled with the old nails
and washers which Rory had taken from a smiddy dump
at Falkirk. The plan had worked perfectly.

The explanation is quite simple—when you know it!
Little Rory had lately got into the habit of going to see a
lassie living on the far side of Beinn an Uaimh. On one
of these visits he had got a hint from the lassie that
rumours were going about that the robbers who had for
the past few years been causing so much trouble in that
part of the Highlands had their headquarters in this mountain cave. It was also said that the Duke's forester, either
from fear, or because of reward, was hand and glove with

them; so that under his protection they were fairly safe.
Little Rory had plotted in secret with a few of his friends to
make a raid on the cave some day. The difficulty was to
get into the cave because of the narrow entrance and the
fact (so it was rumoured) that one of the gang was always
left to protect it. The young fellows decided to keep their
secret to themselves till they saw a way of overcoming the
difficulties and of giving a pleasant surprise to the old folks.
But when Little Rory saw the disaster that had overtaken
his father at the market, and that the load of debt would
break his heart, he decided to let the old man into the
secret in the hope that between them they could think out
some plan that would put an end to their troubles.

It was old Rory who saw how to get rid of the " watch-
dog" in the cave. When Little Rory reached home he
would keep out of sight for a few days, but to trusted
friends he would tell of the big money the Drover had
made at the market; that he would be coming home loaded
with money, but that for safety he would be taking a friend
or two to see him safely through the Bealach Garbh. The
lads (who knew the truth) saw to it that the story went
well round the district; so that it would be sure to reach
the ears of the robbers—and *they* were not going to lose a
rich haul because of Rory having a companion or two.
They would come in full force and clean out Rory as they
had done the previous year. Rory's boasting and drunken-
ness were just good acting.

The lads took turn at keeping watch on the gully, and
on the afternoon before the night on which Rory would
pass through the Bealach Garbh, they saw four men come
down from the mountain and disappear in the birch woods
below. With the coast clear a gang of them climbed to
the cave and found it unoccupied as they had hoped. They
blocked the narrow entrance with stones so that the robbers
could not easily get in. Then they hid themselves amongst
the rocks nearby and waited. The " owl" that had hooted
joined them in the dead of night with the news that Rory

had been " robbed " and that the robbers might be expected at the cave by daybreak.

And so they did arrive; and they were met by a volley from the blunderbuses that wounded two of them and so surprised them all that they didn't even make a fight of it.

The lads took possession of all the money in the cave—the gatherings of years of robbery—and debated whether they should hand over the lot and the robbers to the law—but came to the conclusion that that would not be the satisfactory way. They would themselves restore the money direct to those from whom it had been stolen.

As for the *spuineadairean,* well (Dònull concluded) it would be as well not to inquire too closely about what the lads did to them! But believe you me, they never worked again at their old trade of thieving!

CHAPTER XXII

A Little about a Lot of Things

ABOUT seventy-five years ago compulsory education was introduced into the Highlands of Scotland. One of the first fruits was an organising by the natives of the north, of a political movement for securing for themselves certain fundamental rights in regard to the occupation of their crofts.

A Borderer or an Aberdonian with quite a good case may make strong political protest and is lucky if the press or a Member of Parliament takes any notice of him. But, come a breath of protest from a northern Gael, even on the flimsiest of foundations, and the papers run to headlines, a Minister of State has the jitters—even the Prime Minister may have a restless night; and of course a Committee or a Commission must be appointed to enquire into the matter!

As a Gael I confess to deriving not a little satisfaction from observing this ability on the part of a few countrymen to cause these flutters in political dovecots. It reminds me of an old neighbour of ours, *Mairi Nighean Alasdair Ruadh,* who had the gift of wisdom if not of book-learning. Mairi used to warn us youngsters against rating ourselves too cheaply in the world. "*Dean luideag dhiot fhein ri càch 's cha'n eile 'n còrr aig càch ri dheanamh,*" she would say, which is to the effect: "If you depreciate your own worth to others, others don't need to "—another way of saying that the world is prone to take you at your own valuation, or that "Here's tae us! wha's like us!" etc., is a sound toast. Doubtless the explanation of the concern of the politician to placate the Highlander is the fact that so many natives of the north are imbued with a strong dash of Mairi's philosophy.

With the protection afforded by the Crofters' Act of 1886 came a comparatively quiet period during which many crofters were busily and happily employed in building on their crofts comfortable slated cottages in substitution of the clay-built thatched hovels which previously existed. In fifteen years thousands of such cottages were built by crofters out of their own resources, augmented by the hard-saved earnings of "away" members of their families.

I know that romantic visitors to the Highlands—and some absentee natives—deplore the passing of the old thatched cottage; but, take it from one who knows, the old thatched cottage made a poor place of abode. If any of those artistic people who "simply love the old romantic cottage with the thatched roof" had to work laboriously for a month in renewing the thatch, and within a week of finishing the job had the mortification of seeing the whole of that thatch scattered down the glen by an October gale —as I have had—I'll bet he would view the thatched cottage from another angle.

For the crofter who had known the bad old pre-Act days there was a quiet joy under the new regime: he and his wife were happy in their new security. But they cherished other ambitions for the family. The family must be educated—educated up to the extreme limit of the financial resources. They must be fitted to "get on in the world." They were; and they did—so successfully that soon they were flourishing in every quarter of the globe except the Highlands. Year by year the number of young people left at home grew smaller and smaller. This simple fact has become a burning topic with a certain class of people who are somewhat hazy in their knowledge of the subject and illogical in their attitude towards it. From such comes a wealth of oratorical and journalistic pronouncements in regard to the populous, prosperous, happy Highlands which existed sometime in a past when cultural attainments and piety were the distinguishing characteristics of the Gael. Reference is made to a " glorious heritage " which, it would appear, present-day Gaels are in danger of forgetting or besmirching. So many people have said this sort of thing so often in recent years that a number of other people have come to believe it. There follows a comparison of the magnificent past with the mundane present, and the terrible conclusion is reached that there exists a Highland " problem " which, if not tackled and solved will prove the primary cause of the decline and fall of the British Empire. For myself, while I would be the last to deny or decry the substantial contribution which Highlanders have made to the building up of that Empire, I can find little or no evidence in support of the belief in those Utopian times in the Highlands. True, there arose in the past from time to time in the Highlands men richly gifted with the spirit of poetry and romance. Than, for instance, Duncan Bàn MacIntyre's poems, there scarce can be anything more sublime in any language. It is also true that in those days of illiteracy in the Highlands every parish or community had its Bard or *Seanachaidh* on whom Nature had bestowed the gift of song or *sgeulachd* (story-telling). But to assume from this that the generality of the people lived in an atmosphere of culture, or that socially or domestically they were " well off " is to assume what is far from the truth. The truth is that in those much-lauded old days most Highlanders lived in an atmosphere of endless strife with their neighbours and squalor and poverty in their homes—just as people in the rural districts of southern Scotland and England did; and in any discussion of the state of the Highlands, a simple survey of the relevant facts is more likely to lead to intelligent understanding than a flirting with fiction and sentiment—however sweet!

Having regard to the worship which the past generation offered to so-called " success " in life, it was not reasonable to expect that the comparatively well-educated young men and women who were the product of Highland schools in the past fifty years should have willingly selected as a career the then generally despised calling of crofting. That the popular view may have been unsoundly based in both its aspects mattered little. Youth is ever sensitive to popular opinion and prone to select such careers within its reach as are most likely to result in that success which the world acclaims. This is what happened in the Highlands. That is why the Highland population has gone down.

But it does not necessarily follow, because there are now only about 290,000 people in the official Highlands compared with a peak of 380,000 in the middle of last century, that the Highlands are, even yet, seriously under-populated. True, there are " empty " areas which ought to have people; but on the other hand there are districts heavily congested—where the natural resources of the district fall far short of maintaining the present population at that level of sufficiency which this generation has a right to expect. This anomaly does suggest the need for a better " spread " of population and a higher economic level. But whether the resulting total should be much greater than the present population is questionable. In any case, so far as the state is concerned, the essence not merely of the Highland problem but of the rural problem generally, is how to keep people on the land, and that resolves itself into a question of the number of people that may expect to earn a sufficiently attractive livelihood there when the natural rural resources have been fully developed. In recent times there has been some talk of founding a Celtic College in the Highlands. It is true that man does not live by bread alone, and some day, as a spontaneous growth from the material prosperity it is hoped Gaeldom will yet enjoy, there may arise in the Highlands, Celtic Colleges and Cultural Centres. But as an initial step towards the solution of the " problem " the artificial nurturing of such institutions is of little value. It is starting at the wrong end: putting the cart before the horse. Any remedial measures not based on the practical bread-and-butter point

of view are bound to prove abortive—and, be it noted,
" butter " in these days must include all those extras which
in the old days would be counted luxuries, but must now be
regarded as common necessities. Gone are the days when a
country wife in the Highlands can be expected to fill the
rôle of family slave that was her mother's. For her no :—

(a) living in a damp, insanitary house;
(b) eternal carrying of water from a distant well;
(c) messing with paraffin lamps;
(d) squelching along " roads " ankle-deep in mud.
(e) isolation from neighbours and shops and vans.
    and buses.

And who can blame her?

In a review of the possibilities for a better spread of
population in the Highlands, large farms and the land
presently under deer forests come inevitably to the mind.
As a result of the war-time policy many millions of money
are being paid annually out of the public purse for the
assistance of farmers, and the industry is meantime in a
superficially flourishing state. But even if by subsidy methods
—so unloved by the non-agricultural classes and distasteful
to the best type of farmers themselves—prices of agricultural commodities can be kept to the present high level, on
large farms there would still remain the problem of labour.
For farm labour is fast becoming not merely a question of
wages. There is something much deeper than that. In the
Highlands at any rate it is becoming more and more the
aspiration of intelligent young people of the farm-servant
class to seek emancipation from what, despite recent betterment in the way of wages, hours and holidays, is a hard
life at best, offering little prospect of independence with
advancing years.

Already on many large farms the problem of securing
an adequate supply of labour, even at rates in excess of the
legal (and ever-rising) minimum standard is becoming
acute. That difficulty will spread and intensify. Unquestionably before long, land on such farms will go out of

cultivation and that problem is not confined to the Highlands. Unquestionably, too (so I believe), the remedy is the "family-farm" type of holding, where in the worst of times there is a livelihood and independence, and in good times something more.

As to deer forests, it is a thousand pities that this subject should be such a "touchy" one. As a rule, in interested circles, the mere suggestion of deer forests as a possible field for extension of existing crofters' grazings or for the settlement of new holders evokes such a storm of partisan protests that, for anyone seeking information, it is all but impossible to arrive at an opinion based on cold fact.

On the one hand there is the ardent but patently biased advocate of Highland reform who extols with fanatical enthusiasm the suitability of deer forests for Land Settlement and vilifies the landlord as a greedy, grasping unpatriotic monster. The landlord or his representative, on the other hand, ridicules the idea of any alternative use for his forest and cherishes an aristocratic and contemptuous antagonism towards his traducer. Both may be decent enough fellows, but each seems woefully incapable of achieving that admittedly difficult but so salutary mental transposition commonly described as putting himself in the other fellow's shoes. Even a brief experience there should prove to each that at least to a certain extent the other is right. For instance, the reformer would realise that the conversion of sheep grazings to deer forests was largely attributable to economic pressure. Estate ledgers would prove to him that deer forests, however profitable to their owners in the past, have long ceased to contribute much in the way of free income, and in many cases have become definite liabilities. In short, he might be constrained to admit that, had he been the Laird, he might have acted all along the line much as his enemy the latter did, and found himself in the same sorry mess that most Highland deer-forest owners now find themselves in, and temper the tone of his patriotic wrath as a "reformer."

In the reformer's shoes the landlord might well catch glimpses of wisdom which perhaps prejudice has hitherto excluded from his sight. He would be compelled to admit that, taking the long view, rents from pastoral tenants are a better and more stable source of net income that rents from deer forests; that especially is this the case when rents are derived from tenants sitting under landholders' tenure. For in such cases the burden of maintenance of buildings and other permanent equipment is not a proprietor's obligation as it is in the case of ordinary agricultural tenancies. Nor should there be the nightmare of sheep-stock valuations; so that, however small his rents may be from tenants under the Landholders' Acts, they are not subject to deductions for maintenance and wages—indeed they are more in the nature of a gilt-edged security. In short, he would doubt the wisdom for himself or his estate of a policy of such extensive and exclusive deer forests. It is interesting to note that the truth of this contention appears to have been appreciated by certain Highland landlords who, when recently compelled to dispose of part of their estates, chose for sale the deer forests, and for retention the areas tenanted by smallholders. An accounting review of the profit and loss from the respective sections over the previous quarter of a century left no doubt as to where the losses occurred, and these proprietors were fortunate in being able to cut their losses by disposing of the forests to wealthy industrialists who were not concerned to derive monetary profits from their purchases.

Let it be clearly understood that no kill-joy spirit lurks at the back of this. Far from that! I know that deerstalking can be one of the grandest of sports and that no country offers better opportunities of following that sport than the Highlands of Scotland whose mountains and highlying corries are the natural habitat of the red deer.

The question at issue is whether the $3\frac{1}{2}$ million acres now almost exclusively reserved for deer are being put to their best economic use, or whether a large part of that area could not be made to contribute towards the solution of the Highland Problem (such as it is) without injury to the community, the landlord or the nation. Emphatically—and without a vestige of partisan bias in the matter—I say that much of that area is not being put to the best economic use and could be so used, not merely without injuring any interests, but with considerable advantage to all concerned.

For one of the tragedies of the *exclusive* deer forest vogue is the deterioration in pasture which it inevitably produces. The best arable field in the Lothians, if left in grass, *uncut* and *undereaten* for thirty years, would so alter in appearance and deteriorate in pasture value as to be scarcely recognisable as Lothian land at all. For thirty, forty, fifty years and more a corresponding process has been going on in the deer forests. Draining and heather-burning have been neglected. As a result of insufficient eating and trampling by sheep and cattle and horses the coarser herbage plants have smothered the finer and more nutritious ones, so that a serious depreciation in the pasture value of these areas has taken place, and deer are forced to wander far in the night to seek the more succulent pasturage on the sheep ground, and even to raid the crops on the arable lands. It must not be forgotten that practically the whole of the lands now in deer forests are fundamentally capable of carrying, and in the old days did actually carry great stocks of sheep and cattle as well as naturally restricted herds of deer.

The history of the use as pasture-land of the areas comprising the present deer forests is interesting and instructive, but can only be glanced at here. Prior to the middle of the eighteenth century there were very few deer forests as we know them. Deer were sufficiently numerous over a large area to afford good sport to the "gentry" of that day, but they shared the grazings with the cattle and sheep belonging to the native peasantry. By the middle of the nineteenth century large flock-masters with the better breeds of sheep from the Borders had largely ousted the deer and native stocks. There followed in the eighties and nineties the ruinous prices for sheep and wool. This threw farm after farm into the hands of the proprietor who, in financial straits over the sheep, and tempted by the high rents then being offered for land as deer forests, cleared a great area of the ground for deer. And from that time the depreciation already referred to has gone steadily on.

It was the reserving of the land *exclusively* for deer that caused the tragedy. But even here one should not so readily place all the blame on the shoulders of the landlord. In this matter the arch-criminal was that selfish peppery type of shooting-tenant to whom the sight of a sheep in a deer forest was as the proverbial red rag to the bull. Up to a point one can sympathise with him. How fervently have I anathematised that "old bitch of a ewe" with her snort that ruined a whole day's stalk! But the truth is the old ewe snorts only because there are so few of her kind on the forest, and because she is so unaccustomed to see a human being that she herself is as wild as a stag. If there were more sheep and cattle on the ground accustomed to the sight of shepherds there would be no snorting ewe. Some of the finest stags ever grassed in Scotland were stalked and shot while grazing along with sheep and cattle.

The irascible type of tenant was all too common in the past, and he is still not extinct. But there is a more tolerant view gaining ground. Gradually it is dawning on owners and tenants of deer forests that there is room for cattle and sheep as well as for deer: that, indeed, the grazing for the latter is improved by the presence of the former; and that at most all that is necessary to ensure undisturbed stalking is a minimum of actual shepherding on the high ground during the stalking-season—a mere matter of weeks. Some of the most progressive landlords have for years put this system into practice on their estates, and in that connection the Departmental Committee who investigated the position in 1919 reported :—

"The evidence we have taken shows that in almost

every case the interference with stalking has been less than was expected and that the complaints received from shooting-tenants have been few. Happily, in investigating this question we were not entirely dependent on the experience of the war. It is a fact too often neglected, that in many of the older forests there has always been a considerable stock both of sheep and cattle."

That passage in the report should be in red type. It points the way to correcting an erroneous view which has been largely responsible for the present deplorable condition of an area equal to a third of the whole of the Highlands.

Many deer forests are now let—when they are let at all—at rents which leave little or no net rent to their owners. Managed on more sensible lines there are reasons for believing that after a few years they would yield triple rents—deer forest, grouse-moor and pastoral—considerably in excess of the present single rent.

But the restoration of deer forest lands to a condition which would allow of its being put to best and fullest use would be a costly process; so costly that probably few landlords could face it. Where that is found to be the case it would seem the responsibility for restoration must rest with the State.*

" But," it will be asked, " even if deer forest land can be renovated, and they and large farms are made available for settlement, and the State were willing to foot the bill, would people go there? And could they make a living of it if they did?"

My answer to that is : "Yes, if they are offered 'hirsel holdings' or 'family farms' including the provision of good access roads and good homes with hot and cold water and electric light and power on equitable terms."

* This was written two years before the advent of the Hill Farming Act of 1947, which is mainly directed towards the rehabilitation of hill grazing lands, and offers 50 per cent. State grants of the cost of schemes designed for that purpose.

For in this respect I believe there is a new light on the horizon. In the past few years a remarkable change in outlook has become evident. The more intelligent of country-bred youths are beginning to realise that any betterment the city or the professions may offer them in the way of cash income can be more than counter-balanced by the disadvantages incidental to city life. Rents, rates, tram-fares, school fees, holidays, doctor's bills, which are moderate or negligible items in the country, make a heavy drain on income in the city; and it requires but a short experience of town housekeeping to appreciate the cash and nutritional value of the potatoes, vegetables, milk, butter, cream, honey, eggs, chickens, etc., which the despised croft provided—and which hitherto were taken for granted!

On the other hand, too, there is an ever-increasing number amongst all classes of the community who have got their eyes opened to the fact that truer wealth and health and happiness may be found even in "humble" life on the land—and a truer standard of social dignity and independence too.

So that, in fact, the time and "atmosphere" are propitious for a drive towards life on the land. But that drive must not come in a stupid and condescending manner from people largely alien in character who regard themselves as socially and intellectually superior to "poor crofters." That attitude is always irritating—until one begins to chuckle at the reflection that the poor and curious specimen of humanity which such menders of Highland ills see in the Highland crofter is not nearly so queer and ridiculous a specimen as the crofter sees in his would-be "mender." Any drive to better the Highlands must come from people with a deep understanding of where real human worth and national wisdom lie. It will cost money : yes; money too on which there can be little in the way of direct cash return. The mending of dilapidations due to a century's neglect of the country's most valuable asset—the people on the land—is bound to cost money : but whatever the cost, it would be money well spent and but a trifle in comparison with our astronomical spending in recent years.

Given two years for surveying and planning, a score of practical men, free from the shackles of bureaucratic control, could produce a scheme with estimates of cost for the rural reconstruction of the Highlands. It might take twenty-five years or more to put it into practical operation, but that is not a long period in which to remedy a decay that has been going on for over a century. . . .

But my sorrow and my shame! What I had in mind was to entertain you with another story of a day after the deer, and if the devil and all didn't get into my pen and set me off writing like a preacher or a politician! As if *I* could mend the troubles of the Highlands! . . .

I would like to say, though, that I am not nearly so pessimistic about the future of the Highlands as many people who know less about them. The talk amongst lairds and gamekeepers at the moment is of a desperate gloom. Never, they say, will the forests or moors or fishings be let again. The war has killed all that : after this no one can have enough money to afford such luxuries!

But (as Neil Munro's inimitable Para Handy would say) " Stop you on you! " I'm thinking it will be queer if the resilience and capacity for crawling out of economic quagmires, that are so marked characteristics of our race, do not once again assert themselves. Given a more enlightened policy of estate management, whether private or nationalistic, which will make fishing and shooting available on reasonable terms to people of all classes and creeds that toil to maintain this complex country of ours, and I'm a Dutchman if there won't be people in plenty financially fit and heart-hungry to resort to the mountains and lochs and streams in search of that health of body and tranquility of mind which sojourn in the Highlands so bountifullly bestows.

Part Two

HIGHLAND MEMORIES

CONTENTS

CHAPTER I

CHAPTER XVI

CHAPTER XVII

CHAPTER XVIII

CHAPTER XIX

CHAPTER I

Lucky Escape

WHEN senility first came creeping up on old Elspeth she used to laugh heartily at her stupid little mistakes; but she began to think the thing was getting beyond a joke when one winter's night she carefully set the hot-water bottle on the door-step, and took to bed with her the milk pitcher carefully rolled in flannel and wondered why she felt so cold.

Well, with that sort of thing in mind, while in process of putting together what is now being irrevocably committed to public exposure, every now and again there would come to me the shattering fear that in trying to write another of my story-books I was merely piling up proof of advancing senility. And as (so it would appear!) I am not yet so far gone as to be quite indifferent, the thought would so effectively scotch all zest for literary achievement as to put the pen idle for days; indeed it might take weeks to recover morale if, during such days of punctured vanity, I found myself putting salt in my tea or, when homeward bound, wondering vaguely why the shops seemed so strangely unfamiliar until I realised my No. 16 car was nearing the Crematorium instead of Morningside Station.

Just to what extent I have managed to conceal evidence of advancing years must be left to readers to decide; but at least I can assure them that in that respect this book is not nearly so bad as the sort of book I was itching to write—and of which indeed I did write several chapters. For I have to admit the sad fact that there is growing within me the foolish ambition to turn preacher.

Looking round on a world of humanity gone stark mad, like Omar I find myself ambitious

> " To grasp this sorry Scheme of Things entire
> And then remould it . . ."

Dash it all! am I not crawling up to the seventy? And in that time isn't any average person bound to have gathered innumerable wrinkles in the art of avoiding trouble? So I wrote what I hoped would be regarded as clever sentences, laughing at the philosophers who had propounded for the guidance of humanity " systems " so profound as to be but vaguely comprehensible to themselves and of no earthly use at all for ordinary people. I listed some of the commoner causes of troubles and from my pharmacopœia of experience prescribed a cure or at least a mitigation for each.

Take matrimony, for instance. In principle one of our best institutions ; but what a gamble as usually approached! And what a mess it can make of lives! I was eloquent on the folly of young folks entering so solemn and intimate a state with no firmer foundation for future accord than that provided by the transient and treacherous promptings of wildly beating hearts. I made a list of the less romantic but more stable dictates of commonsense, so desirable when computing the chances of success in the Matrimonial Stakes.

Then on the folly of taking offence, losing one's temper, quarrelling! Highlanders came in for a special roasting here—the fiery sort of creature who, when called a coward or a cheat or a thief, deems it the first duty of a gentleman to draw dirk or sgian dubh in defence of honour. Honour my foot! Instead of getting red at the neck and snatching at the sgian dubh, why not consider the charge calmly? If as a result of calm and honest reflection he knows the charge to be true, why should he take offence at being told the truth? On the other hand if it is not true, why not express regret that his accuser should be so misinformed—and smile—and suggest a dram together? And so on through a long list of human follies and failings and stupidities. With modest pride I read some of the best bits to the family critics, savouring on my literary palate the sentiment and style. Their verdict was kindly candid : they didn't approve. . . .

Yet when I got over the first disappointment it became rather obvious that not many would want to live in the dreary tedium of my Utopia. So I again fell back on Omar and decided to

> ". . . leave the Wise to wrangle and with me
> The Quarrel of the Universe let be,"

and make another raid on the recesses of memory for a few stories which may, I hope, help to pass an armchair night.

CHAPTER II

A Study in Languages—A Qualified Stalker

How prone most of us are to think that foreigners who neither speak nor understand our language must of necessity be of a lower grade of intelligence than ourselves! Personally, although I know it is absurd, I can never quite overcome that instinctive assumption—and should therefore be not too critical of our English visitor who, on his first contact with the Highlands, is apt to jump to an equally erroneous conclusion in regard to native Gaelic speakers, who either speak English not at all or only slowly and brokenly and with a Gaelic lilt. True, accounts are squared in that each is under the same misapprehension in regard to his superiority over the other; and many a time have I wished that the "superior" visitor to the Highlands knew just what the seeming-stupid Highlander thinks of *him* and his intelligence! As one with some knowledge of both languages and people, and weighing up the matter without bias, I give it as my opinion that, by and large, there is little difference in the standard of natural intellectual endowment between *Gall* and *Gael*; but that if there is any difference the superiority lies with the latter. Certainly there is a gift for natural philosophy and a rock-bottom commonsense quality about most Gaels that sometimes is profound to the point of genius. If only I could adequately reproduce in a book or play what happened soon after the first big war at a hearing before an arbiter in Edinburgh, where the principal witnesses were old crofters who had never previously given evidence in any court of law or arbitration, I would make a fortune! The whole tale is too long to tell here, but I must try to give a sample of some of the high spots.

In that war, as in the next, our food supply was the most vital question. To minimise the danger, drastic powers were given under D.O.R.A. to various Government departments and Ministers. Amongst these was power to authorise the grazing of sheep and cattle on deer-forests and the killing of deer. In the recent war such measures were, in the main, taken for granted and heartily co-operated in by deer-forest owners, but in 1914 so unprecedented an encroachment on the hitherto private and sacrosanct rights of the landowner evoked not a little resentment in certain quarters. But, in accordance with the usual British scrupulous concern for fair play, due regard was had to a right of compensation in respect of any proved loss consequent on the operation of such powers; and it was when an aggrieved deer-forest owner was trying to substantiate before an arbiter in Edinburgh a compensation claim for several thousand pounds that the crofters were brought into the case as witnesses; for it was to them and their neighbours that the right of killing down the deer on this particular forest had been granted.

The case came before an eminent legal gentleman in Edinburgh. It was a full-dress affair of wigs and gowns, with senior and junior Counsel on either side, and might well be thought likely to strike the layman's heart with awe. The Department's solicitor, astutely questing for some advantage which might tend to counteract any inferiority complex which so impressive an occasion might produce in his witnesses, conceived the idea that their evidence should be given in Gaelic and translated by a competent interpreter. With this the witnesses heartily concurred—and this notwithstanding the fact that for two or three years they had conducted a voluminous correspondence with the Department couched in the best of English! They were warned, however, that for the purpose of this hearing they had *no* English.

But as this ruse had not been thought of earlier, and as the case was now due to commence, nothing could be done about having an interpreter there in time for the start. So it was decided that, when the time for evidence-taking came, Department's Counsel would ask permission of the Arbiter to have the crofters' evidence taken in Gaelic. The request was duly submitted, and the Arbiter, obviously somewhat flattered by the rather unusual " tone " which such a proceeding would confer on the case, readily assented. *An duine bochd!* (Poor man!)

Immediately there arose the question of a suitable interpreter. Some of us present who might be otherwise qualified were ruled out as " interested parties," so :

10.30 A.M.—Court adjourned to give opportunity of finding interpreter.

Phoned most likely man in Edinburgh—not at home— gone to Glasgow by morning train.

Phoned two others in succession—not available.

After much phoning got in touch with the man who had gone to Glasgow. He would return early and be available at 2.30 P.M.

11 A.M.—Court resumed.

Report on hunt for interpreter submitted.

Court adjourned till 2.30 P.M.

2.30 P.M.—Court resumed.

The first question seems a simple one, but Eoghan (who understands it perfectly in both languages) must sense a snag, for he asks the interpreter for further elucidation. This is given—generously. Eoghan wants further enlightenment before committing himself to a reply—and more, and still more, so that he and the interpreter have animated exchanges in Gaelic, prolonged for several minutes; and the answer when it does finally come is just " *Tha* " (" Yes ").

The next question necessitates the same cautious approach and produces the same answer. The third requires even more exhaustive study ; but this time Eoghan is able to avoid monotony by giving a firm negative, " *Cha'n eil.*"

4 P.M.—Arbiter beginning to doubt the efficacy of a system of examination and " crossing " which, in an hour and a half of much conversation but monosyllabic replies, does next to nothing towards getting on with the case. Besides, having found amongst his papers a copy of a three year old letter addressed to the Department—and purporting to have been written and signed by Eoghan— his temper is getting frayed at the thought of possible deception. At last he can stand it no longer: he raps his hand on the desk and fixes on Eoghan the stern optic of the law.

" Come, come ! This is just a waste of time. I suspect you have a very good knowledge of the English language? "

He is speaking direct to Eoghan and obviously expects a direct reply. But Eoghan remembers his lesson : he has no English this day. So he turns to the interpreter and asks, " *Ciod e tha e ag ràdh?* " (" What is he saying? ") The interpreter proceeds to enlighten him, but his Honour will have none of it.

" No, no ! We have had enough of this ! Read that " (passing the letter on to Eoghan). " You wrote that letter did you not? "

" *Ciod e tha e ag ràdh?* " Eoghan again asks.

This time the interpreter is allowed to explain; so Eoghan must do something about it. He does. He slowly searches all of his six capacious pockets for his spectacles—which he ultimately finds and adjusts very carefully on his nose. He picks up the letter, has a look at it, but at once lays it down again. The spectacles need wiping. He takes them off, has a prolonged search for his big bandanna, breathes audibly on each lens and polishes it with the hanky. Again the spectacles are carefully mounted for action and again Eoghan picks up the letter.

For one devoid of a knowledge of English he looks at it for quite a long time. Actually he reads every word of it—twice over. Then he lays it down, removes the spectacles, lays them reverentially in their polished tin case—which he deposits in the appropriate pocket—and turns towards the interpreter. There is an expectant hush in Court.

" *Abair ris nach do sgriobh mise am print tha sin!* " (" Tell him that I didn't write that print ! ")—What Eoghan has been reading is only a typed copy of the original letter !

This—after what seemed an hour of waiting—when interpreted to his Honour fairly gets his Honour's goat.

" I'm not asking if you wrote that print," says he quite testily. " I'm asking if that is a copy of a letter—in very good English—which you wrote to the Department? "

But Eoghan is taking no chances on that : the most that can be got from him is that he " didn't write that print."

So there is nothing for it but a search amongst the barrow-load of official files for the original letter. And as that will be a long job and it is now late in the day, at

5 P.M.—Court adjourned till 10.30 A.M. to-morrow.

NEXT DAY. 10.30 A.M.—Same scene, same actors.

Eoghan is given the original letter. He goes through the same elaborate process of cleaning his spectacles, scrutinising the document and finally putting everything in its proper place. Then he cogitates deeply for quite half a minute.

" Did—you—write—that—letter? " asks his Honour

rather balefully; which awkward question is duly translated for the witness's benefit.

Eoghan takes a deep breath—"*Cha'n eil mi ag ràdh nach do sgriobh.*" ("I'm not saying that I didn't.")

HIS HONOUR. I am not interested in what you are *not* saying. What I want to know is: did you or did you not write that letter?

EOGHAN (to interpreter.) "*Ciod e tha e ag ràdh?*"

Again the interpreter translates the question to which his Honour demands an answer. But the most that Eoghan can be bludgeoned into admitting is "*Feudaigh e bhi gu do sgriobh—ach fhuair mi cobhair.*"

INTERPRETER. My Lord, the answer is: "It may be that I did—but I got help."

HIS HONOUR. Oh! Who helped you?

Eoghan duly waits for the translation. He gazes stolidly at the ceiling for quite a while, then searches for and finally finds the big bandanna, buries his face in it, blows a blast like the Misnish fog-horn, returns the hanky to its lair and in most respectful but firm accent:

"*Abair ris (le chead) gur e mo bheachdsa nach eile còir aige air sin fhaighneachd, agus nach fhaod mise freagairt thoirt dha.*" ("Tell him—with respect—that it is my opinion that he has no right to ask that question and that I do not require to answer it.")

A roar of laughter throughout the Court—in which his Honour joins heartily; he frankly admits the correctness of the reply and thoroughly enjoys the joke against himself. Later, on the adjournment for lunch, he compliments Eoghan on his ability as a witness—although admitting his evidence did not further the case much in any direction! Then says he, "It's a grand language the Gaelic! Do you know that as a boy in Argyllshire I used to have quite a smattering of Gaelic—but I'm sorry to say I have forgotten most of it."

" Chist like me weeth the Eengelish ! " affably agreed Eoghan—his only venture in that language throughout the two days.

.   .   .   .

On the evening of the second day of the deer-forest compensation case the Department's solicitor—while jubilant over the success of his ruse so far—was inclined to be apprehensive as to the wisdom of persisting with it: it might tend to irritate and antagonise the Court to his ultimate disadvantage; and so, after much deliberation he finally decided that the remaining two witnesses must know sufficient English to give their evidence in that language on the morrow: from them the " no English " ban was lifted. Nor was their self-possession and skill in the " box " in the slightest degree impaired by this circumstance.

A strong averment in the Claimant's case was that so many deer had been killed, or died of wounds as a result of inexpert shooting, that the stock of beasts on the forest had been seriously depleted. Seumas, as a crofter and ex-deerstalker had been deputed by the Department to pay a special visit of inspection to the forest in question so that he might be in a position to give expert evidence on the point. He is now giving the appropriate evidence, and is somewhat surprised and not a little hurt that Counsel for Claimant appears to doubt his word. On the contrary, the impudent fellow has actually suggested more than once that Seumas is not telling the truth !— which indignity causes Jimmie to turn red at the collar. But, of course, he must conduct himself as a Highland gentleman : must be patient with this ill-bred person ; so he continues to be calm and polite.

But presumably this is an attitude which Counsel

misinterprets as weakness and indecision, for he continues to press in a most ungentlemanly way the suggestion that, on the occasion of his inspection of the forest, witness must have seen many dead deer and very few living ones. At last witness can stand it no longer: this *creutair* must be put in his place!

" I—wass—not—eenterested—in—dead—deer—and— I—deet—not—see—any. I—was—eenterested—in—the— living—and—I saw—plenty—of—*them*."

It is quite impossible to convey in a book the dignity, deliberation and finality with which this pronouncement was made. Clearly, his last word had been said on the matter. And so Counsel must have sensed, for he dropped it like a hot coal so far as Seumas was concerned.

But later, when Farquhar was giving his evidence, Counsel made another attempt to make capital out of the (allegedly) many deer that had got away wounded as a result of inexpert shooting and subsequently died. He presses Farquhar on the point very hard:

" Did you let many of the deer away wounded? "

Evidently a comparative admission is advisable here:

" Och! a few beasts might get off right enough—*but not so many got away from us as will be getting away from the chentlemen that will be shooting at them*."

" It's a very difficult matter, is it not, to shoot the proper beasts in the proper way? "

A long reflective pause, then:

" Yiss—but not if you haff knowledge of the work."

" And do *you* claim to have knowledge of the work? "

Very modestly: " Well, I sink I do."

" Ah! You *think* you do, but you are not *sure*? "

Evidently another case of misinterpreted modesty. Through shaggy brows gleam eyes blue and keen as an eagle's, and:

" Well! *If that iss what you are saying!* Feefty years

aco, when I wass a boy, I went ass a gillie for five years at Glencuoich.

" Then I wass under-stalker for other five years.

" Then I wass stalking for ten years at Guisachan.

" After that I wass more than twenty years head-stalker on two of the best forests in the country.

" And I wass a while wiss Maister Weennans.

" And I stalked for two black Preences from India—and for the Grand Tuke Michael—and for King Edward— and for a lot of other pick pucks—*If that is what you are saying!* "

And that was that!

CHAPTER III

Island Cargoes—Coming of the Motor Car

As is the case of all island communities, the most magnetic spot on any of the inhabited islands of the Hebrides is its pier—a *cheithe* ; that fascinating centre at which the mail-boat discharges and takes on board its intriguing medley of human beings and merchandise. If only the pier master at any one of these places weren't so engrossed with the doing of his job what rare material for a book couldn't he gather in the course of a year from a systematic noting of the ebb and flow of the life of the community !

To an island people their mail-boat is not merely a structure of hull and masts and funnels and holds : " she " is a veritable sentient thing. On a sunny day and a calm sea, or when the breeze but ruffles the surface so as to catch and reflect the light as in a million mirrors, she is a thing of joy and gladness. When wind and tide combine to rouse to rage seas that threaten to destroy her, for a few awful moments in the trough she creaks and groans in agony—to rise again, trembling and shuddering, but grimly ready for the next round. And so—late indeed it may well be—at long last she rounds the headland to give the anxious watchers on the pier the first sight of her masthead light.

" *Sin agad i! tha i direach air nochdadh!* " (" There she is ! she is just showing ! ")

And who and what will she bring this time?

As she glides in towards the pier, and while official concern is directed to the sometimes tricky business of getting her safely tied up, there is a sharp exchange of scrutiny between the passengers and folks ashore. Most people are looking for someone in particular; and glad are the eyes that catch and look into each other, perhaps for the first time in years; for wide are the wanderings of the sons and daughters of these islands, and warm, warm is their welcome home.

But not even sentiment can long stand in the way of satisfying the robust island curiosity to know what the boat has brought.

There is an amazing variety of general merchandise, but certain things catch the eye. Boxes and boxes of baker's bread from Glasgow—stale trash compared with the *aran coirce* and *bonnach eòrna* that their mothers used to make!

There are bags of carded wool and yarn for the making of the world-famous *clò* (Harris Tweed) that will help even *Sasunnaich* to look like ladies and gentlemen!

Large barrels of beer—and wee, wee cases of whisky— *mallachd air an t-àm a th'ann!* (that that should be the way of it!) That a decent *bodach* cannot get as much of his native *deòch* as will cheer his heart in the evening of his day!—that he would have to insult his palate and his stomach with that trash! Can you wonder that in the islands the occasional wreck of a whisky-laden vessel is ascribed to the benevolence of an all-wise Providence?

The motor car tied on the deck is the subject of considerable conjecture. Will it be for the hotel—or doctor—or merchant—or shooting tenant? But next moment in some mysterious way the name of Erchie Chaluim is on every tongue. Well, well! Erchie with a car! What would his grandfather say if he had lived to see this day?

Not a bad-looking second-hand either; if he takes care of that one it will be years before it joins the ever-increasing regiment of derelict cars that bestrew the island's roadsides.

A Dhia! and do you remember yon day not so many

years ago when the big crowd came to see the steamer landing the first motor car that was ever on the island—yon time that the new shooting tenant, not knowing that he was to make history, decided to bring his car with him for the shooting season?

The word went round like wild-fire that a " mortar " was coming by the steamer on a certain day. There was some apprehension about how the horses would look on this innovation, but curiosity overcame fear, for when the great day arrived never was such a gathering of horses and carts and family parties seen on the pier, waiting for the boat that was to bring the " mortar."

As per custom, each horse on arrival was solemnly backed into a place in the pier yard and loused out of the cart. Then—as per custom—the bit was removed, a *taod* (rope) tied round his neck and to a spoke of the wheel, and a sheaf of *arbhar* (corn) placed on the ground for him to munch, while the family packed on to the pier to get the first glimpse of the new arrival.

Soon the steamer hove in sight and as she approached the pier there, sure enough, was the " mortar " tied firmly on deck !

Like so many things in an island community, due consideration had been given to the state of the tide; with the result that when the boat arrived her deck and the pier were practically on a level. Two strong planks were laid from pier to deck, and with considerable shouting and shoving the car was soon on the pier. A blue-coated brass-buttoned gentleman went to the car, opened a " lid " near the front of " her " and did something to the inside. Excitement was intense. The man with the brass buttons inserted a handle in her nose and " whirled " two or three times. Nothing happened ! Sarcastic doubts were expressed about the possibility of the contraption ever doing anything. Brass Buttons again lifted the lid, tickled her inside and again whirled the handle.

"Brrrrrrrrrr——" said the "mortar," and her shaking and trembling like she was alive!

This astounding development caused the crowd on the pier to back so suddenly that two boys near the edge were pushed over into the sea—but quickly scrambled to safety on the under-beams. Soon all eyes and interest were again on the "mortar." The driver, now in his seat, pulled and pushed things, and slowly, very slowly and quietly, without help of horse or man, she began to move forward!

All this had happened in front of a shed which screened that part of the pier from the horses who were happily munching their sheaves round the corner; but when the car went to turn the corner and the driver saw a dense crowd of people still in front of him he suddenly squeezed the rubber bulb, and "Dhoat! Dhoat! Dhoat!" said the "mortar."

Now the horses were accustomed to the ringing of bicycle bells, to the sound of a ship's siren and of the breakers on the rocks; but this was a new one on them entirely! On the instant each horse shot his head high into the air—and broke the *taod* that had tied him to the wheel!

Momentarily mesmerised by the sight of a hideous monster creeping stealthily towards them, the horses could only stare in horror. Then another "Dhoat!" from the car and the spell was broken! With one accord every horse dashed for the gateway. But the gateway was only nine feet wide and nearly fifty maddened horses were striving to get through it at the same moment. Saddles, breechings and bridles—and even collars and hames—were torn off in the mad scramble. As each horse got clear of the mêlée and pelted off up the road at the gallop he held his head high, turned it this way and that as frightened horses do, and trumpeted his mixed fear and contempt of the awful thing that had come to the island.

The owners' whoa! whoas! were futile in that mad stampede. Not a horse stopped until he reached the safety of his stable—and that in some cases was seventeen miles away. Never was such a scattering of harness. Each man did his best to collect his own, but at the end of two years many a bridle and *briogais* was still missing and some were never recovered.

Gléidh mise! And now the beasts on the island will hardly get up from their siesta on the warm sandy road to let your car pass; the cow, whose granny the sight and sound of the first aeroplane drove frantic from the machair, is annoyed if you disturb her cud-chewing bliss by shooing her away to allow a bomber to land!

CHAPTER IV

Harris Show-day Troubles

WE were dead out of luck with the Harris Agricultural Show. It had always been held on the same day of the last week of August. Meteorically its experience had never been too happy, but now, for three years in succession, it seemed that a sinister Weather Clerk had been balefully determined to make clear to the Committee his disapproval of that particular day. His first effort was just bad enough to make show-going unpopular to the extent that there was only about half the usual turnout of people. Next year, as if offended by the Committee's failure to take the hint, he put on a more wrathful turn that left groups of drenched sheep miserably huddled in corners, too dispirited even to chew the cud, while cattle and horses, with tails to the storm, humped their backs and, with a pathetic look in their bright brown eyes, perhaps questioned the sanity of their masters.

At the after-rally in the inn that evening it was generally agreed that there appeared to be a case for considering a change of date; indeed most of the members of the Committee, in informal talks through the ensuing winter, tended to favour the idea. But, when it came to the formal meeting to arrange for the next show, the Committee were badly shaken by Uilleam Thormaid's strongly-voiced prediction that the chances of getting a storm on the same day three years in succession were so remote that their safer course would be to stick to the same old date. And so it was decided. And, to make a painful story short, this year the storm deity really let them have it. He did scurvily, too, in giving them a bonnie morning; so that every person that could walk set off in high glee for the show; the ladies in their lightest

26

and brightest of frocks, and carrying umbrellas or parasols only for that little extra bit of dash so favoured by the feminine mentality. Having thus lured his victims to the stake our sadistic despot proceeded to do his dirty work with a malevolence which soon achieved the complete ruination of a big percentage of all frocks, parasols and umbrellas on the island.

The Agricultural College marquee with its so beautifully arranged display was wrenched from its moorings to come down a sopping, flapping canvas on our heads. Literally a blow-out as well as wash-out of a day, and the reputation of Uilleam Thormaid as a wise man slumped badly.

Next year the decision was prompt and unanimous: that fiend of a week was given the go-by. The Show was fixed for the first week in September.

With a perversity characteristic of Hebridean weather the old Show date turned out to be a beauty of a day: a day of sunshine and singing larks and quiet blue seas. Well, well! However, the portents were good. It was firmly believed that genial conditions would continue for perhaps a fortnight. Certainly it couldn't break by next Wednesday, the new date for the Show.

On the Friday prior to this Wednesday the usual crowd was waiting on Lochmaddy pier for the arrival of the S.S. *Lapwing,* that in those days left Portree every Monday, Wednesday and Friday morning for Harris—Lochmaddy —Dunvegan—Uig, and did the reverse run on Tuesdays, Thursdays and Saturdays. This Friday afternoon we saw her approaching from well out the Minch. The sea was like glass. Soon the *Lapwing* disappeared from our view while passing behind one of the Maddy Rocks—the " dogs " or Maddies which stand sentinel on the loch and give it its name. In a few minutes she would appear again, passing the Maddy. Soon we began to wonder why it was she wasn't yet showing. What on earth was delaying her? She should have shown minutes ago! Ah! Here she comes at last! But excitement and speculation ran high as we saw an obviously crippled *Lapwing* crawling crab-wise towards the pier.

We could see that her bow was bashed in. Her engines didn't have their usual rhythmic beat. The captain stood sphinx-faced on the bridge. Donald MacAskill was wiping his bleeding face with his hanky. It was from Donald we got the first inkling of explanation.

"Talk about a slip between the cup and the lip!" said he with a grin that cracked his face and started the bleeding again. "I was down in the saloon having a last *deoch an doruis* with Erchie. 'Well, well, *slaint*!' said Erchie to me. '*Slaìnte mhòr*, Erchie' said myself, and me lifting it. But never a taste did I get! I had just got the length of putting the glass to my nose for a sniff when *bang* she went! and the next thing I knew was the tumbler smashing between my face and the mirror, and the stuff in my eyes and running down the outside of my neck. *A Dhia!*"

The story as we gathered it on the pier was to the following effect: The man at the wheel on the *Lapwing* in those days was so stanced that it was impossible for him to get a clear view forward, in consequence of which circumstance he was entirely dependent on the officer on the bridge for steering orders. The previous night the mate of the *Lapwing* had been superintending the loading of cargo and working hard till the early hours of the morning and was consequently so tired that he was momentarily overcome by sleep on the bridge that warm and drowsy afternoon. Normally the ship passed quite close to the Maddy. She was being steered on her usual course. Had the helmsman been in a position to see where the ship was going, he would of course have given

the wheel that shade of a turn required on this occasion
to counteract the effect of a slight tide drift. As it was,
and with no instruction coming from the bridge, instead
of just clearing the Maddy, at a speed of some eleven
knots the ship hit the rock square on. No wonder Donald's
drink went astray !

.   .   .   .

It had been our intention to go from Lochmaddy to
Harris by the *Lapwing* the following Tuesday so as to
get our demonstration tent and agricultural exhibits all
fixed up and ready for the opening of the Show on the
Wednesday forenoon. In her crippled state the mail-boat
was of course unfit to proceed on her rounds; but that
the mishap to her should involve us in any trouble over
the ill-fated Harris Show never crossed our minds: we
were confident that another boat would be sent to take
up the run without delay. So we got all our stuff down
to the pier to be ready for the relief boat when she came.
But Saturday came and went, and no word of another
boat. Sunday—Monday, still no word ! We began to
get uneasy. We would have to get to Harris by hook or
by crook not later than Tuesday evening. Frantic inquiries
at the pier and post-office yielded no ray of hope of a
relief boat coming in time. Then it was I did one of
the most foolish things I have done in my life; and this is
how it happened.

Willie Urquhart, the local Excise Officer, was my
greatest friend on the island. Although a most efficient
Officer of His Majesty's Customs and Excise his special
love was reserved for the sea. What he didn't know about
boats, big and little, and of every make, wasn't worth
knowing. And, as is the way with such experts, he rode
his hobby enthusiastically. His 12-foot rowing boat—it

also carried a sail—was the smartest thing of its kind.
At this time he happened to be courting the lassie who
ultimately became his wife, and some of us used to annoy
him by arguing in his hearing whether it was the boat
or the lassie that held first place in his affections. Actually
he was a first-rate boatman and used to do things with
his little craft that made ordinary land-lubbers' hair
stand on end. Now, a delightful characteristic of the
man with a special love of that nature, be it for horse or
dog or boat, is his abounding confidence in the object
of his affection and in what he can do with it. In an
access of such faith and affection my friend had on more
than one occasion asserted that, in reasonably fair weather,
he would think nothing of sailing his boat from Lochmaddy
to Rodil in Harris. As this meant a good twelve miles
by sea and included the crossing of the treacherous
Sound of Harris—known locally as *Caol an Fhuaim* in
reference to its ever-turbulent waters, due to the meeting
of opposing tides—I had ventured to doubt the practica-
bility of such an achievement. But of course that merely
confirmed him in his faith: that *his* boat couldn't do
a thing like that! He would prove it to me some
day! It was with this background and the urgent
need for getting to the Harris Show that, on the
lovely morning of Tuesday, I did that foolish wicked
thing.

" Man, Willie," I opened, " there's not a sign of a
relief boat yet, and I'm fair stuck for the Harris Show—
and it's going to be a grand day ! "

As I had suspected, Willie was far too good a seaman
not to appreciate the risks of trying to cross to Harris
in so small a boat even on a good day, and if he suspected
what I had in mind (as I am pretty sure he did !) the
offer which I was angling for didn't come : he merely
expressed sympathy with hard luck.

" If only that boat of yours was a bit bigger do you know I believe we could make Rodil of it on a day like this," I goaded.

" My boat is big enough as she is," he bridled, " but I'm to be far too busy here to-day."

" Just that ! " said I most unkindly. " That's what I always thought ! "

" What is it you always thought? " said he challengingly. " Do you think I'm afraid to go? "

" No, no ! " says I; " but you're not going ! you're too busy ! " Even yet I blush at the unfairness of the form of attack.

" Well," quietly retorted my gallant friend and boat lover, " if that's the way of it, I'll go; and we will start from the old pier in two hours from now."

But then it was my courage that failed as I thought of the load we would have on that little craft and of *Caol an Fhuaim*. In addition to a litter of smaller items there were boxes and hampers containing bottled samples of fertilisers and feeding meals; there was a large barrel churn, a wide-legged butter-worker and a cream-separator, as well as a large marquee-tent with poles and furnishing all complete. Then between crew and passengers we were five: Miss Bannatyne, the dairy and poultry expert, John Rose and myself as passengers, and Willie and wee Ewen the stable-boy as skipper and crew respectively. By the time we had piled everything on to the boat it was all too obvious there wasn't going to be much freeboard when passengers and crew got in. Meantime the news that we were setting off for Rodil in the exciseman's wee boat caused consternation in the village. The venture was universally condemned as hare-brained—suicidal ! One friend after another implored us to give it up. In an effort to stop us the hotel lady refused to supply us with sandwiches and beer. The police inspector quite seriously considered whether he should not place us under protective arrest.

Rose entered into the plan in zestful spirit. Miss Bannatyne showed of danger an utter disregard, born of ignorance of it, and of a simple faith in the skill of the superior sex. Personally, but for consideration of loss of face I would gladly have backed out of the whole business; but in any case, even if I had the courage to advise in accordance with the dictates of my now faint heart, such a course would but incur the contempt of the skipper, who was now as one inspired to high adventure. Thus caught in the grip of circumstance, the hotel lady relented and tearfully gave us a bottle of whisky and a generous supply of beer and sandwiches; and off we set at one o'clock of the afternoon.

.   .   .   .

We had already carefully thought out the course and distances and had a neatly prepared time-table. From the old pier to a little beyond the Maddy Rock is a good two miles in an easterly direction. There was hardly a breath of wind, but what little there was came straight from the direction of the Maddy towards the pier. That meant we could not hoist sail till we got clear of the Loch outside the Maddy. We had allowed an hour for rowing out to that point. Then we could hoist sail and get the help of the gentle easterly breeze to waft us along on the straight north-easterly course that would take us to Rodil some ten miles off. We even dared to hope that out in the Minch the breeze might be enough to be of real help, in which case only the helmsman need keep awake; the rest of us could sleep in the sun till we arrived in Rodil about five o'clock. Failing such luck the four men would take spells of rowing in pairs, and at very latest we would be there by six.

Meantime, with Rose and Ewen at the oars, in dead calm we rowed out the narrow channel below the doctor's house and, after clearing the various islets and *sgeirean*, kept her heading straight for midway between the Maddy and Weaver's Point that towers at the north side entrance to the loch; from there it would be literally plain sailing.

But—as so often happens!—when we got clear of the small islands and out into the open loch we soon found that the water which had seemed so calm and still from the shore wasn't so calm and still: in fact there was quite a jabble; also, there was a quite perceptible breeze. But of course this latter was what we had been hoping for, so in short spells each pair pulled lustily at the oars to get at the earliest moment to the point where we could lie back and leave it to the breeze.

Just then a seemingly innocent wavelet broke on our bow and treated us to a surprisingly generous shower-bath. We moderated speed to lessen the risk of repetition, but despite every precaution every now and again we had another substantial splash. The churn had to be shifted—a delicate operation!—to let us get with the baler at the now considerable water in the bottom of the boat. Under such handicaps it took us nearer two hours than one to reach the longed-for point where we could up-sail; and then—would you believe it?—when, wet and weary, we did at last arrive at that point, there was the wind blowing, not from the east but from the nor'-nor'-east!—straight in our teeth from Rodil!

It was a bitter blow. Commonsense urged the wisdom of making back for Lochmaddy. Stubborn foolish pride prevented everybody from voicing it. Then after a few thought-packed moments:

"Not a hope of getting to Rodil to-night," firmly announced the skipper, "but the wind is going more to the north, and by keeping close inshore we should have a little shelter and will try to make Hermetray of it for the night. If the wind goes down we may still get to Rodil in the morning in time for the Show."

Hermetray is one of the larger of the many small uninhabited islands to the south of the Sound of Harris. It was still a long three miles from where we were. The hoped-for shelter on the way to it was from the towering black rocks that form the coast northwards of the Weaver's Point. With an easterly breeze the back-surge from this bastion can be highly dangerous to small craft. In a gale the breakers there are stupendous. Our hope was that the wind would not go round to the east; and in that flimsily-founded hope we started pulling slowly and grimly for Hermetray.

Even now, as I write, the recollection of that desperately slow and dreary pull in a heavily laden cockle-shell below yon fearsome rocky ramparts makes me shudder. The shelter fell far short of what we had hoped: there was indeed a dangerous back-wash from the base of the cliffs, and but for the exciseman's superb handling of the little craft this story would certainly never have been written—by me or anybody else. If (as it happened) Willie Urquhart never took us from Lochmaddy to Rodil in his boat, in tribute to his memory and skill I am bound to record that on that awful afternoon he displayed twice as much of seamanship as would be required to do so on a moderately fine day.

The wind had increased ominously and I have a shrewd suspicion that for a while the amount of courage amongst us—always excepting the trusting lady and the intrepid skipper—wouldn't have amounted to as much as a half-pint. For my own part I know I was scared stiff. Yet I soon found that the quality of courage can be as infectious as that of fear: that courage is largely the fruit of faith in something or someone—including oneself. In this case, after our skipper had again and again saved us from being engulfed, it seemed that the seed of faith in him and his seamanship was planted in our minds; and as it grew and flourished, fear took a back seat and courage came to the front. Thus guided and encouraged, at long, long last we got to safety in the lee of Hermetray. Soon we would be ashore on that desolate island and would put into effect our plans for passing what was bound to be a rather uncomfortable night in the best open-air shelter we could find. Half the sandwiches were already well and truly eaten and only strict self-discipline had saved the other half. There was most of the bottle of whisky and half a dozen of beer. But if the storm continued and increased (as now seemed all too likely) it might be long enough before we got off the island. However, we were safe! and we would manage to subsist somehow for a few days.

. . . .

In the main we were intent on looking for the best spot to make a landing on Hermetray, and it was more by good luck than presence of mind that some of us didn't fall overboard when Eoghan Beag yelled excitedly in Gaelic. " Look at this, boys! A vessel making for Lochmaddy! "

And sure enough there she was, a sturdy if rather rusty-looking craft, heading straight in for the loch. The possibility of relief came on us so suddenly that for a few moments we were dumbfounded. But soon the wits got going again. In half a minute we were in complete agreement: this must be the ship sent to take up the *Lapwing's* run. She would pick up the mails and stranded passengers, and be out and passing us again in less than an hour on her way to Rodil! We would pull back in the direction of Weaver's Point to be in a position to intercept her when she came out, get the Show party and paraphernalia hauled on board to be landed at Rodil, and leave Willie and Ewen to row themselves back in comparative safety to Lochmaddy. As simple as that! What a relief! How incredibly lucky!

So great was our delight at escaping the misery of perhaps three hungry days and nights on the island, we did not mind rowing back over the course we had so strenuously covered in the past two hours. Besides, it was much easier going with the wind, even if hoisting sail was out of the question. Soon we were half-way back to Weaver's Point and hoping every moment to have our surmise proved right by a reappearance of the relief ship. Nor had we long to wait for that!

"Pull like blazes, boys, to get right in her course and we will keep position there," came the order from the skipper. We obeyed so effectively that soon the ship was bearing straight down on us, and we were being yelled at in broadest Buchan by an angry man demanding to know what sort of bloody fools we thought we were, and adding some picturesque but quite unprintable opinions of his own on the subject. Also, to avoid running us down, the engines had been practically stopped.

"We want you to take us to Rodil," I yelled down wind.

"Rodil?" he bawled back. "Where's that?"

This came as a shock; but of course he could only be bluffing; so I countered, "Your first port of call in the south of Harris."

"Never there in my life, and am not going there now. I came to Lochmaddy to pick up a stranded shooting party and am to land them at Uig in Skye. And get out of there!" came angrily from the captain, who had now come to conduct the conversation.

This, coming from so authoritative a source, rather

punctured us. There was only one line left to us now, and we took it. We spoke portentously to the captain. We pleaded urgent business of State. The Secretary for Scotland would be a disappointed man if his highly placed officials should be unable to meet him at the Harris Agricultural Show because of the refusal of the captain of the *Moray View* to render them a courtesy that would cause a delay of less than an hour—and for which they were prepared to pay a reasonable fee. (May we be forgiven! The Secretary for Scotland wasn't going to the Harris Show that year, and we knew it. But, anyway, this turned out to be an occasion on which that distinguished Servant of the Crown proved really useful.)

After a brief consultation with his mate the captain protested, " But I don't know the course to Rodil, or the way in."

" Mr Rose," I bawled, " knows this coast from end to end and will take you safely there." As a matter of fact John knew the coast sufficiently well to do that on a clear day, even if he might not have passed muster with the Board of Trade.

Further consultation, then, " How much will you give? "

" How much do you want? "

" Five pounds."

" Right-o ! " yelled everyone in our boat in chorus.

Then the *Moray View* was manœuvred so as to allow us to get in on her sheltered side. Not till we started the job of transferring the boxes and ourselves to the ship did we fully realise its difficulties. One moment the wee boat would be away down near the keel of the ship and the next up so high that we were looking down at her deck. That half of our stuff—and of ourselves— didn't find a watery grave was a sort of miracle that must be largely attributed to the skill and strength of the men on the trawler, who were experts at snatching a box or a body at the right moment and holding on to haul it safely aboard.

In a surprisingly short time the desired amount of transfer was complete. Willie and Ewen backed out and headed their boat straight for the shelter that would be between the Weaver's Point and Lochmaddy pier. I passed over a cheque for five pounds, for which I got a duly stamped receipt in the name of David Main of the *Moray View*. Rose was put in charge of the ship and against a rousing nor'-easter directed her course to Rodil Bay, where we were safely transferred to the ferry boat and finally landed at the slip.

As we refreshed and warmed ourselves at the hospitable Rodil hotel that evening I'm not saying but there might have been a bit of being rather well pleased with ourselves. After all, you know—well, it did take a bit of doing!

Virtuously we retired at ten to be ready for the early start in the morning—and the Show.

.   .   .   .

Somewhere in the small hours we were wakened by the rattling of windows and various other indications of an uncommonly rough night. Nor was there another wink of sleep. With morning we got up, to realise that we were experiencing one of the great storms of the Hebrides. A howling, shrieking wind from the east that drove the waters of the Minch to break against the rocks and toss their spray two hundred feet higher than the headlands. A storm that continued all day and is still spoken of with awe. . . .

And there was *no* Show in Harris that year after all!

CHAPTER V

Orkney—A Rude Awakening

HAVING regard to its natural disadvantages of latitude, climate and severance from the mainland, it might be supposed that Orkney would be one of the most backward farming counties in Scotland; in fact, it is perhaps the most progressive and successful farming county in the whole of Britain. A stranger motoring there for the first time, on seeing a very fine lot of cattle in a roadside field, might well conclude that this must be a lot collected for competition at an agricultural show. But as he proceeds on his journey he becomes puzzled; for in the next field there is a similar lot of cattle—and in the next and the next! Gradually the truth dawns on him: they cannot *all* be going to a show! They are not: they are just Orkney's ordinary cattle.

Then he would notice that the whole countryside is peppered with poultry houses. Fifty years ago Orkney was at least as backward as its neighbours in this branch of farming. The first stimulus came from an Aberdonian who, with characteristic foresight, saw a fortune in Orkney's cheap eggs. This pioneer inaugurated systematic egg-collecting, first on the " mainland " and later throughout the islands. The eggs were promptly tested, graded and despatched to the markets at Leith and Aberdeen. Soon the reputation of Orkney eggs (hitherto rather unenviable) improved. They commanded a better price—which enabled the Aberdonian to pay a higher price to the producers, who were thus stimulated to greater and still greater production efforts. The number of poultry rapidly increased. Now a croft of no more than five acres may have on it up to a thousand hens; and not any old hens, but every bird well bred

39

and carefully selected from healthy heavy-laying strains.
Between the two big wars the annual value of Orkney's
eggs was estimated at nearly £200,000. Now it has
topped the half-million mark and is still rising.

In this matter of the general high standard of farming
it may or may not be a significant fact that nearly
two-thirds of the 3,250 agricultural holdings in Orkney
are owned by their occupiers. How this came about is
rather interesting. Soon after the termination of the
1914-18 war the Zetland family, to whom the greater
part of Orkney belonged, decided to sell out. The first
offer to sell in large lots did not attract a satisfactory
response. The next move was to offer each holding to
the sitting tenant at a reasonable price. This proved
highly popular. Orcadians had prospered exceedingly
during the war and were flush of cash. The great
majority of them bought their holdings—and so became
landlords! And a political cynic may find amusement
in the reflection that, not many years after, for the first
time in history, a hitherto stubbornly Liberal Orkney
returned the Conservative candidate as their member
of parliament!

Before the coming of the air service—that is, up till
about fifteen years ago—the only way of getting to or
from Orkney was by sea, and the shorter crossing was
between Scrabster and Scapa. I read in the papers the
other day that a new boat is being built to take the place
of the *St. Ola*, which for over fifty years has been on that
run. It is easy to imagine a vessel providing more
luxurious accommodation than the old *Ola*, but it is
mighty difficult to believe that anything tougher and
safer than that little craft can be provided.

She wasn't by any means a new boat when I first
crossed in her in 1902. The fact that she has never had
any serious mishap in all these years and is still going

strong, despite the marine hazards of two world wars and the turbulent tides and screaming storms of the Pentland Firth, is a remarkable tribute to those responsible for her and her passengers' safety. That first time I crossed was also the first time I had ever put to sea in a boat. I had heard so much about the Pentland Firth that I was prepared for an unpleasant experience. However, despite some considerable heaving and dipping at the bows (which in my ignorance I accepted as evidence of a rough crossing), neither on the outward nor homeward voyage did I feel the slightest sensation of sickness. As others of the family who had previously visited Orkney had returned with tales of the humiliating toll of the Firth, I was inclined to brag a bit and explain that sea-sickness was largely a result of apprehension. In fact, no one need be sea-sick who thought the right thoughts about the thing. Look at me! The suggestion that I must have had a good crossing was refuted by a reference to the heaving bows, and I was eager to show proof of my theory next time I crossed when, I hoped, it might be really *very* stormy. Well, next October I was Orkney-bound again. When the train arrived at Georgemas Junction (where normally passengers for Orkney take the branch line to Thurso and thence bus for the boat at Scrabster) there was the platform porter bawling: " Passengers for the *Ola* carry on to Wick."

When that happens it means that the weather is so wild that the *Ola* can't make Scrabster and has to run to Wick instead. Good! It was to be a really rough crossing. I would have a chance of proving my theory!

In less than an hour we were in Wick, where we found the few people in the streets chasing hats and dodging slates and chimney-cans that rioted through the town. With difficulty we got to the quay where the *Ola* was berthed.

At that time she was commanded by Captain Robertson, a spare, white-whiskered, keen-eyed man with a local reputation as an intrepid seaman whose place it would be hard, if not impossible, to fill. But when the time for that came the owners were fortunate in that they had ready to hand one who in every respect was soon to prove a worthy successor—the late much loved and lamented Captain Swanson, who was then a young fair-haired, blue-eyed Scandinavian whose great seamanship was matched by his unfailing courtesy and his gift for friendship.

This day at Wick, no doubt after much anxious reckoning of risks, old Captain Robertson finally decided to sail. Of sixteen intending passengers, nine decided not to go. Only seven—four never-say-die " commercials," one elderly woman going home to Orkney, one very portly gent going north for some rough shooting and my indomitable self—were prepared to risk it. In a matter of minutes the ropes were let go and we were under way.

The lady passenger proved an immediate casualty; as soon as she came on board she turned a pale green colour of countenance and crept to oblivion down below. The corpulent sporting gentleman and two of the commercials also quickly disappeared. The other two and myself manfully paced what small strip of deck there is and inhaled the stimulating salt sea breeze.

Going up the Caithness coast we were in comparative shelter, although, after my previous experience, this seemed to me a very stormy day indeed. But there was that grand feeling of physical well-being and the subtle joy that comes from demonstrating a theory. Then all of a sudden one of my companions appeared to lose interest in our conversation, gurgled a throaty " 'scuse me! " and dived for a companion-way.

" What's wrong? " I asked.

" Poor Davie ! He's signed off ! " the remaining com-
mercial explained.

" Dear me ! Very strange ! " said I.

" Oh well, of course, it's not too good even here," my
companion expounded, " but believe me it's a mill pond
to what it will be when we round Duncansby Head and
get into the Firth ! " Then he added, " And as that
will be in the next few minutes I'm going while the going
is good." So there I was, the proud sole survivor on
deck ! Just then the mate came along and suggested I
should go below as soon it might be " a bit dirty."

" Oh, thanks " I said, " but that is what I want. This
is grand ! "—as the bows rose higher and plunged lower
than before. The ship also began doing other queer
delightful things ; squirming side-ways like a crab ;
heeling over this way and that, plunging and bucking
violently. While I was enjoying all this, and mid-way
in a deep inspiration of ozone, there came over the side
with startling suddenness a monstrous mass of solid sea
that just didn't sweep me overboard. But it did lay me
prostrate against the rails and drenched me to the skin—
and it wasn't warm ! I had also, involuntarily, swallowed
a salty pint. With more of hurt pride than apprehension
I clutched at the rails and pulled myself to my feet.

" Get down below. We don't want you to get washed
overboard," commanded the mate.

It was only when I started to descend the steps to the
saloon that there came to me the first premonition of the
possibility of the theory breaking down. Nor was I left
long in doubt; in seconds there was within me a complete
transition from the jolly outlook to hitherto uncharted
depths of physical and mental misery as the first moiety
of tollage cascaded down the stair and a violent lurch of
the ship pitched me after it.

Sitting at the bottom of the steps in what had so

recently formed part of my personal content, I made desperate efforts to anticipate the direction of the next lurch so that I might reach in safety a vacant part of the cushioned bench which surrounded the saloon. But always I guessed wrong: the next move of the ship was quite unpredictable and my every attempt at reaching the desired spot violently frustrated.

My objective was the vacant space between where one of the commercials and the sporting gentleman lay stretched and strapped to the bench. Fatty, on the near side of the vacancy, lay on the broad of his back, and sound asleep. By now I had arrived at the fireplace in the middle of the saloon and was grimly hugging the stove-pipe, waiting the chance of one last dive to where I longed to lie. Just for a moment the ship steadied, and I sprang for it! But alas! who can foretell the puckish ploys of a plunging ship? Anyway, just as I jumped, the *Ola* did something which lifted me clean off my feet; instead of plunking down where I meant to, my stern, with all my considerable weight on top of it, came plunk down on the highest round of Fatty's tummy! One can hardly conceive of a ruder awakening, and certainly his yell did justice to the occasion. In his wild physical reaction, too, the strap which bound him to the bench broke, and the next heave of the ship had us both sprawling and slithering helplessly over the floor of the saloon.

But hold! enough of a pitiful tale and an exploded theory. In forty-six years I have crossed the Pentland Firth in a boat one hundred and twenty times; occasionally—very occasionally—in comparative calm and comfort. But, weather fierce or fine, it's a grand country to visit, and the courtesy and friendliness of officers and men of the *Ola* unfailing.

CHAPTER VI

Locked Out—Fire Brigade—Phantom Funeral—William
Wallace from Australia

FROM infancy I was brought up in an atmosphere of
hot hostility to, and contempt for, landed estate factors.
Such we regarded as the natural enemies of crofters;
much more so than the lairds! Tales of their tyranny
and turpitude were in prime favour at the ceilidh, and
many were the stories of that kind that I listened to in
the long winter evenings as we sat in semi-circle round
the blazing peat.

That there was solid foundation for some of these tales
was undoubtedly true. It appears that, until towards
the end of the nineteenth century, many Highland lairds
and factors alike—just as in the case of manufacturers
and their factory hands—failed to grasp the vital fact
that their own and their tenants' interests were identical:
that a régime of rack-renting and harsh treatment—
which discouraged improvement of land and buildings
and engendered hatred—must in the long run inevitably
react detrimentally on the laird himself as well as on
his crofter tenant. Doubtless, even in these bad old days,
there would be a proportion of decent lairds and factors
who were far-seeing and humane in their dealings with
their smaller tenants, but he would be an unpopular
member of the ceilidh circle that made mention of such!
Reared in that creed it can be readily believed that
when my official duties first brought me in direct and
frequent contact with estate factors I was prepared to see
an ogre in every one.

Here and there, indeed, I did come across the genuine
monster, but after many years I am happy publicly to
avow that of the scores of estate factors I have had dealings
with—and not infrequently hotly contested dealings—the

45

term " gentleman " would apply to the great majority; the ogre is the exception. And I am also happy to think that in most cases (while the ceilidh circle may be reluctant to abandon their century-old right—and duty—of anathematising the arch enemy !) crofters now know in their inner hearts that their factor is quite a decent, kindly man, and that in any ceilidh censure of him they are merely chanting the refrain of an old song that has lost its sting and meaning.

Personally, I have been privileged to enjoy the hospitality and friendship of crofter and factor alike in every part of the Highlands and Islands, and have not hesitated to take full advantage of that circumstance to promote their mutual interests. With that in view I usually make a point of calling to pay my respects at the local factor's house or office. One day in Skye, rather late in the evening, I went over to the factor's house for a chat and to get the low-down on Skye affairs generally—in regard to which, for one who seldom goes far from Portree, he is amazingly well-informed.

As was not unusual on such occasions, " the time flew by with tentless heed " and we were surprised to see the clock creeping to 1 A.M. I had said nothing at the hotel about the possibility of being late; it would be awkward if in ignorance of my absence they had locked up and gone to bed. The assistant factor, who was with us and lodged down in the village, hurried off with me. It was bright moonlight without a breath of wind. Not a creature—bar a prowling cat—did we see as we hurried to the hotel—to find its massive door well and truly locked ! With guilty conscience I pulled the bell. It clanged like a fire alarm. Goodness gracious ! that would waken everyone in the house ! The assistant factor stood by and we waited for deserved reproach. But minutes passed and nobody came. The assistant factor suggested I should go with him to his digs and sleep on a sofa. That was very kind—but dash it all surely that bell should waken someone! I gave it another tug—which caused it to set up a frightful clangour sufficient to waken all but the dead. Another shrinking wait. Not a sound of anybody moving.

We went to have a look at the windows. Every one on the ground floor was securely shut. There was one on the first floor slightly open. That was the window of a private sitting-room which was converted into a bedroom only occasionally under pressure of demand. The hotel was now fairly full, but this private sitting-room had not been commandeered; at least it had not been earlier that evening as I happened to know.

If only I could reach that window our problem was solved. But it was twelve feet up, and all attempts at scaling the wall proved futile. Then the assistant factor remembered about the Fire Brigade ladder. This ladder was kept in a long shed up near The Knock. In the gable of the shed there was a hole through which, in case of emergency, it could be pulled out for action.

So off we set to investigate on the spot. There was the shed right enough, but there was a rank growth of nettles obscuring the hole. These we trampled down sufficiently to allow of one getting a grip of the butt end of the ladder to pull it out. Not a move! Presumably there had been no call on its service since it and the shed had been put there some twenty years earlier. Only one pair of hands could get a proper grip of the ladder, so for our next effort the assistant factor took that grip and I gripped him round the waist.

One—two—heave! . . . and the ladder came away so suddenly that we were both laid flat among the nettles . . . nor were we long in getting to our feet! Then more cautiously we proceeded to extract it through the hole, my companion standing close to the shed and I at the outer end going farther and farther away with every pull, until we began to wonder how that shed could possibly contain so long a thing.

We had soon noticed that what we were extracting was really a sort of Siamese Twins arrangement of two ladders firmly lashed together. At long last the extraction was complete: the Twins were lying among the nettles. We untied the lashing to free them and then—the assistant factor near the front end and I at the rear—with ladder hoisted on shoulders we marched in step towards the hotel.

On arrival below the open window it was soon all too evident that our ladder was much too long for our modest purpose. Set at a safe angle for climbing, it reached up to beyond the second-floor windows and at that slope did not come within six feet of the wall passing the window we wanted to get to.

On the other hand, when we set the top of the ladder against the sill of our window, the bottom of it was far away out in the roadway and the slope so flat that it seemed very doubtful if it would carry my rather substantial weight. But there was no alternative : we must test it. Cautiously I began to go forward step by step. When I had got to nearly half the length of the ladder, but still a long way from the window, there was an ominous down-sway followed by a loud crack ! I jumped to the ground just in time to save the ladder from a complete break in two ! And that was that; so we shouldered the confounded thing again, marched it back to The Knock and left it to lie in the nettles with its futile fellow.

It was now after two o'clock in the morning and we made straight for my friend's lodging—which happened to be the house of a local tradesman and away on the other side of the hotel. As we were about to enter at the door what should we see lying against the garden wall but a twelve-foot ladder! Well, I'm blest! The very thing we had been looking for! So (in the same order) we shouldered this one and marched off down towards the hotel.

But now the moon had retired behind a mass of black cloud and there was an eerie gloom over the village. As we were passing along the main street what should we dimly discern coming up the steep harbour brae but the form of a notorious village worthy who had had a riotous night, and was now making heavy weather of it coming up that hill. But gamely he rose to his feet again prepared to carry on. The top of the brae could not be far away? With somewhat bleared vision he tried to gauge the extent of effort still required to reach level ground. It was then we heard his moan of horror as, miraculously sobered on the instant, he fled down the hill again as if pursued by Evil Spirits—a conviction in which he was doubtless confirmed by the howls of our laughter which pierced the stillness of the night. Later we learned that for months the poor man went about sober and in daily dread of the death of which he had had so dreadful a prevision that night at the top of the pier brae. For, out of our marching along with the ladder in the gloom of the night, what easier for a scared and imaginative Celt than to construct a phantom funeral procession?

As we had guessed, the ladder proved just right for our purpose. Up I scrambled and pushed the window up another foot to allow of an easy entry. By now there was no light from the moon, so that the room was in darkness. I did listen for any sound from within just in case it might be occupied; not a sound! But of course the noise I had already made pushing up the window couldn't have failed to waken anyone there might be! So I gave the O.K. and a good-night to the assistant factor, who marched off home with the ladder on his shoulder.

I knew that the door of the room opened on to the

corridor, not immediately opposite the window, but away at the far corner. In order to avoid a collision in the dark with a table which usually stood in the middle of the room, I decided to feel my way along the west wall and then the south wall to the door. Now, as a test of the power of observation, I cannot think of anything stiffer than trying to steer a noiseless way in the dark through a room with whose every item of furniture you may consider yourself to be familiar. As I groped along in the dark my feet and my face came in violent contact with quite unexpected objects. The coal scuttle did not seem to be in its usual place ; on the wall, pictures and crockery arrested my hands in most unexpected places, and with alarmingly noiseful results. Then, when half way along the south wall and not far from the much-desired door, my heart misfired several times before starting to race at high speed. The cause was the faint but unmistakable sound of a human snore ! I stood stock still—there it was again ! Peering back against the modicum of light coming from the window I could dimly trace the outline of a bed with a hump showing beneath its counterpane. No head or any other part of a human being could I make out; but there was the bed—and there indubitably was the hump ; and the hump rose and fell rhythmically with the gentle snore. Perspiration oozed from every pore. Good heavens ! Was it a male or a female snore? But how could man or woman sleep through all yon din? If a man, and he suddenly wakened up, he would be justified in doing bodily hurt to the now boneless intruder ! If a woman she would probably scream and perhaps incur permanent injury to her reason !

This was clearly a place where it would be good for me not to be. Cautiously I edged in what I judged to be the direction of the door. Mercifully I encountered no clattering impediment. Soon the knob was in my hand. Gently I turned it, stepped softly into the corridor and pulled the door shut. At that moment I thought I heard a voice say " Eh ! What ! Who's there? " But perhaps it was just imagination? Softly I crept to the electric switch at the stairhead and got light to see the way to my room. It was quite a while before I could compose myself and go to sleep.

At eight o'clock Katie came in with a cup of tea. " Och," says she, " so you got in all right ! I was off duty last night and forgot to tell the mistress to make sure you would be in before she locked the door and I was afraid you might be locked out ! "

" Katie," I said, " was it a man or a woman who was in No. 4 last night? "

" A man—a man of the name of William Wallace, from Australia. Why? "

" Do you know if he is alive—or dead? "

" Dead ! No indeed ! He went off with the boat this morning."

" Was he quite all right? "

" Yes ! He was quite all right as far as I could see; but he was asking me if there was a ghost in the house. He thought he heard one going about in the night ! "

" Listen, Katie . . .," and as I proceeded with a brief outline of the night's happenings Katie's mirth mounted to hysteria. " Stop you," says she, " till I tell the mistress ! "

And so, should any of the Portree police force of that day still survive and happen to read this, they will at last have the solution of the " ladders-in-the-nettles " problem that puzzled them for so long. And should William Wallace from Australia by a more remote chance see it, he will have the explanation of his ghost-disturbed sleep. But it would be too much to hope that he can still sleep as soundly o' nights as he did as a young man in Portree so many years ago.

CHAPTER VII

Crossing the Fords

ONE day we travelled from Lochboisdale to Lochmaddy. The distance is only a matter of forty-two miles, but in that are included the two famous fords of the Hebrides— the South Ford of about a mile, between the islands of South Uist and Benbecula, and the North Ford of fully four miles, between Benbecula and North Uist. Now a beautiful bridge spans the former, and hopes are high in the Islands that before long they will see a similar bridge over the North Ford. When that happens even the presently diminished travelling time between the two capitals of the Uists will be further diminished; then, without moving out of your comfortable seat in a car, you can do it in a matter of an hour! Well, well! and there was yon time we went " over the fords " on a day some thirty-five years ago.

Of course we had it carefully planned out in the hotel the night before, timing all our movements to synchronise with the immutable laws of the tides.

" With this wind from the west you cannot depend on much time between the opening to the closing of the fords," declared the genial old autocrat of the hotel, whose dictum on such a point no sane traveller dared dispute ; " you can get the first of the South Ford at Carnan at eleven o'clock and you must be over the North Ford and at Carnish not later than half-past two. That means that the wagonette will leave here in the morning at eight o'clock prompt. You will be at Carnan before eleven. MacLean will put you over in his cart to Crea-gorry where you can get a bite of food. The Creagorry wagonette should be at Gramisdal not later than half past one to give the Carnish trap a chance of getting you over in time. If the Lochmaddy brake is waiting for you at Carnish at three, you should be at the end of your journey by five o'clock at latest."

Splendid! and so it was arranged. Various telegrams were despatched in the hope of ensuring the necessary transport.

With a bit of luck here and there the journey sometimes did actually work out that way in those days. But the crossing of the fords was always an adventure, subject to the qualification which we usually referred to as " D.V. and W.P."—and this day the gods and the weather were in all-out opposition.

How fortunate that often the morning gives little indication of the troubles that the day may bring! We left with spirits in keeping with the wine in the air and the beautiful high-stepping pair of greys. Past Daliburgh (where in this land of leisure not a smoke yet showed) and on by Askernish, Bornish, Howmore and Crogarry with their spacious machairs stretching out to infinity in the west and their hundreds of highland cattle; over the causeway that straddles Loch Bee (that rendezvous of the white swan and Princess of fishing lochs!), and, well on schedule, pulled up at Carnan—where the greys were to eat and refresh preparatory to taking a party from Crogarry to Lochboisdale later in the day.

But now we had our first spot of trouble. One of the Carnan carts had gone over on the night ford and had waited in Creagorry to take another party back at mid-day. Following on receipt of our telegram the lad had gone to the hill to search for the other Carnan horse, which had just come in with a cracked hoof and a broken shoe—which condition could be remedied only when the smith could be retrieved from where he had gone to work at peats nearly two miles away. The lad was now away for the smith—who did turn up half an hour later and wasn't long at his job; but as we entered the South Ford we were already an hour behind schedule. The ford near the north shore was none too good, but we managed to splash through with the horses' feet still finding bottom.

At Creagorry came a real shock: a telegram from Carnish saying all conveyances otherwise engaged and advising us to take the Creagorry wagonette right on to Carnish.

Our friend at Creagorry was not for this plan at all. For one thing the sun had gone to hide behind banks of black clouds that had gathered up and now raced overhead; and then, if he did put us to Carnish he would certainly not get back home by the same ford—which would mean either his staying at Carnish till afternoon tomorrow or returning by the ford in the middle of the night. But these men of " The Fords " never let travellers down if they can possibly avoid that; so at the back of one o'clock we started off in the Creagorry wagonette with its two tough ponies that knew too well what was in front of them to make any show-off other than flattened ears, indicating a determination to get on with the job.

The North Ford is really a double one: there is one water channel near the Benbecula shore and another near the North Uist side. In the most favourable of crossings there will be anything up to three feet of water in these channels. After negotiating the first, for nearly a mile you are on dead flat firm sand (if you are careful to keep to the course marked by a row of wrack-covered boulders !) till you reach the notorious Caigean Rocks through which, over the vilest of tracks, horses, harness and carriage twist and groan and creak most alarmingly. After this liver-stirring in the Caigean there is another stretch of firm sand till you come to the Carnish channel— and the feature of this ford is its inconstancy ! here this tide, there the next, and goodness knows where it may be safe to chance it another time. At one hitherto " safe " place, a tide of the week before had scooped out a hole eight feet deep into which Donald Archie's good horse stepped, dog-cart and all. That was the end of a gallant beast, and it was only by the grace of God that it wasn't the end of Donald Archie too.

This day when we came in sight of the water in the Gramisdal ford even Angus the driver was taken aback. Instead of twenty yards wide or so it was nearer a hundred yards, and the water was dark and ruffled ! Bad—very bad looking ! Was the tide still receding or was it already on the turn?

The horses stopped. Angus got down and with his boot streaked the sand parallel to the water's edge. Anxiously we waited to note the result. The mark in the sand filled with water.

" She's on the turn already. I don't like the look of it," pronounced Angus. " Even if we get through here we will have to race for it to get over the Carnish ford."

There was some talk of discretion being the better part. Angus made another mark in the sand—from a study of which he seemed to gather some slender hope.

" Take your bags on your knees and keep a good grip; we'll try it," came the commander's decision.

Pluckily into the dark water stepped the ponies. Down—down—to knees !—to bellies !—to ribs ! Up rushed the water into the box of the wagonette; up went our feet to escape the flood. Only the horses' backs were now above water. In a moment they were down to it and swimming strongly. The wagonette swung round in the current, but the ponies with only a few quiet words of encouragement from Angus held gamely on. Soon they got bottom again and clambered out to the other side.

" Good boys ! " said Angus, patting the pair, " just a minute to get your wind." And then we were off at full gallop for the Caigean.

While winding through the Caigean what should we meet but another of the Creagorry drivers leading a horse and carrying a bundle of gig cushions.

" What's wrong with you, Donald? " inquired Angus.

" Went into a new hole in the Carnish ford and snapped the axle," Donald explained. " I'm putting the cushions above high water, and then I'll have to ride like the devil for Gramisdal and swim for it. But where on earth do you think you are going to? You'll never make the Carnish ford of it with the water like yon."

" And I cannot get back to Gramisdal in time: the horses haven't the breath left in them for it," said Angus quietly after a moment's reflection. " Where exactly is the hole? "

" It is right on the track that we were using yesterday— but for heaven's sake watch yourselves ! I must be off ; " and Donald astride the black horse made off like the wind for Gramisdal. Quite right, too : by waiting he could do no good and would but add to the list of possible casualties.

We set off for our own problem—and I cannot recollect the slightest effort on the part of any of us to get a joke out of the situation.

One glance at the state of the Carnish ford was enough to appal anyone. Here was no narrow channel of water with firm sand bottom, but a wide expanse of surging sea which blotted out all the usual landmarks and guide-stones.

" Not too good at all," was Angus's masterly under-statement of the situation.

We got a glimpse of Donald's dog-cart floating past a rock on the now fast-flowing tide. All trace of its wheel-marks had vanished. Angus did his best to decide where yesterday's line of ford had been and drove the pair into the water on a line calculated to clear us of the danger. That was the most fearsome drive I have ever had. The bottom was fiendishly uneven. One moment the horses would be swimming; the next they would be stumbling on submerged banks of sand—while all the time the distance to the other side seemed to be increasing instead of lessening. We were too concerned to keep our backsides out of the water to bother about our soaking cases. Out of the black sky came a real snorting shower of sleet. It was in the middle of that that the near-horse almost all but disappeared, while the off, in comparatively shallow water, struggled desperately to keep clear of the hole which had swallowed his companion. There was some confusion of pulling and drawing to no purpose; the traces got ravelled. The near-horse was being held under by the pole. Angus threw aside the now useless reins, scrambled on to the back of the off-horse and with a small hatchet and strong knife contrived to cut traces, etc., so as to give both horses their freedom. Immediately the horses made back for the safety of the Caigean; nor were we long in following their example.

But for the substantial flask which one of us happened to have in his pocket there might have been serious consequences to our wretched stranding on these dreary rocks for four hours—till a boat from Carnish came to take us off and to retrieve what we could of our sodden cases. It was after seven when we got to the little window and the big peat fire at Carnish—where the Lochmaddy conveyance had been waiting since three o'clock; and between one delay and another—largely taking appropriate " precautions " against pneumonia—it wasn't far off midnight when we pulled up at Lochmaddy hotel.

Usually there is a streak of consolation in the most adverse of circumstances. One of the party on that memorable crossing was one of my big shots from Edinburgh to whom I had been telling some tales of the Fords and who, having crossed them for the first time only two days before under perfect conditions of white sand and sunny skies, had left me in no doubt as to his opinion of my veracity !

CHAPTER VIII

Court of the Dogs—Many Clients—Keeping the Peace—
The Shah

In regard to the keeping of dogs, farmers and shepherds in this country are in a favoured position: provided the dog is kept for the purpose of tending sheep or cattle, no licence fee is payable in respect of it.

Up till about forty years ago such exemptions were granted rather promiscuously. Each year the Inland Revenue people sent to every farmer and shepherd a printed form setting forth that the dog (or dogs) was kept solely for the purpose of tending sheep or cattle. This statement was signed by the owner, and without further ado official exemption from tax payment was granted.

Very likely there would be a smattering of such exemptions held on very thin grounds! Certainly, in some parts of the Highlands there was an inordinate number of dogs which—not being strenuously engaged in the vocation in respect of which their master benefited in the matter of taxation—found their highest joy in life in chasing motor cars, and thereby proving a perfect menace to drivers in the early days of motoring. The first hoot of a motor was the signal for every dog in the township—and what swarms there were of them!—setting off hell-for-leather for the roadside to attack this monstrous thing that had come to disturb the peace of the countryside. They would yap and bark furiously at the front wheels, and seemed never to understand why the monster did not, like a sheep or a cow or a horse, turn tail and flee instead of carrying straight on. Some of them would follow for a mile, keeping up their puzzled but futile yapping at the thing that would neither stop nor turn. Then, what was left of them would go back to their homes, with tails erect, consciously proud of having done their best; and in no way dismayed or discouraged at the sound of the next motor horn.

You will notice I have said " what was left of them." That is because sometimes the casualty list was heavy. I remember one occasion when my driver bagged seven dogs in less than four miles. Another day he had a record bag of nine in the one run. I was not his passenger on this occasion, but in subsequent Court proceedings the sheriff, instead of imposing a fine, complimented the driver on his valuable service to the public. It appeared that his Honour had himself experienced considerable inconvenience and annoyance from the alert and vociferous dogs of the district. Nor am I as callous in this matter as may seem. To me, as to every decent motor driver, the avertable killing of a dog is a most reprehensible and distressing occurrence. But in those days very few of the owners made any effort at controlling their dogs: the latter were allowed to chase motors to their heart's content. It was mostly the really wily ones that ran to the roadside well ahead of the car and lay concealed in a side-drain to make a surprise all-out spring at the front wheels when they came along that got run over. With such, no driver had a ghost of a chance of steering clear.

It was probably as a result of this trouble with the dogs that there was then introduced a more discriminating régime in the matter of granting exemptions from tax. It was now open to any responsible citizen to lodge with the authorities an objection to the granting of exemption in any specified case or cases; and following on such objection no exemption was granted unless the dog-owner proved before the sheriff that he was legally entitled to it.

Throughout the Hebrides such objections were lodged

in hundreds; and the perturbation and anger which this further threat to their rights and privileges caused amongst the island crofters—every one of whom regards his dog with utmost pride and affection—will be readily appreciated. Not even the crime of murder could have created wider concern and indignation. In every ceilidh house from Loch Seaforth to Barra Head the threat of being rendered dogless—for so the refusal of exemption seemed to be generally interpreted—was the one and only topic. For it was in this area that all the landlords (advised, it was alleged, by the " Factor Dubh " of vivid memory, who was also a lawyer) had acted as one, and lodged objection to every dog-tax exemption on their estates. This involved 1,542 dog-owners and 1,679 dogs. To what extent the Factor Dubh was in fact responsible for initiating the campaign can never now be ascertained, but there is no doubt in my mind that it would be difficult to find a pair with a stronger sense of puckish humour, or more ably equipped for such a ploy, than himself and his friend and legal opposite number Alasdair " Iain " (MacDonald)—who, as I write, is still going strong. Be that as it may, the gauntlet was now in the ring: the battle was joined. The Factor Dubh—hitherto champion of the crofters in their Land Law " Reform " battles—was now acting for the landlords! Alasdair—then a young and ardent antagonist—acted for all of the 1,542 dog-owners.

The case was put down for hearing at Lochmaddy on a Wednesday at 10 A.M. The great majority of the owners determined to appear in person to promote the cause of justice so far as was possible in a wicked world. Other members of the family came in support. Wednesday's boat would be too late for the people from Barra, and as there was no north-going boat on the Tuesday, they travelled by the Monday's boat. There was a strong representation from Harris on Tuesday, many crossing the Sound in sail-boats. On Tuesday morning, too, the trek from the south end of South Uist started and gathered strength as it went north over " The Fords." Finally people from all over North Uist came in on the Wednesday morning. The resulting crowd was the biggest ever seen at Lochmaddy and is likely to hold that distinction for a long time to come.

In anticipation of so large a gathering the Chief Constable had arranged that there should be at Lochmaddy for two days a full muster of the Islands' police force. Presumably the underlying idea was to ensure the maintenance of order. Anyhow, it didn't quite work out that way. Actually, while there was a good deal of dramming and some candid expression of opinion in regard to the intelligence of " them that wass at the bottom of all this troupple," there was nothing approaching a disturbance of the peace; with the result that seven genial policemen found themselves staying in an hotel and with very little to do: a positive gift, as one might say, for the old gentleman whose proverbial concern is to provide mischief for idle hands.

They were good fellows and friendly towards humanity, and so many people wanted to offer them good fellowship and hospitality. Besides, there was considerable conviviality amongst themselves. Moreover—and most unfortunate of all—they made the Highlander's usual mistake on such occasions: the mistake of depending entirely on liquid refreshment and scorning to eat solid food. So it was that in more than one instance the respective rôles of police and public were reversed. In particular one member of the force gave considerable concern to four of us who had got away from the general turmoil to the smoke-room and were enjoying a quiet game of solo. Somehow this policeman had got it into his head that we were far gone in drink and that it was his duty to stand by and see us safely to bed; a complete inversion of the facts. So he lay down on a sofa on the broad of his back to be ready to do the needful by us when the game finished. But there was a " kitty on," and as is the way with kitties, it took a long time to clear. When at long last the game ended, our guardian angel was sound asleep. Nay, more: he was dead to the world! We shook him. We gripped his nose. We rubbed his ears. We put cold water down his neck. He snored on. The idea of carrying sixteen stone of inert humanity up a twisted stair was pondered, but dismissed as impracticable. He must be wakened up and induced to contribute some measure of self-transport.

It was the exciseman who had the brain-wave. A cherished pet of the lady of the hotel at that time was an out-size half-bred Persian cat; an affectionate creature delighting in more warmth than was always available in the wind-swept Hebrides. Its favourite couch was a chair-cushion which its mistress had warmed at the fire. On that it would squat and purr and purr in a physical ecstasy. Soon there would come the peak-period of bliss when some obscure feline instinct caused it to dig its claws into the cushion at every purring intake; a habit which, when indulged on human knees instead of a cushion, had often caused yells of anguish and some profane language. For this poor cat the stir caused in the hotel by *Cuirt nan con* was sheer nightmare: every room and corner of the place crowded with noisy human beings occupying not merely its favourite chair but all the other chairs as well—and even the steps in the stairs! A dozen times that day we had heard the anguished yell of " the Shah " when coarse tackety boots came crashing down on his tender toes. Thus battered and kicked from pillar to post, with that extra instinct cats have for ensuring their own comfort, the Shah had at last found his way into the comparative quiet of the smoke-room and was doing his best to retrieve his dignity on a corner of the hearth-rug while we went on with our game. But the fire was getting low. By the time we cleared off the kitty the last bit of peat was reduced to ashes, and the poor Shah was faced by the horror of a cold and comfortless night. Imagine, therefore, his surprise and joy at finding himself being lifted by gentle hands and placed on a cushion warmer and more delectable than he had ever known! It was the bare, expansive lower abdomen of the arm of the law, which we had discreetly but adequately exposed as a cushion for the distracted Shah. Expert that he was, it did not take that intelligent animal long to realise that he was on to a good thing. Down he squatted, " purr, purr, purr," in rapid crescendo, while we stood clear for action. Nor did we have long to wait. Within a minute the Shah's eyes were closed in a delirium of delight. Soon the big bramble-bush claws would . . . " Baaaa! Oooich ! " . . . And on the instant there was the widest-awake policeman imaginable; nor was he ever clear as to the cause of his rude awakening, for we assumed an air of utmost innocence, while the Shah, scared at the astounding reaction to his loving embrace, had vanished out of the door as if scalded by boiling water.

On the Wednesday morning nearly every one of fifteen hundred and forty clients was anxious to have a personal interview with Alasdair Iain before the Court would open. There were, of course, many of them who were strangers to him, and as he and I had neighbouring offices in the old Temperance Hotel building there was a good deal of confusion in regard to names. Dozens pushed their way into my room, each anxious that his man-of-business might understand his case at first hand; and even when I managed to explain that I wasn't the right

MacDonald for his purpose I still had to hear the rest of the story—partly perhaps, because there wasn't a hope of getting near Alasdair anyway. Soon the demand for him was so overwhelming that Alasdair decided he must go out to the road and give a short open-air address. The crowd extended along the road nearly from the hotel to the bank. A table was carried out and placed in position. Alasdair mounted the rostrum. His intention was to give them a short résumé of the points in the case. It proved to be, surely, the shortest speech on record, and I am terribly sorry that the story of it is so utterly incapable of adequate translation that I am not attempting any and must leave it in the original for the more fortunate readers to savour. Below is all that was said—and the merriment evoked in a crowd so appreciative of humour was such as to effectively kill any further attempt at serious talk. None appreciated the humour more keenly than Alasdair, who, shrewd psychologist that he is, and having got his audience in the best of spirits, warmly complimented the old man on his shaft of wit and assured all that he would do his utmost on their behalf.

ALASDAIR (in yon firm impressive voice of his). " *A'Chairdean! Mudheighinn Cuirt nan con tha'n so. . . .* "

BEARDED BODACH FROM BARRA (slowly, distinctly and with hearty emphasis). " *Mata! B'e sin Cuirt nan galla!* "

.   .   .   .

The Court room had normal seating for about a hundred people. This morning it had three times that number packed into it. The bulk of the crowd had to content themselves on the landings and stairs and out on the front green.

After some preliminary sparring by the lawyers the Factor Dubh outlined his case briefly and brightly as was his wont. In his view there had been gross laxity in the granting of exemptions. There were ten dogs on the Islands for every one required for the purposes which earned exemption in terms of the Act. These dogs were a menace to sheep and cattle, and a public nuisance. He would argue before his Lordship that the vast majority of dog-owners in the Islands, being merely crofters, could not qualify for tax-exemption as *farmers* at all—and he would ask for judgment accordingly.

But Alasdair Iain has had a busy over-night session fortifying himself against just such an attack. He has studied carefully the wording of the Act. He has also consulted an agricultural dictionary and the relevant sections of a ponderous and newly published encyclopædia of agriculture—all of which authoritative tomes he respectfully placed at the disposal of his Lordship (and some of which I did not recover for a very long time!).

His case was quite clear and logical:

A. Every farmer who keeps a dog (or dogs) for tending sheep or cattle is entitled to exemption from payment of tax.

B. There is no essential difference between " farmer " and " crofter " in regard to the right to exemption. Essentially and legally all crofters must be regarded as farmers so far as the right to exemption is concerned.

C. Therefore, all his clients who are crofters are entitled to exemption, not necessarily in respect of one dog only. The Act says " dog or dogs." It also says " sheep *or* cattle " (either of which, Alasdair conceded, must be read in the plural—but in a minimum of two!)

" And so, m'lord," Alasdair concluded, " my submission is that such of my clients as are crofters—and the great majority are—are, *ipso facto*, farmers, and every one of them, if he keeps on his place even no more than two sheep *or* two cattle is entitled to exemption from tax in respect of a dog *or* dogs for tending such sheep or cattle."

His Lordship was so impressed by this logic and argument and the authoritative tomes that the case—which we expected might not finish that day—was over in half an hour, with a verdict in favour of the crofters. Only a few dog-owners who, for one reason or another, fell short of the legal status of crofter were refused exemption. Well over fourteen hundred duly qualified. It was a great victory for them and for their lawyer. Moreover, as the latter was awarded expenses against the objecting parties in respect of each of his clients, there was just cause for a little celebration amongst us at the hotel that night.

CHAPTER IX

Agricultural Confusion—American Beef—Training in Diplomacy

On my appointment as a member of the Scottish Land Court quite a number of people phoned my wife to say they were delighted, etc.—but what exactly *was* this Scottish Land Court? What did it or they *do*? The poor woman did her best to explain, but soon even she found herself rather tied up in knots about the respective functions of it and its several related bodies. Although not insensible of the common human aptitude to take less intelligent interest in the work of others than in one's own, I confess to a little wounded dignity at such widespread ignorance of the functions of the august body that was now to have the inestimable advantage of my wisdom. Frankly, though, it is perhaps not surprising that, even in the minds of normally intelligent people, there should be some ambiguity; for, in addition to the Scottish Land Court have we not also got a Department of Agriculture for Scotland, Agricultural Colleges, Agricultural Executive Committees and the S.A.O.S. (Scottish Agricultural Organisation Society)? Indeed we have, and a Farmers' Union and a Farm-Servants' Union, and the great Highland and Agricultural Society besides innumerable lesser Unions, Associations and Breed Societies; all charged with some statutory duty or corporate responsibility in connection with the good of the land and of the people living on it—and therefore, of course, of the good of the country as a whole. So perhaps it is not surprising that, in trying to grasp the exact nature and functions of so many bodies, some people " lose the place."

A complete treatise in this book on the subject of such

associated but distinct agencies would make dull reading, but perhaps a passing glance at some of them may prove interesting.

The Breed Societies. The main concern of every breed society is to foster in the minds of the rest of humanity the idea that their particular breed of cattle, or whatever animal it is, is the best in the world. In pursuit of their ideal they are tirelessly (one might say tiresomely!) diligent and surprisingly resourceful. Actually their concern is not really necessary, for the fortunate fact is that Scotland, by reason of the nature of its soil, climate and the sort of grass we grow, is by far and away the best stock-breeding country in the world. That is why shrewd men from the great ranching countries come to Scotland year after year and pay incredibly big prices for bulls of various breeds. Nor is this gold mine likely to peter out in a foreseeable future; for the other delightful truth is that in these great ranching countries, because of the deleterious effect on live-stock of climate and other conditions, a fresh infusion of the vigorous blood of the Scottish-bred bull is and will continue to be an annual necessity. In this connection, I remember in America some years ago visiting one of the big abattoirs and being treated to lunch by the management in the restaurant of their gigantic premises in Chicago. Including the then head of the firm there were about a dozen of us seated at a circular table. Suddenly, as the roast beef was being served, a peculiar silence became quite noticeable and developed into a strained atmosphere that I just could not understand. Then someone made an obvious effort at conversation and I started in to my roast beef— a noble helping equal to nearly half a dozen of our present weekly rations. To myself I soon had to confess that this lovely looking beef was a disappointment. In flavour it wasn't too bad—in fact it was all right; but it was mighty tough! Just at that moment came the shock: it was the President speaking:

" Say! Mr MacDonald, would you mind telling us straight just what you think of our roast beef? "

Having regard to the aforementioned self-communing, and to my innate horror of all but unavoidable lies, the question caused some momentary embarrassment, but, pulling myself together, I hedged brightly:

" Well, isn't that interesting?—that you should ask that question at the very moment I was thinking to myself ' What grand-flavoured beef!—beautiful! ' "

" Yes," he said, " and what else? "

This was decidedly awkward for a guest. For three seconds I searched frantically for the right answer, but even that slight hesitation was enough. The great man came kindly though devastatingly to my relief: " Let me tell you what you'd say if you wasn't so darned polite; it would be: ' flavour beautiful, but *texture mighty tough.*' "

" No, sir! " he continued, " we've gotta face the fact. We have tried this breed and that. We have had all sorts of crosses. We have experimented with scores of varieties of grasses and in kinds and ways of feeding. No, sir! It's got us beat!—and the man who can put us on to the secret of prodoocing yon marly tender texture you get in your Scottish beef won't have to work no more! "

So let our Breed Societies be of good cheer.

.   .   .   .

The Highland and Agricultural Society of Scotland, as it was known for well over a hundred years, was founded at the instigation of an energetic and far-seeing Caithness man and ancestor of Sir Archibald Sinclair. The Society is best known to the public through the medium of its great show—" The Highland "—which moves round in rotation annually from one centre to another. But " The

Highland " is not merely a show of the cream of our farm live-stock and the latest agricultural machinery. It is also a big social event in the countryside, sometimes graced by the Royal Presence, and affording grand relaxation to the care-worn workers on the land.

In more recent times this Society has acquired some political force and thereby serves as a training ground for the Secretary of State for Scotland and the Society's principal officials in mutual toleration. Annually there is elected a new President, who in new-broom fashion sets about the business of making sweeping demands for governmental assistance for the industry. He can be a sore thistle in the thumb of the Secretary of State and his assistants and permanent officials whose primary duty is to say NO to all such demands. But, of course, both sides have to be polite! And the way that works out as the year goes on provides an edifying example of the British way of government and people making the best of things: how the one has to be satisfied with less than his original demand and how the other finds it expedient to take some weight off the breeching. By the end of the tussle they have acquired much mutual respect, and each has a livelier appreciation of the other's difficulties.

. . . .

The S.A.O.S., or to give its full title—Scottish Agricultural Organisation Society—has for about forty years been active in an effort to instil and foster the spirit of agricultural co-operation—particularly amongst small-holders; and, considering the markedly anti-co-operative and pro-individualistic nature of the crofting population, S.A.O.S. are entitled to respect for the measure of success they have attained. That such small tenants should benefit substantially from co-operative action in purchasing their requirements and selling their produce seems theoretically watertight, but the fact remains that, for one of those psychological or other obscure reasons by which the Celt is apt to be guided in his practical affairs, he is not by instinct an ardent co-operator. Is that a fact to be deplored?—or is it not? I go no further than to suggest it might be an interesting study.

.   .   .   .

College of Agriculture. There are three of these : Edinburgh and East, Glasgow and West and Aberdeen and North of Scotland. Their function is purely educational. Each has its training centre, in association with the University, where young men and women study for degrees and diplomas in agriculture. To each College has been apportioned an area of country in which it has the responsibility for providing a full advisory service covering every aspect of Scottish agriculture and ensuring that the latest discoveries and developments in agricultural science are placed at the disposal of the practical man in the field. The usual team for each county, or part of some of the larger counties, is a County Agricultural Organiser (with sometimes an assistant) and a Dairy and Poultry Instructress. In addition, there is a service of " specialists " available from College Headquarters.

When first this service started—about the beginning of this century—there was a quite understandable tendency on the part of shrewd practical farmers to scoff at a service which savoured so strongly of lessons to granny in the art of sucking eggs. Dandies in breeches and polished shoes ! And henwives dressed like ladies ! But gradually it was borne in on the old farmer that the youths of the breeches brigade and the smartly-dressed henwives knew lots of things about farming that he didn't know—and would be much the better of knowing. It was a grudging recognition, but ultimately grew and spread all over the farming community. Now the best farmers normally seek the College man's advice on any problem that may arise. On the other hand the wise College man learns much of the more practical side of the business from his farmer friends—a mutual questing and learning relationship resulting in advantage to both.

CHAPTER X

Department of Agriculture: Some of its Doings and Troubles

The Department of Agriculture for Scotland is by far the largest of our family. It was born a Board in 1912, but (?) promoted to the status of Department in 1928. Travelling the country in its service as I did for many years I found it impossible to escape the feeling that in the opinion of the people the chief function of this great Department was the irritation of the rural community. Of course that was an exaggeration. All the same, by the very nature of its duties and of the powers statutorily conferred on it, some of the Department's operations were bound to cause considerable irritation to a number of people. For example, one of its primary duties was the provision of enlargements for existing small-holdings and the creation of new ones. That involved the procuring of land for such purposes, and to that end the Department was invested with powers to acquire land—compulsorily if need be. The shock caused by such a violation of the hitherto generally accepted notions of the sacred rights of private property may easily be imagined!

In a few cases hard-up landlords were glad to sell. In some cases they bowed to the inevitable. In many instances they strongly opposed the Department's schemes; and almost without exception (but not quite) all cases developed into long legal battles over the question of compensation due to landlords and disturbed tenants. In addition to its power of acquiring land—that is, entering into full ownership—for its purposes, the Department also has power to impose schemes of new holdings and enlargements on land belonging to private owners, subject, of course, to the latter being adequately compensated. Now, one of our maybe illogical but certainly pronounced British characteristics is always to regard a Government Department as fair game when it comes to a question of extracting compensation. That despoiled landlords and disturbed tenants should be compensated adequately and even generously was very much in the minds of those of us who were directly concerned with land settlement schemes, and with a view to avoiding the expense of needless litigation our policy was to advise the Department to offer to settle privately at a figure considerably in excess of what the mere values in the case warranted. But for the first number of years most of such offers were scornfully rejected in favour of the chance of a higher award resulting from the legal battle. Nor did claimants often have reason to regret such recourse to the law. In cases where the Department did not purchase the land, but merely imposed a scheme on the private owner, a strong contention put forward by the latter in support of his claim for compensation was that, *because of his now having on his estate a number of small-holdings instead of a large farm, if and when he came to sell that part of the estate, he would not get so high a price for it in the market; there was thus a potential loss in selling value for which he must be compensated now.* The theory was that small-holders were undesirable tenants who would scare intending purchasers. In the final result the law and the arbiters supported that view and solemnly assessed the scare-value of small-holders on an estate at seven years' purchase. That is to say, that while a purchaser would be prepared to pay for the property a sum equal to say twenty-one years of its annual rental *as a farm*, he would not give more than fourteen rents for it as cut up into small-holdings, *e.g.*—take the case of a farm rented at £500.

Its selling value would be £500 × 21 = £10,500
As small-holdings would be £500 × 14 = 7,000

Thus leaving the landlord with a loss of £3,500

Actually many thousands of pounds were awarded under that head of claim. Yet some years later, when a property which had been " mutilated " by small-holdings came to be sold, not only was there no loss to the landlord, but there was a very substantial profit. The demand for the small-holdings was so keen that in some cases they sold at rates 50 per cent. higher than that paid for large farms. After that experience amending legislation was introduced to bar such claims in future.

Another heavy item of claim was in respect of damage to sporting rights, especially where grouse-moors were involved. Here the general line was to assume that all small-holders were poachers, or at least careless of the value of the shootings to the landlord. Under the scheme they would have access to the moor to look after their sheep. There would be disturbance to birds by dogs and men. Nests would be destroyed. The grouse-bag would slump. The landlord would be ruined.

Despite carefully gleaned figures given in evidence to show that no such calamities resulted from small-holders having access to grouse-moors, for many years arbiters persisted in awarding substantial sums in compensation for a contingent loss which might never materialise; and it was probably the openly declared attitude of the late Sir Edgar Horne towards this matter which in the end was largely instrumental in disposing of the bogey.

At Lairg station one day, into my compartment in the south-going train came a large elderly gentleman with the assortment of bags, gun-cases, fishing rods and tackle and kindred impedimenta that usually denote the sporting gent. He was a stranger to me, but as he appeared to be quite genial I immediately set about satisfying natural curiosity.

And had he had a good holiday?

Indeed he had—a great holiday. He always enjoyed his stay in Sutherlandshire!

I agreed: indeed it was a grand sporting country! Had he been long in the north this time?

He had been for six weeks—and was still sore at having to tear himself away—but he would be back at Lairg again soon—perhaps within a month!

Good!—At Lairg? He wasn't by any chance Sir Edgar Horne of whom I had heard such a lot?

Indeed he was—and hoped his reputation wasn't as bad as all that! And who, might he ask, was I?

It was far from bad!—and I counted myself lucky to meet him—I was a minion of the Department of Agriculture—of whom he might not be enamoured but who might not be nearly as bad as they were painted. From then on we " southered " fine. At Inverness station, just as the train was about due to start, my companion, searching in his bags, got quite bothered about something. Though an abstemious man he required to have a small drop of stimulant occasionally. But he couldn't take naked whisky—and if he hadn't stupidly come away without a glass and without the usual diluent! While he was still deploring the oversight I bolted out at the door. Later I learned he had assumed it would be to speak to someone I must have seen on the platform.

As usual, the Edinburgh coach was right at the front of the train. I had to sprint back the full length of the platform. The guard had the green flag in hand ready for the starting wave.

" Don't let her go for two minutes," I pleaded with a desperate earnestness; " something very important."

" But the time is up! I can't wait . . .! "

I waved back at him significantly.

Then to the lady in the refreshment room—" Two

tumblers and a bottle of soda!" I gasped. "Quick, *please!* I'm going with this train."

She demurred about the glasses—but stemless glasses would do, or chipped ones—anything so long as the business end was intact!

She was a nice lassie, sympathetic and smart. As I rushed towards the rear of the train an angry but loyal guard waved the green flag and yelled at me to jump in—I could get along to the front by the corridor. Which I did as the train was actually under way.

Five minutes later I found my companion much distressed. My platform friend had delayed me too long! I had missed the train! Now he was happy again. He proceeded to tell me what he had been explaining when I ran out. No soda! no glasses! Most annoying.

"I sometimes carry a glass in my pocket," I said, pulling one out—and then another—and then the bottle of soda water from the hip pocket.

His eyes had opened wider with each extraction. "Good God! Do you always go about with glasses and bottles of soda in your pockets?"

Not always, I protested; just sometimes; and it was lucky I had them now!

After that we had a mutually delightful journey to Edinburgh, and it was then he told me of his experience with grouse-moors and crofters. It was to this effect:

When his London friends learned that he had bought an estate in the Highlands, having on it a large number of crofter tenants, they were sorry for him. It was a dreadful mistake! These crofter fellows were incorrigible poachers. They would ruin his moor. He would require to get two or three extra gamekeepers at once; very expensive, and doubtfully effective, but without extra keepering the position was manifestly hopeless.

He had his doubts about all this, but could not help

being somewhat impressed by what those experienced friends said. However, he would go canny till he had put the matter to some test. For the first two seasons careful note was taken of the favourite nesting places and of where every bird was shot. A study of the collected facts showed that by far the best beats of the moor were those which formed the crofters' common pasture and to which they and their dogs and sheep and cattle had full right of access. He was so delighted at this emphatic repudiation of a belief widely held amongst tenants of grouse-moors that he invited all his crofter tenants to a supper and social evening where he had the pleasure of telling them the story of his friends' fears and his own apprehensions, and of his test and its wholly satisfactory result. That evening was the beginning of much friendly intercourse between landlord and tenants which promoted goodwill and mutual understanding and respect.

Nor did Sir Edgar often miss an opportunity of relating the story of his experience of crofters in relation to grouse.

Here have I been blethering quite a lot about my old Department, and still haven't said much about its manifold activities. Nor of these will I say more than that they extend to a concern to guide, control and encourage every conceivable measure calculated to promote the welfare of the industry, including the specialised activities of the subordinate or associated organisations aforementioned. But before leaving the subject there is one peculiar aspect that I just cannot resist having a look at; and if in doing so I give some of them a dig in the ribs, I trust any surviving old colleagues and friends will be big enough to take it in good part. I feel sure they will. Anyway, dash it all, I am entitled to my joke.

A simple-minded person might assume that a sound knowledge of agriculture would be an essential qualification for anyone charged with responsibility for directing the affairs of an agricultural department. But the matter is not so simple as that; and for long it has been the official view that for the satisfactory direction of a department's business in association with the responsible minister, administrative experience is the most essential qualification. There is an element of political discretion in the official view which may justify its general application. But, be that as it may, there is no doubt that at times a lack of understanding of the technicalities of the subject under discussion can be embarrassing and disadvantageous to the unfortunate official concerned; and personally, at meetings with farmers, I never ceased to admire and marvel at the dexterity and skill with which such officials, when all but bogged in bewildering idiomatic terminology, skated to safety over the thinnest of thin ice.

Perhaps it was the sheep department which caused their worst nightmares. And after all, what could the uninitiated make of an animal that might be one of so many things?—a lamb, a hogg, a gimmer, a maiden ewe, a ewe, a fine ewe, a yeld ewe, a cast ewe, a milled ewe, a dinmont, a wedder, a keb, a piner, a pallie, a peelie, a straggler, a tup, a top, a mid, a shott—and heaven knows how many more shapes that this blasted beast can assume! Worse still: the confounded things wouldn't stay put! It is fatal to assume that what is a gimmer this year must still be a gimmer next year. In all probability she will not—although confound it! she *may* remain a gimmer, but with the prefix " Eild "; and so on with those alarming and elusive female classes.

In face of such a fluid and treacherous nomenclature how on earth could anyone, whose knowledge of sheep was hitherto limited to the beast in cooked form, be expected to make head or tail of the matter or to check up on the honesty of the technical officer in charge of the farm?

I remember an early sheep-stock case which caused

much perturbation at head office. We had taken over a large sheep farm in Sutherland for the purpose of breaking it up into a number of new small-holdings and enlargements for several groups of existing crofts. As is usual in such cases, most of the old arable land that had lain uncultivated for many years as pasture for sheep would, under the new régime, form the arable land of the new holdings, with a consequent diminution in the number of sheep which could be kept, but with more than a compensating increase in crops and cattle and people. This meant that, after the small-holders had taken over the number of sheep which the diminished grazings would carry, there would be a surplus which must be sold off. But nearly all the farm leases in Sutherlandshire have their termination at a Whitsunday term; and it was at Whitsunday that we took over this place with its sheep-stock numbering nearly 5,000 head. It was at that same Whitsunday term the new holders and crofters got formal entry to the land and, " on paper " at least, took over their respective lots of the different classes of sheep.

But Whitsunday is just about the worst time for splitting up a sheep-stock or for disposing of a surplus. The lambs are then too young to be driven off their home hirsel or trucked to a sale—and in any case that is not the normal season for marketing ewes or lambs. So the holders and myself agreed that by far the most sensible plan would be to carry on the stock as an undisturbed unit till the back end when, lambs, cast ewes, wool, etc., having been duly disposed of at normal sales, a complete trading account could be prepared on a basis for a pro-rata allocation of profits and stock. With that in view we made at Whitsunday only a " paper " allocation of stock, and it was left to me to carry on in the management and prepare the statement for final settlement in November.

With so many new holders and resident crofters (in addition to the Department) as shareholders in the venture, anyone with knowledge of such matters can readily appreciate the highly complicated and delicate handling entailed in the preparation of a statement satisfactory to all parties. Here I need only say that for weeks of nights I sweated blood over it and was more than a little pleased with the final elucidation; dead sheep, lost sheep, sheep transferred to holders, lambs sold (tops, mids and shotts), ewes sold, (ditto and also broken-mouthed), wool sold (fleece, skins and broke), cost of fence repairs, marketing, clipping, dipping and all the rest of it worked out to the third decimal point per head of sheep. There it was; the perfect exposition that was bound to impress the fellows at head office with the manner of man its composer must be! . . . Well, they weren't favourably impressed at all. Indeed, I rather gathered that in so involved a series of intromissions they suspected there might well be the possibility of an opportunity for improbity. Of course they didn't quite put it that way; but I did receive on two sheets of foolscap no fewer than twenty-two demands for more light on specified portions of my masterpiece. The questions were neatly numbered down the left half of the page. Opposite was ample space for reply. I couldn't decide whether to meet this blow with tears or profanity. I know there was a little of the latter. Then I just laughed when I tumbled to it that what had inspired most of this catechism was the inability of the people at head office to make head or tail of the technical terms which of necessity bestrewed my report. One of the questions was priceless—and it was in my favour! Here it is:

" It is observed that at the Whitsunday valuation you reported having taken over 914 wedder lambs and 941 ewe lambs. You further reported on 6th June having taken over 12 additional lambs classed as ' stragglers,' which together make a total of 1,867 lambs taken over.

" It is further observed that according to the statements of your intromissions, the number of lambs sold, retained for holders and listed as dead, total 1,878—or 11 in excess of the number you took over. Please explain this discrepancy."

And I was cruel enough to write opposite that one just two words: " Grit ewes."

NOTE.—Grit ewe is the name applied to a ewe which has not yet lambed on the day of the valuation. I had duly listed such in my valuation report.

CHAPTER XI

Friendly Official—Modest Native

In its earliest years—1912 to 1918—the Board of Agriculture for Scotland (as it then was) was assiduous in the work of creating new holdings and enlarging existing crofts: so much so, that for this purpose one large estate after another had been acquired at a rate which far exceeded the possible speed of settlement. As a result we had in hand during the years of the first world war a large number of farms and estates for whose management people like myself were held responsible. Under conditions obtaining at that time—war-time restrictions and an indoor clerical staff innocent of agricultural knowledge, but exasperatingly ingenious in putting spokes in practical people's wheels!—it was bad enough to be landed with the ordinary work of management in addition to the essential work of interviewing applicants for holdings, framing new schemes for development and supplying munitions for frequent legal battles between the Board and landlords; but when on top of this was added the responsibility for keeping accurate accounts to be rendered monthly, the thing became a nightmare to most of us whose skill in accountancy was not our strong point. Every month it was a nightmare trying to get the darned things straight; nor did it help to know that if one did make a mistake it might be a year after the event that head office financial pundits would discover it and call for an explanation. It was terrible to be going in constant dread of being shown up as a thief or embezzler. At long last my often-urged request that someone from head office should pay periodic visits to give a hand with accounts at the provincial offices was given effect to. To most of the out-door officers this leg-along was a mighty relief. Incidentally, the job of travelling to the provinces became highly popular amongst those of the indoor staff with any pretensions to a knowledge of the obscure art of accountancy. For such slaves of the pen it was sheer heaven to know that to-morrow they would discard the shiny blue suit. They would habit themselves like men; for three to four days, perhaps for a week, they would breathe the untainted air of the countryside; they would come into close and prideful contact with stots and sheep; maybe even the honey-scented breath of the heather might permeate their lungs. Of course, they would have to come back! But they would come back with the tan of the sun on their faces, the song of the burn in their ears and a joy and hope in their hearts that would enable them to thole their chains till the next time.

That was how my old friend and colleague Gemmell felt that time he went to check up on the accounts at the Portree office. Maybe he had caught a trout or two, also; I wouldn't put it past him. But, anyway, he was enjoying himself—as he has a grand capacity for doing. Even when the joke is against himself no one enjoys it better—as I think you will sense from the fact that it was from himself I got this one.

On the way back from Portree, in consequence of a not unusual disaccord of boat and train movements, he found himself at Kyle of Lochalsh with a couple of hours to spare before the south-going train would start. But it was a grand day! And there were so many things to see from yon lovely view-point in front of the hotel. Across the shining water rose the frowning hills of Skye. Down at sea-level that gem of Highland hamlets that is Kyleakin. The ruins of Caisteal Moile, onetime stronghold of the MacKinnons, who it is said used it as a base from which to sally forth to demand toll from ships passing up and down the waters of the Kyle. For centuries Caisteal Moile has been a roofless ruin of massive walls and gables, seemingly on the point of disintegrating and tumbling into the sea, but still held together by a mixture that can be no ordinary mortar! And the ferry-boats, shuttling this way and that, packed with strangers from the south seeking the quiet of a Highland holiday; the gracefully gliding gulls—when they weren't in screaming squabble over the ownership of a discarded herring or some other fishy titbit. Then in the village itself the shops with their open doors and unhurried customers. Huge rolls of home-spun, in golden crotal and the blue of the sky, stood invitingly out in the roadway in front of the shops—at three-and-six a yard!

Having feasted his fill on such scenes and with still an hour to spare he set off for an inland walk. Soon he found himself passing not far from an old white-whiskered man working at the peats. With the infectious sociability born of pleasant contact with the country my friend hailed the ancient:

" It's a grand day for the peats! "

" It iss that: och yiss, a peautiful tay," the old gentle-man agreed. " And dit you hear the news of the war? "

In those days our latest war news came through the medium of a telegram displayed in the post office window. At once my friend diagnosed this to be the case of an old man anxious on account of a son or grandson away at the war. He had read the telegram at Kyle and passed on the gist of it to the dear old fellow.

" And how are they getting on at Galipolly? " inquired the native.

That's where the son or grandson is, the informer was convinced; and he was sorry he could give no more reassuring report of that sector of the struggle. " But mind you," he added, " it isn't easy for our fellows to get at the Turks, and it's very difficult for our ships to get up behind him through the Dardanelles."

" Aye, aye ? " obviously much interested.

" Yes: you see it's like this ": and with his Edinburgh walking-stick my friend sketched on the road a rough plan of the Dardanelles and proceeded to enlighten ignorance. " The Turks have a fort with heavy guns right here " (a dot on the road), " and then another on the other side here " (another dot), " another here, and here."

The interest evinced by his audience encouraged him to give a full and graphic explanation of the difficulties then besetting the British Forces in their attempt to overcome the Turk.

" Yiss, yiss ! I am understanding it fine ! And you will haff been oucht there yourself ? " the old man asserted rather than inquired.

" No, no ! " (modestly, but proud of the compliment). " I just saw it on a map in the newspaper."

" Well, well now ! Inteet, you made a ferry goot chop of it ! " came the compliment.

" Oh, thank you ! I'm very glad I helped you to understand."

" Yiss, yiss ! you make it ferry goot inteet—chist as like it iss ass anysing ! "

It was only then a glimmer came to the instructor—but no ! impossible . . .

" You—you—you were never out there yourself ? " he ventured incredulously.

Then, very modestly, " Och inteet yiss, I wass oucht there when I wass a young man. I went up the Strights seven times, but I only came down seex times because the last time I wass up fever broke oucht in the sheep and I was put into a hospital in Constantinople and I wass seex weeks there and then travelled by a traine to jine another sheep at Fiume. You will haff heard of Fiume ? "

CHAPTER XII

Land Court: Constitution and Peregrinations—Oath
Evasions—Waterloo!—Economy in Words—The Right
Time—Biblical Quotations

AND now about that august body, the Scottish Land
Court. In the main its function may be described as
"judicial." It acts as judge, arbiter and friendly inter-
mediary in the wide variety of cases of dispute, disagree-
ment or uncertainty in regard to things agricultural
which have a habit of cropping up between owners of
land and their tenants. I shall not attempt to enumerate
the cases of different type and nature that come, or may
come, before this Court in the course of a year—they
are practically innumerable. But whatever the point at
issue, the Court's solemn responsibility is to keep the
balance even.

Its roots go back to 1886, in which year, as a result of
a decade of alarming agrarian unrest throughout the
Highlands, there was put on the statute book that measure
which has so crucially and intimately affected the lives
and circumstances of our Highland people—The Crofters'
Act. From then on, all differences of opinion as to whether
the rent of a croft was fair or whether a crofter could be
removed from his holding, with or without compensation
in respect of permanent improvements he may have
carried out on it, ceased to be a matter for wrangling and
ill-feeling between factor and crofter. For under the
new Act was set up a judicial tribunal called the Crofters'
Commission before whom all such disputes could be
brought, and to whom each party could give relative
evidence on oath. And the Commission, having considered the evidence and inspected the subjects, duly
issued their findings and pronounced their decision—and
that was that.

Under the wise administration of the Commission and the protection afforded by the Act, crofters proceeded apace with improvements to land and buildings, and the " Land Question," so long the source of bitter feelings and conflict in the Highlands, gradually lost its venom. In course of time the advantages of the new régime became so obvious all over the area to which the Crofters' Act applied—Shetland, Orkney, Caithness, Sutherland, Ross, Inverness and Argyll—that in 1911 further legislation was enacted which provided for the extension of similar and additional advantages to the whole of Scotland. This was the Small Landholders' (Scotland) Act which gave birth to the Board of Agriculture for Scotland and substituted the Scottish Land Court for the Crofters' Commission.

The present authorised establishment provides for five Members of Court of whom one—a senior member of the Scottish Bar of not less than ten years standing—shall be chairman. The ordinary Members of Court are deemed to be men with a wide knowledge of agricultural practice and values, and one of them must be a Gaelic speaker. In control of the office and staff there is the Principal Clerk to the Court.

The present set-up is:

> Chairman and three Members.
> Principal Clerk.
> Three Legal Assessors.
> One Surveyor.
> One Accountant.
> One Keeper of the Rolls.
> One Grazings Officer.
> Four Clerical Officers.
> Two Typists.
> Two Messengers.

And—I am bound to say it—an astonishingly small team to overtake the volume of highly responsible and delicate work which they are called upon to do.

To each ordinary member is allocated a section of the country within which (with the assistance of his legal assessor when necessary) he normally deals with and decides all cases that may arise. Against such a decision, though, there is the much prized right of appeal. The Chairman along with the other two Members of Court and the Principal Clerk hear appeals. Their decision is final and can only be referred to the Court of Session in a stated case on a point of law.

In its high degree of mobility the Land Court is unique. Instead of hauling far-away applicants into Edinburgh to have their cases heard—and thereby involving them in considerable expense and inconvenience—this most sensibly designed tribunal goes out all over the country to issue its decrees and dispense its justice; sometimes at the local Sheriff Court, but it may be the village hall, a school, a crofter's kitchen, a barn, a byre or even a stance on the open moor which serves the Scottish Land Court's purpose and is for the nonce imbued with all the dignity and solemnity of a Court of Session. The mere process of putting a witness on oath goes a long way in producing this atmospheric metamorphosis and when supported by the awe-inspiring effect of the Chairman's gorgeous robe the transformation is complete.

Not that the Highlander, as a rule, is anxious to take the oath. Sometimes, indeed, he refuses to do so even when warned that by so doing he may be prejudicing his case. It has been suggested to me that this reluctance is due to his awareness that the disclosure of the truth, the whole truth, and nothing but the truth, might not be to his advantage anyway. But I incline to the view that the real explanation lies in the fact that the mere extraction of so solemn an undertaking has in it the insulting inference that otherwise he might tell lies ! Times without number I have seen and heard my brother Celts instinctively and anxiously seeking to evade the awful affirmation in the oath. Many of them just slither the essential words, hoping that it will be attributed to a defective knowledge of English; and one venerable old gentleman did it so well that he actually got off with " the truse, the whole truse and everysing but the truse ! "

Neither could one fail to admire the ease and dignity with which many of those who appeared before the Court conducted themselves; a circumstance due in part perhaps to the reputation of the Court for giving every suppliant's case patient and fair consideration, but certainly largely the result of independence of outlook and self-confidence characteristic of a people living in security on the land.

Away back in the eighteen eighties at a hearing before the Crofters' Commission, the Chairman—Sheriff Brand —was so much impressed by the quality and clarity of the evidence given by a very old man in English, despite his limited knowledge of that language, that at its conclusion he felt it incumbent on him to express his appreciation and thanks. He added: " And it is all the more remarkable that such evidence should come from a man of your years—for you are not now so young as you once were, Mr Cameron ! "

" Och indeed, no sir," Mr Cameron agreed with a smile.

" Just how old are you, Mr Cameron, can you tell me? " inquired his Honour.

" Och, chist *me* to-day, *Waterloo* to-morrow ! " came the cryptic reply.

In another chapter I tell in some detail of the result of taking evidence in Gaelic and having it translated by an interpreter. Recently it was rumoured in official circles that the necessity for having a Gaelic-speaking member of the Land Court no longer exists. With that I do not agree; and that not merely because of the indignant protests which would certainly come if the suggestion were given effect to. While it is true that a good knowledge of English is now widespread throughout the Highlands—better English, indeed, than you will find in any other rural community in the British Isles—the fact remains that when it comes to making a verbal statement before a tribunal like the Land Court, the native Gaelic speaker prefers to do so in the native tongue. Thus it is that every now and again, particularly in the Islands, a witness asks to be permitted to give evidence in Gaelic. Nor is this surprising. He could probably prepare a *written* statement of his case in flawless English, but his evidence must be given by word of mouth—and that is a very different matter. Besides, on the tongue of the master, the finer shades of expression in the Gaelic can be so much more effectively applied to his purpose.

At a sitting of the Court in Skye only a few years ago the Chairman was somewhat surprised when a well-dressed young lady, who was known to have lived for several years in Glasgow, asked to be permitted to give her evidence in Gaelic. In reply to his Lordship's suggestion that in her case such a procedure might not be necessary, she explained that while it might not be altogether necessary, she still felt she would be able to give her evidence more adequately and clearly in Gaelic. She did not wish to inconvenience the Court in any way, but if her evidence was to be taken in English could she have the Court's permission when answering questions to refer to a written statement in English which she had prepared in anticipation of such an eventuality?

Not only was the desired permission granted but the witness was invited to read the statement if she so desired. She did; and that statement could not have been bettered by a D.Litt., LL.B.

As the story in another chapter shows, when an interpreter is brought into a case the opportunity for supplementing exchanges between interpreter and witness is quite considerable. It's all very well to have fired at you a crisp question in a foreign tongue which in the mind of the originator needs a " yes " or " no " reply! But a " yes " or " no " is terribly committal! A Highland gentleman must have delicate regard to the dreadful possibility of unwittingly stating—on oath!—what may not be quite true by so drastically limiting his reply. So, even when he may have a shrewd idea of the purport of the question in its original form, he must ask his friend the interpreter for elucidation. And his fellow Gael, quick to appreciate the need for such, proceeds to supply it. But the elucidation, because of the wealth of nuances in the language of the Garden, in all probability discloses within it matter for further grave consideration which in the interest of absolute truth must be investigated. So it is that in such cases the Court or an arbiter or legal gentleman is apt to conclude either that the witness is a downright twister, or that as a medium for concise expression the Gaelic language is of low degree—and that possibly there is an element of both responsible for the protracted procedure! But, of course, so uncharitable a conclusion is rooted in ignorance.

I recall one Chairman of the Land Court who was profoundly sceptical of the necessity for those five minute conversations between witness and interpreter which were ultimately translatable in a syllable. Nor did his Lordship miss many opportunities of twitting some of us about the the shortcomings of the Celt and his language. But one

day we got our own back on him—in full! This same
Chairman, anxious to ensure that applicants should not
merely understand what the Court's decision in the case
was, but also the reasons that led to it, not infrequently
announced the decision from the bench and then proceeded to give the reasons annexed at considerable
length! On this occasion the decision was to the effect
that the applicant (who, through an interpreter, had
pressed hard for a certain advantage) had failed to make
good and was thus left in *status quo*. . . . No doubt with
a view to blunting the sting of disappointment, the Chairman launched what developed into a long-winded and
somewhat tedious explanation of causes. The interpreter,
who had heard the essential verdict and was expected to
garner a few of the crumbs of comfort for passing on to
the applicant at the finish, unfortunately fell sound asleep
at an early stage of the monologue. Not until the silence
which followed its termination did he waken up! His
Lordship was waiting for the interpreter to administer the
bitter pill with the sugar coating. The interpreter rose
to his feet, adjusted his spectacles, looked solemnly towards
the unsuccessful applicant and said, " *Thà thu mar bhà
thu*." * He then bowed respectfully to his Lordship and
resumed his seat!

No one who visits a Celtic community even for a short
period can fail to notice—and envy—the philosophic
decorum of the people in their attitude towards Time; for
to them that rushing to do this or that with the unseemly
haste so characteristic of slave-driven city people, whose
lives and actions are governed and inhibited by the
blaring of factory horns and railway time-tables, merely
discloses an irreverent lack of appreciation of one of
Nature's greatest gifts to man. As if Time were a commodity that came gushing through a tap from a cistern

* Highland-English equivalent : " You *are* as you *was*."

that will soon run dry! No wonder, therefore, that a stranger desirous of fixing up a meticulous holiday itinerary during his visit to the Highlands may find the Celt somewhat elusive; but to conclude from such evidence that laziness and lack of business acumen are qualities inherent in the Highlander is often but evidence of the visitor's less mature philosophy.

Even people who ought to know better, fresh from the stir of the city, are apt for a day or two to forget to tune in again to the serener tempo of the north. There was yon time the flight of the aeroplane from Renfrew to the island was delayed by fog and I was getting apprehensive about the possibility of being late for a sitting of the Court. On arrival at the hotel (several miles from the place of meeting) I was indiscreet enough to voice that fear to the hotel-keeper. My host looked at me pityingly. Surely I should know the islands better than that!—as if an hour here or there mattered!

I apologised; but after all, punctuality had some legal significance where the Land Court was concerned, I pleaded.

And when I got there (he ridiculed) I would probably find they were going by the sun and I would be far too early.

He declared I was no better than an Englishman he had recently staying in the hotel. The English visitor had a friend staying in private lodgings some miles away. One day the pair arranged that on the morrow they would go out with the land-lines for a fry of codlings. They would meet at a bay, where there was a boat and tackle, at eleven o'clock next morning. It was to be a grand outing and was much in the mind of the hotel guest that evening. He would have to be up in good time and warned several people of the necessity for an early knock.

But that night there seemed to be an unholy conspiracy against the poor man:

Item. The hotel-keeper hadn't possessed a watch since the beginning of the war.

Item. Every one of the dozen or so clocks decorating the various mantelpieces and lobbies had observed a profound silence for years.

Item. In his excitement the visitor had over-wound his wrist watch so that it had stopped at the moment of winding and he hadn't noticed.

Item—and last straw: the wireless battery had run done.

Not that this row of unfortunate circumstances disturbed in the slightest degree the tranquillity of the hotel-keeper and his staff. But to the fisherman it was very disturbing indeed. He might be far too early. But he might be too late! Good heavens! What a place! And nobody seemed to bother, and their repeated assurance, " Och! you'll be there time enough, right enough," was just an aggravation. He had a hurried breakfast—or at least as hurried as breakfasts happen there—and set off for the rendezvous in a mood mixed of annoyance and apprehension.

Ha! Here was someone coming who might have the desired information! It was an elderly Celt, ample in form, in blue guernsey and sea-boots, and in contemplative mood smoking his pipe.

" Good morning," said the Englishman.

" Good morning," cordially responded the Celt, but making to pass on, still deep in contemplation.

" Excuse me, but can you tell me the time? " anxiously inquired the Englishman.

" Time ! " said the Celt, jolted out of his reverie and desperately pulling his beard in anxiety to oblige the stranger. " Time? Time? I think it's *Tuesday*, isn't it? "

. . . .

In the hearing of a case a certain Chairman of the Court was always quick to seize any opportunity of quoting scripture to illustrate a point in the matter under discussion. On one occasion in Lewis whilst a venerable Islander was giving evidence his Lordship had freely indulged this pet propensity. But it would seem that his recourse to Holy Writ was more frequent than accurate. For a time the witness suffered in silence but at last was goaded into protest:

" If your Lordship will be for using the Holy Word at all in a case of this kind it would be better if you used it correctly. Indeed, I am thinking myself you would be wiser to take any quotations you need from your law books, with which no doubt you will be better acquainted than you are with your Bible."

CHAPTER XIII

(Being Extracts from Diary)

River Inspection—A Wet Day

FOR nearly a week we have had the most glorious of summer days. It's grand to see the early morning light stealing over the whin bushes of the Braids, as I am lucky to be able to do, from my bedroom window; a glimmering grey at first, but quickly changing through varying hues of indescribable beauty till at last the sun himself appears in regal splendour to proclaim another day.

There is endless interest, too, in observing the doings of the denizens of the rookery near the tennis courts at the Braid Burn; for, be it fair weather or foul, and whatever the season of year, just about half an hour before sunrise out sally the crows in their daily search for breakfast; they know precisely, too, where to go for the best rations.

Every spring and early summer there is a recurring battle of wits between crow and farmer for the potato sets which the latter has planted to produce that year's crop and which the former strives to steal as his favourite morning titbit. At the farmer's most realistic tattie bogle the crow—so to speak—soon puts his claw to his beak. During reasonable daytime hours the farmer usually has the upper hand: what between dykes and hedges behind which he can sneak in on them, and that grossly unfair and fatal instrument he puffs at them with such terrifying noise, a potato field is a chancy place for crows in day-time. So Mr Crow, wise by experience (and without a single " caw " !) slips over to snatch his favourite breakfast while his arch-enemy is still abed.

For his protein diet the crow has a passion for Leather-jacket, an ugly grub begotten of the harmless-looking

Daddy-Long-Legs, which in dry weather plays the very devil with the young oat-crop after old lea. The war-time plough-up of golf courses and other tough old pasture land made high holiday for the crows in their neighbourhood, for there, under the surface clods left by the harrows, are leather-jackets in their thousands; and there will be the crows in regiments, morning, noon and evening, turning over clod after clod with their bills as expertly as you could with your fingers and gobbling down the grub in incredible quantity. A few of the more sporting farmers allow in their reckoning a spot of credit to the crow on this account—but I'm afraid the great majority remember only the stolen potatoes!

To-day has been yet another of those lovely days. It's rather interesting to realise how many good days we do have when one begins to take note of them—and it is also interesting to note how prone many of us are to remember only the bad days: a sort of dour Calvinistic trait which seeks joy in gloom. One morning not so long ago there was a deluge of rain being driven along by a gusty wind as I entered the office. Now, while we did have rather more than a fair share of rude weather earlier on, that was positively the first rain we had had after a week of genial sunshine. Yet the greeting of a colleague that morning was: " Isn't this awful! Rain! Rain! every blooming day without a halt! "

Well! but as I started to tell, to-day really has been one of those lovely days that live in the memory; a blazing sun, a blue, blue sky artistically flecked with white wispy clouds, and just that breath of cooling breeze. On such a morning we step out blithely, even on city pavements that but lead to the shop or office.

But och! if only we could be out among the broom bushes on the brae or picking our steps along the banks of a moorland burn and here and there stopping to try to tempt the trout from beneath its green banks! And yet, look you at what can happen!

Wednesday—that was the day before yesterday—it was just another such day as this. The Court were " sitting " in state, uncomfortably dolled up in dark and ancient garments and with a richly robed and bewigged chairman, all complete. Learned Counsel, also dressed in the sombre habiliments of their sordid trade, were doing their clever best to get their own witnesses to say the right thing in support of their case and to get the witnesses on the other side to corroborate; so that the " learned judges " were in danger of being bamboozled by being pulled this way and that. All through that weary day of trying to reconcile irreconcilables the sun was high in the heavens and the earth was gay—and this lugubrious investigation might go on for days!

In the late afternoon, before rising, and as by a common impulse, there was a whispered consultation on the bench: what about going to *see* this wretched river that we had heard so much about, which had or had not been so efficiently cleaned that the adjacent farm lands had or had not been improved? Never was decision more quickly taken: we would go and see the *locus* to-morrow. That was the obvious thing to do; we could then listen to and talk about the case intelligently. Splendid! that suited everybody. Of course, nothing was said about the joy of walking among the corn and barley rigs or of strolling by the side of the murmuring river in the glorious summer's sunshine, but anticipation ran joyfully, if silently, high.

Next morning (yesterday as ever was!) a first glance through the window made it all too obvious that the " sunstoker " was on strike. A smooth rain was falling and the sky was leaden grey.

Ach! but wasn't that the usual prelude to a bright and

bonnie day? It would clear up by the time we reached the rendezvous by the river; so we ate heartily and hurried to the station in high hope.

After an hour in the train, learning from the daily press of the singular lack throughout the world of that brotherhood of man which our national poet was so optimistic about, we got out at a station where cars were waiting to take us for the out—ahem—inspection.

It was too bad that the sun had not yet come out; in fact there was quite a business-like shower as we drove off.

Passing by the farms we could see that much rain had fallen in the night: field after field of timothy was as flat as if steam-rollered. Unfortunately for us the wheat and oats, as well as the thistles and couch and knot-grass, were still standing sturdily erect, and as we began our inspection, believe me, every blade of grass—and oats and wheat and thistle—kepped its ain drap o' dew!

Being British we couldn't retreat, so we plodded on and on, weary and uncommonly wet, for over two hours. Learned Counsel, somewhat inadequately clothed, were there in force, and manfully stuck to their unusual job. The non-technical side of the Court, including the Chairman, shrewdly saw there was no necessity for *them* to inspect the river; so they discreetly retired to a barn while the heroes bent to their task.

By noon we concluded we were as wet as we could possibly be—and, right enough, we were far from dry. But most things are relative. Just then a black overhead cloud that we hadn't particularly noticed had a stab of lightning through it—and down it came in torrents. We were still half a mile from the cars. Between us and them was a perfect jungle of water-laden cereals and weeds to negotiate. Were we wet?

At the nearest hostelry—six miles away—even some of the semi-teetotallers didn't shrink from the fire-water which we coaxed from the bar-lady at five shillings a glass.

Now the sun is resplendent again; the larks will be singing, and the cereals will be whispering lovingly in the gentle breeze—while we again sit in the Court listening to the lawyers!

Yet, we are not sorry—and we *are* more intelligent. And after all, whatever unkind things we may say about our Scottish weather we cannot say that it lacks variety.

CHAPTER XIV

(Being Extracts from Diary)

Flying to Barra—The Importance of a Will

Last Tuesday, having breakfasted in Glasgow, we left at 8.25 in a bus for Renfrew. Scottish Airways have fairly spruced things up. No more standing in a draughty shed waiting to be weighed: a polite official invites you to use one of several well-upholstered chairs and couches in a luxurious lounge. This fosters a feeling of affluence which tends to soothe the sore of having had to part with all of ninety shillings as the price of personal transport from Renfrew to Barra—not that I should grumble! Hasn't His Majesty's Lord Treasurer's Remembrancer for nearly forty years faithfully reimbursed me for such expenditure? Moreover, I felt quite guilty in the knowledge that the rate for self and luggage worked out at 4½d. per lb., while the rate for a nice wee seven-stone wifie who crossed by the same plane must have been about 10d.

It was her first flight, but she soon forgot her first-flight apprehensions in the wonder of gliding smoothly over strange-looking towns and toy farmsteads, and then over loch and mountain and deep blue sea.

There—there near the north end of Jura is the swirling Corryvreckan; and there, right below us is Iona, the Scottish very cradle of Christianity.

In exactly an hour she was again on solid earth on the Reef of Tiree. Then off again on a final flip and there she was, in an hour and a half from Renfrew on the snow-white cockle-strand of her native Barra! *Dhia gle mise!* And then from old friends those words of welcome that are so warm on the Gaelic tongue. Here for a fortnight the soot and fog of the city are forgotten in the joy of the silver strand, in the greens and blues and purples of the ever-changing seas. . . .

Oh, yes! There will be a bit of a shower there sometimes, too; and there will be times when the wind will blow the blue colour from the seas that will roll and roar and burst heavens high against the rocks. But isn't that, too, the grand sight?

.   .   .   .

Every year there comes from the Highlands to the Land Court in Edinburgh a crop of requests for local investigation of complaints and difficulties, and " craves " for their settlement. A frequent cause of trouble is the question of march fences or the boundaries of the croft. Pity you the man who, either innocently or covetously, when laying down his crops encroaches by even a foot-breadth on his neighbour's land! Nor is the question so easily settled as one might suppose, for the march may be up to a mile long and anything but a straight line or on level ground. What between the ups and the downs of it, the little rocks and the big rocks that intersect the alleged line of boundary, and the *feanagan* and *baic-mona* (lazy-beds and peat-hags) that abut on it from every angle of the compass, the man who has to decide between the hotly hostile disputants would need to be a bit of a Solomon as well as a surveyor. On one occasion when, as usual, the truth got thoroughly bogged in a mire of contradictory verbal evidence, it was decided to inspect the *locus* in the hope of getting some light there—one witness having sworn that he knew the boundary well, and could show it to the Court by walking it from end to end. So out to the open went the Court and the crowd. In such circumstances it had been Mr Norman Reid's custom to remind the boundary-walker that although not now in the witness-box he was still on oath. This time by a mischance he forgot at the outset to give the usual warning. After the man had walked about a hundred yards—in a direction that presumably raised some doubt in the judge's mind—Norman remembered the omission and immediately corrected matters with an admonitory bawl that sounded like the island's fog-horn:

" Sandy! Sandy! Mind now! With every step you take your feet are ON OATH! "

Then in a case where the crofter dies intestate there is the question of deciding who has the right of succession. For the information of those who do not know (and there are many even in Scotland!), let me explain very briefly that one of the great features of the Crofters' Act of 1886 (now incorporated under the more comprehensive title The Small Landholders' (Scotland) Acts, 1886 to 1931, which have done more for the Highlands than any other legislative measure in the past hundred years) is the peculiar form of tenure which gives the holder the undisturbable right to remain in occupation during his life-time and the right to pass on a similar right to anyone within a specified circle of relationship. But if he wants to be sure that the person of his choice shall succeed he had better do something about it: he should either " assign " the holding or " bequeath " it. The former process requires the sanction of the Land Court and results in the assignee taking occupation of the holding while the old holder is still living, but usually with a friendly understanding that he will stay in his old home and get bed and board—and respect and *ceilidh* rights and privileges till the end of his day. But here's the rub! The crofter who philosophically contemplates his own demise and makes sensible arrangements for the time subsequent to that event is rather exceptional. In fact the great majority of crofters are most reluctant to make a will or an assignation, and most of them never do—often with lamentable consequences to those whom they most love. Take the sort of case that not infrequently comes before the Land Court.

Donald, the holder, and Mary his wife have been in the place since they married. They have suffered sore bereavement by the death of their only child. They are now middle-aged; there will be no more family. But they are still both hale and hearty and have many years of happy companionship to look forward to. Then Donald, out at the lobster creels, gets soaked to the skin, catches a cold which develops into pneumonia—and Mary, still scarcely realising the fact, is already Donald's widow.

Perhaps the greatest mitigation of her grief comes from the knowledge that at least she has her beloved home— the home that was Donald's father's and grandfather's and great-grandfather's before him—and the house that Donald had improved and made so cosy after their marriage so many years ago. Nor is she quite empty-handed, for Donald was a hard-working provident man; so that between his lobsters and herring-fishing, and the Government subsidies of £10 per acre for potatoes, £3 an acre for rye, £7 per cow and stirk (they had two head of each) and seven and sixpence a head for their twenty sheep, and Mary's own earnings from the world-famous Harris tweed, there was the tidy sum of £700 in the bank. Moreover, her favourite nephew from the croft on the other side of the bay—young Donald who had always been so mindful of herself and Donald, helping them with the work on the croft and with the sheep—would look after her affairs; and she would see to it that the croft would go to him after her day—*a laochan!*

So Mary settles down to make the best of what is left to her in life.

But within a month comes a shock in the form of a letter from a lawyer:

" DEAR MADAM,

" Acting on the instruction of Mr John MacEachan, 87 Millburn Street, Glasgow, I now beg to intimate to you as relict of the late Donald MacEachan that my client has lodged with the Scottish Land Court an application for an Order finding and declaring that he is heir-at-law of the said Donald MacEachan.

" As there does not appear to be any question of my client's right to succeed, and as he intends to take early personal occupation, I shall be glad to learn that you can make arrangements to quit the holding at an early date—and in any case not later than the term of Martinmas next."

" What lawyer's nonsense is this? " Mary asked indignantly of young Donald, but with a mind ill at ease.

Young Donald has to confess that he does not know—but surely it *must* be nonsense—didn't the croft belong to Uncle Donald? And wasn't it him that built the new house—and wasn't Aunty Mary going to have what belonged to her man?

" Of course the croft was his; and wasn't it himself that lifted the new house so that I would have a nice home to come to; and it was Donald that made the garden and put up the fences—and all that was Donald's is mine ! This letter, and that about Johnnie MacEachan must be a sort of cruel joke."

But poor Mary soon learns from the Land Court (before whom she had laid her trouble) that it isn't nonsense but sound law !—just an example of the application of the law of primogeniture. A man's widow is not his heir-at-law. As compared with the heir-at-law she has only limited rights of participation in his estate; and that, in the case of a crofter's widow, does not include the right of succession to the croft—unless her man has willed it to her. Donald had not done so—and that was the cause of all this heart-breaking trouble. Had Mary's son lived *he* would have succeeded as heir-at-law of his father; as it was, there was no doubt at all that Johnnie MacEachan (a son of a brother of Donald's) was heir-at-law, and as such entitled to get possession of the croft.

Nor is the law such a " hass " in this respect as might at first appear. For instance, suppose Donald Mac-Eachan had not been so lucky in his selection of a wife: suppose his wife had turned out a tartar or thoroughly bad egg (that does happen occasionally and there are many instances of a crofter deliberately " willing " the croft past such a wife); the sort of rank outsider that it would have grieved the heart of everyone in the Mac-Eachan family, male and female, to see established for life in their ancestral home—and with the right to pass it on, *not* necessarily to a MacEachan but to another of her own execrable brood! The thing is unthinkable! so into operation comes the law of primogeniture.

On the other hand there is legal protection and justice for the like of Mary in the Intestate Husbands' Estate (Scotland) Act, 1911-19, which provides that, in the event of there being no family and the total value of the estate not exceeding £500, the widow has the right of succession to the croft. And of course Mary's own man had it in his power all along to make sure that she would never be put out of her home—Och! if Donald had only the sense and decision to make a will, but he didn't—and he left more than £500 and so Mary was disinherited!

CHAPTER XV

Hill Farming—Road Hogs—The Hirsel—The Year's
Round—Snow Storm—A Man's Job—Harvest of the Hills

SOME of my hill farming friends may wonder why I write
this chapter at all. Well, they can skip it. But the fact
remains that things which to them must seem but the
very ordinary A B C of their lives (and therefore not worth
writing about) are to the majority of " outsiders "
involved in mystery and full of intriguing interest. How
often have I not seen (in days of plenty petrol) visitors
to our Scottish Highlands or the Borders enjoying for the
first time the glorious sensation of haring along a moorland road, with the honey scent of heather going like
wine to their heads, and with not a human being or even
a house in sight to break the serenity of the hills? Only
an occasional sheep, maybe with her lamb, by the roadside
or quietly browsing on the brae face and emphasising the
essential rusticity and peace; and just then!—a screech
of brakes and a sudden swerve—too late to avert tragedy:
a mother ewe or her baby or both horribly mutilated and
wriggling piteously to death. It takes a hardened motorist
to contemplate such with indifference. I have met some,
but thank goodness they are rare. The ordinary decent
man is acutely distressed, and if only he had a real
appreciation of the enormity of what he has done, surely
never again would he be so careless as to allow such a
thing to happen. Unfortunately, though, of the art and
intricacy of hill farming many of our summer visitors
are profoundly ignorant. Of the general extent of sheep-
raising in Scotland or of its importance to the country
they have but the faintest conception. It might surprise
such people to know that of the nearly 7,000,000 sheep
now in Scotland, about $4\frac{1}{2}$ millions are bred and reared

on hill land, or " mountain and heath " as it is described in the official documents. Over 40,000 farmers and small-holders are in this industry—considerably more than half of all the agricultural tenants in Scotland—and the individual interest varies from around 10,000 to less than 10 head of sheep. Thus the capital value of sheep-stock on our hills must be in the neighbourhood of £20,000,000, and when to that is added the value of farm and croft equipment in the way of houses, steadings, fanks, fences, etc., some idea may be had of the substantial nature of the industry as a whole and of its vital interest to those who make their living in it. Actually, there are people so ignorant as to have the vague idea that that sheep they have killed by their speeding car is just one of those scattered beasts they see on the hillsides and probably not owned by anyone in particular! But, indeed, it has an owner who will be definitely out of pocket by its death; and a local shepherd could tell at a glance at the " keels " and " buists " and " lug-marks " not only the name of its owner and his farm, but its age and the very hirsel of that farm to which it belongs.

For the business of hill farming is not the haphazard thing that so many people imagine it to be. Indeed, there are hazards in plenty, but the farm and stock are run to a pattern and on a definite system, disregard of which would soon bring chaos and disaster. To get a rough idea of the set-up and rhythm on a hill farm perhaps the simplest plan is to take a typical hirsel unit and note the main happenings on it in the round of the year—and starting our survey in November. But first let us have a few definitions and explanations that will help in getting a grip.

A *hirsel* is that particular section of the farm and the sheep on it which it is the primary duty of one shepherd to look after. Sometimes it is a " double " hirsel, in which case the senior shepherd will have an assistant. Other varieties are denoted by their distinguishing prefix of " ewe," " eild " (or yeld) or " mixed."

A ewe hirsel is one on which only breeding ewes (" stock " ewes) and their lambs are kept.

A yeld hirsel carries, of the breeding stock, only sheep of younger ages and in particular the one-year-old females (ewe hoggs) and the rising to two-year-old females (gimmers), neither of which is yet deemed sufficiently matured for mating. On the bigger farms this hirsel usually carries the young females of several ewe hirsels from the time they come home in spring from wintering at a low-ground farm perhaps a hundred miles away until, as young ewes they are returned to their native hirsels to take up the serious business of their lives. In the majority of Black-face stocks this return to the native hirsel takes place in November, when they are aged roughly a year and a half; but in the case of Cheviot stocks, particularly in Sutherland, the gimmers are not thus promoted until they are two and a half years old; and as the period of gestation with sheep is five months it follows that a Black-face ewe usually has her first lamb when she is two years of age, while in the case of Sutherlandshire Cheviots the ewes are three-year-olds when they drop their first lambs.

It might be as well to note here, too, that in the case of both breeds the *theory* is that no ewe is kept on the hill after she has reached the age of five and a half years. Thus it will be seen that at that age the Black-face ewe can have had only four lambs (barring twins), and when she has reared her fourth she is sold off as a cast ewe to be taken down to a low-ground farm to be crossed, usually with a ram of heavier breed for the production of cross lambs (often twins) for the early market. After that gruelling experience her title is changed to the less

honourable one of " milled " ewe.   Finally, in a year or
two, she is converted into what in choosey days might
be regarded as sausage mutton but which to-day would
be prized as prime gigot.

In the case of the Sutherland Cheviot ewe, as she is
a three-year-old when her first lamb is born and as she,
too, is cast at five and a half years, it follows that in the
course of her life on the hill she can have only three
lambs—again barring twins, which on a hill farm are but
a mixed blessing anyway.   Her post-hill history is much
the same as that of her Black-face sister.

And now to go back to early November for a very
sketchy glance at the principal events of the year—for by
then all sales of sheep and wool are over for the season.
The rams, since September, have been strictly segregated
within flawless fences; the ewe lambs have been sent off
to wintering, the October dipping (statutory) is over, the
ewes have had time to recover from the strain of rearing
lambs—and the stage is set for the next round.

We will assume a Black-face mixed hirsel.   At this
time the stock belonging to the hirsel including lambs
away at wintering numbers, say, five hundred.   Now if
hill sheep did not die of disease or suffer death by violence
in one shape or another, the age grouping would be quite
simple—there would be:

100 four-and-a-half-year-old ewes	⎫	
100 three-and-a-half-year-old ewes	⎬ 400 stock ewes,	
100 two-and-a-half-year-old ewes	⎭ on the hirsel	
100 one-and-a-half-year-old ewes		
100 half-year-old ewe lambs	at wintering	

———

500

But the causes of death among hill sheep are many.
Trembling, braxy, sturdy, pine, liver-rot, drowning in

bogs and burns, snow-smoor, falling over precipices, foxes, marauding dogs, Black-backs, Hoodie crows, couping and careering motorists are some of the things that play the very deuce with the mathematics of age-grouping of a hill sheep-stock. Even on the " healthiest " of farms and in the luckiest of years an annual death-rate of 6 per cent. would be considered fortunate. Ten per cent. is much more common, and in some districts more than twice that is not unknown. The comparatively moderate figure of 10 per cent. means a loss by death of the equivalent of the whole of your original stock in ten years: a risk far exceeding that in any other type of Scottish farming. In fact, if our average lamb crop is 70 per cent. and our average annual death-rate only 8 per cent., after selling-off female lambs below standard quality, our age-group structure at November would be approximately:

88 four-and-a-half-year-olds ⎫
95 three-and-a-half-year-olds ⎬ stock ewes 400
104 two-and-a-half-year-olds ⎪
113 one-and-a-half-year-olds ⎭
124 half-year-old lambs   at wintering

524

or nothing more than is required to maintain the stock ewes at the four hundred level. And we know many places where the ewe lamb crop is lower and the average death-rate higher. And that is why it is that the theoretical and much desired " casting " of five-and-a-half-year-old ewes is so difficult in practice. Often farmers are faced with the alternative of keeping on their old ewes to maintain their breeding stock or of selling them off and letting their stock diminish. It is a sort of Hobson's choice which usually ends by over-age ewes being retained; and that is apt to set agoing a vicious downward spiral

8

in the number and quality of lambs, and ultimately of ewes, which it is mighty difficult to arrest.

The first active step in the year's round is the putting out of the rams to the ewes—roughly in the proportion of three to one hundred—on a date somewhere in the third or fourth week of November. Towards the end of December the rams are taken in and again segregated or sent to low ground for wintering. In some cases they are allowed to summer on the hill along with the ewes and lambs but again relegated to enforced celibacy in September until required the following November.

In *February* there is a gathering of sheep for the *spring dipping*. This is not one of the statutory dippings, but is now generally favoured because of the immunity it gives to the ewe from irritation by skin parasites and consequent betterment in milk supply during the period April-August when she is rearing her lamb. The spring dipping is nicely timed with a view to maximum destruction of parasites and minimum of risk to in-lamb ewes; and in this connection our Scottish weather can be very trying!

Look out for the first lambs twenty-one weeks from the day the rams were put out in November. That will be just *about the same day of the month of April*. From then on for a month, for the shepherd and his specially hired "lamber" assistant, there is hardly any sleep at all. From dawn to dusk, and often through the darkness, their job is to keep watch and ward over their four hundred ewes scattered over a hill range of perhaps two or three thousand acres and now, in the throes of birth-giving, exposed not merely to the normal physical risks and mischances associated with that function, but to the horrible attacks of ruthless Black-backs and Hoodies, scouting overhead to spot the mother in labour, and then sitting on adjacent rocks in fierce mutual jealousy, waiting for the moment the lamb is born to pick from their sockets eyes that have scarcely seen the light of day while the mother is still too weak to protect her baby. Those ghoulish creatures know from experience that their best opportunity is before that man with his dog—and maybe a gun !—comes along. So they come while it is still dark and wait for the first peep of day. Well does the shepherd know that, and he comes early too. But his hill is wide and his pace is relatively slow. He cannot be in half a dozen places at the same time. A few minutes halt to help a ewe in distress, or to give a drop of warm milk to a weakly lamb so that it may get strength to seek its natural source of sustenance, may result in tragedy on the other side of the ridge only a hundred yards away. . . .

And the red fox ! that can break the neck of a well-grown lamb and carry it off regardless of mother's pathetically futile fury. . . . And if, from a hundred ewes, sixty to eighty lambs may seem a poor crop, having regard to the nature and variety of difficulties by which he is beset, even that measure of success is no mean achievement.

Truly the hill shepherd's is a job that demands all of a man's loyalty and effort and courage and skill; and truly with these virtues our Scottish hill shepherd is richly endowed. Those who imagine the life of a hill shepherd as a romantic strolling over sunny uplands with spy-glass, collie and crook should see him on a night in February when, from a day that gave no warning, there bursts one of those swirling, blinding, choking, terrifying snowstorms which from time to time cause such havoc in our moorland flocks.

His heft of ewes on the far slope at Alltdearg (some three miles across the moor) so seemingly safe when he saw them but a few hours ago, will be driven helplessly towards that deathtrap of a burn ! Never a hesitation as to what must be done—and done instantly. On go the old coat and leggings; the warm woollen gravat is wound round neck and ears; the crook is grasped from its corner; a " Come on, Roy! Bess! " to the dogs; a " Don't expect me till I come " to the wife, and a very gallant trio, without fuss or fear, go forth into that awful night to battle along the trackless treacherous moor with but one thought in mind—to save the ewes from being smothered or drowned at Alltdearg. Yes—not a few shepherds have given their lives that way.

Towards the end of May or early in June there is a big gather for the " marking " of the lambs. All male (wedder) lambs (with the exception of a few specially selected to serve as future rams) are castrated, and the tails of both sexes are docked, *i.e.*, shortened by a few inches. All lambs are also marked (buisted) by having the distinguishing mark of its farm and hirsel tar-stamped on the wool over the appropriate part of the body. Sometimes, too, the female lambs get " ear-marked " to the farm and age-marked as well; but often this distinction is deferred until all inferior and any surplus ewe lambs have been sold off.

Later in June there is a gathering-in of eild sheep for *clipping*.

In July the milk-ewes are clipped. One of the most important events of the year, and, as most of the shearing is done in the open, much at the mercy of the weather; for not even a fleece that is but slightly damp dare be rolled or packed. For catchers, clippers, buisters and packers it's a hot, hard job, which in other days was marvellously lightened by a generous libation of spirituous liquors that inspired tales of old experts and much competition. It's grand to see two experts who happen each to get a sheep from a catcher at the same moment pretending not to notice, but each striving to be the first to snip that last tassel from the tail, and so entitled, a fraction of a second before his neighbour, to get in a stentorian " BUIST ! " to the boy in charge of the boiling tar and buisting irons. And woe betide that youth if he is slow to respond ! By the way, it will save a lot of trouble later if at clipping the five-year-old ewes due for casting in the autumn are specially marked with a " pop " of tar.

As for the ewes and lambs, it is a time of baaing and bleating by day and by night. When at last the penned-up lambs are released to find their newly-shorn mothers the row is beyond belief. There is sometimes the odd lamb or two which refuses to believe that that bleached bleating monstrosity can be mother; but on the whole it is marvellous how quickly and completely the process of mothering is satisfactorily adjusted.

Not so many years ago the getting away of the wool from outlying hirsels and farms was a matter of considerable difficulty. Often it was a case of carrying only a couple at a time of those monstrous wool bags over the moor by pony-back or cart to the junction with a road, from where, in loads of half a dozen bags, it would be carted to the nearest railway station or pier, perhaps forty miles away. Now, with the aid of jeep, caterpillar and motor lorry the annual problem of getting away the wool is a thing of the past.

August, September and October are strenuous months with a continuous succession and variety of jobs. Within this period are due the two statutory dippings—one in August and the other in October—and in parts of the country where autumn hill mists are frequent a " clean gather " for the dippings is often impossible—with consequent irritating hold-ups.

From early August to late September—according to district and custom—come the speaning of the lambs, the expert sorting of the wedder lambs into " top," " mid " and " shott " classes for presentation at the sales, then driving of the lots to the various sale centres—sometimes so far distant as to necessitate an " on drove " period of several days.

Towards the end of September and throughout October the selling of the cast ewes goes on. The ewes, before leaving for the sales, undergo a process of " dressing "— an art in which some shepherds have a skill equal to that required for the achievement of a modern lady's coiffeur.

So, through storm and sunshine and the vicissitudes of the year, to the sales. And what an absorbing climax is this harvest of the hills ! In these few weeks will emerge the earning value of their year of strenuous toil; for in that time they will know the value of their wool ; and every ewe and lamb and other beast surplus to requirements for the maintenance of the flock will come under the hammer. In respect of all of them the owner will experience that poignant moment which, with a final " Going ! Going ! Gone ! " and a bang of the auctioneer's book, transfers the ownership to another.

Och ! it has its ups and downs—mostly downs, according to themselves. But it has its compensations. In truth it's a man's life, and be times good or bad they wouldn't have any other.

CHAPTER XVI

Valuations—An Old Ewe—A Long Lunch

On many hill farms the sheep-stock is "bound to the ground." None but the annual quota of lambs and cast ewes and rams may be sold off the place. An outgoing tenant is bound by the terms of his lease to deliver over the breeding stock in regular ages to the incoming tenant (or, failing such, to the landlord) so that the advantages of better health and strongly developed homing instinct of a home-bred stock may not be lost to the farm. The method of determining the values is also ruled by the terms of the lease. It may be at "fixed prices"; it may be on a "market-value" basis; or it may be on a full "acclimatisation value" basis—which, prior to recent restrictive statutory enactments, afforded considerable scope for imaginative effort on the part of the experts. Quite recently there has died out an interesting custom which from time immemorial dictated the terms of the award in a sheep-stock valuation. That was the custom of valuing the sheep not at so much *per head* but at so much per *clad score* (a clad score being twenty-one); the proportion of shotts (inferior sheep) in the lot was stated per score (twenty) and fell to be taken over at one-third less than the price stated. Leaving out rams (which would be valued individually or in age groups) a typical award would run thus:

1057 Ewes and lambs at £57. 10s. per clad score;
shotts 2¼ per score at ⅓ less.

122 Yeld ewes at £45 per clad score;
shotts 1½ per score at ⅓ less.

317 Gimmers at £47. 10s. per clad score;
shotts 1¾ per score at ⅓ less.

325 Ewe hoggs at £35 per clad score;
shotts 1¾ per score at ⅓ less.

To arrive at the correct total from an award in such terms was a first-class exercise in arithmetic. Often it was beyond the prowess of both outgoing and incoming tenant. Even with the help of their legal agents the best that could be achieved sometimes was agreement to split the difference between their respective totals that represented hours of laborious calculations. It was the late William MacLennan, for many years factor for Lord Zetland, who about forty years ago first made such calculations easy by the tables in his ready reckoner, *The Flockmaster's Companion*. To arrive at the sum payable in the case of the award quoted above all you had to do was to multiply the total number of sheep in each class by the appropriate figure.

			£	s.	d.
For Ewes and lambs it is	$1057 \times £2\cdot635416 =$		£2785	12	8
„ Yeld ewes	„ „	$122 \times £2\cdot089285 =$	254	17	10
„ Gimmers	„ „	$317 \times £2\cdot214781 =$	702	1	8½
„ Ewe hoggs	„ „	$325 \times £1\cdot618055 =$	525	17	4
			£4268	9	6½

William did not visualise any figure above £70 per clad score for ewes and lambs. In 1920-21 and again recently ewes and lambs were going at over £200 per clad score and we had to juggle with the tables.

No wonder that old-time hill farmers sometimes animadvert on present-day nursery-maid methods: of laws that will not allow of men standing on their own feet, and must always be guiding them from chair to chair, so that their lives are robbed of adventure and romance! For them a sheep-stock valuation was a day to be enjoyed and remembered. To it would gather farmers from all over the county, and some from beyond. The neighbouring ones brought their shepherds to give a hand to ensure that every sheep in its class was properly shown to the valuators. Usually there were two of these—one representing the interests of the outgoing tenant and the other of the incoming. There was an oversman in case of non-agreement ; and, as each valuator was all out for his own side, non-agreement was frequent, and the oversman was the person who really mattered. This highly important person was " mutually chosen " by the parties to the valuation. Not infrequently it took many months of mutual and highly diverting sparring for position before the choice could be announced. When no agreement could be arrived at, the appointment of the oversman was remitted to the Sheriff of the county. But the knowledge that in the end they would almost certainly have to submit to the oversman in no wise damped the valuators' ardour in promoting the interests of their respective clients, and their ingenuity and resource in that direction was always a thing to marvel at. In a case where the incoming tenant's expert gives it as his emphatic opinion " before God and with a good conscience " that the gimmers would be dear at £4 apiece, and the expert for the outgoing, under similar solemn guidance and restraint, is equally emphatic that they would be cheap at £6, there is obviously considerable scope for persuasive argument. Variety in technique was infinite. There might be audibly expressed horror at the other's awful position *vis-à-vis* his Creator ; or it might be a whispered (but just audible) concern that neighbours should never be allowed to know the sort of fool he is making of himself in suggesting so absurd a price.

Nor is partisanship always strictly confined to the valuators. If one can do a good turn by a remark which happens to reach the valuator's ears, but does not appear to be made with that end in view at all, should one refrain from making it?

One old worthy I knew was a master of that sort of

innocent soliloquy. On this day the valuator with the incoming tenant's interest at heart had suggested that amongst the ewes presented for valuation was a number of over-age animals whose presence seriously detracted from the value of the lot—an outrageous suggestion strongly repudiated by the outgoing tenant's man. There followed a hot exchange of contradictory assertions which promised to end in a laborious inspection of lug-marks in search of truth. It was just then that old Angus (who was friendly disposed towards the incoming tenant but appeared not to have taken the slightest interest in the point at issue) took advantage of a momentary lull in the brawl. He was looking at a venerable ewe which had lain on a nearby hillock and, regardless of all the fuss, was placidly chewing her cud. In a voice charged with sentimental emotion Angus addressed the ewe:

"*A ghalad! Tha thu 'n sin air an tomain cnamh do chi're direach mar a bha thu 'nuair bha mi so seachd bliadhna bho 'n diugh!*" ("My dear! There you are on the hillock, chewing your cud just as you were when I was here seven years ago to-day!")

Generous hospitality was a feature of old-time sheep-stock valuations—in the dispensing of which the wives of farmers and sometimes of shepherds came in for a strenuous time. On one such occasion I was greatly impressed by the efficiency of the managing shepherd's wife (whom I had not previously met) who, with the assistance of one neighbour and a lassie in her teens, cooked and served in the one day 22 breakfasts, 46 lunches and 34 high teas. She was a pleasant, good-looking woman, and though very stout could have given points to some professional waiters I have known.

The valuation was on a Wednesday. On the following Saturday I called again at the shepherd's place to take delivery of some "stragglers" that had come in since the valuation. The door was open, but I got no response to a knock. I went round to the back to see if there was anyone about the byre or barn. I heard the sound of milking. There in the byre was a stranger milking a cow. She was a tall slim girl and gave a pleasant greeting as she continued at her task.

I explained that I had called to see the shepherd but found nobody in the house. Could she tell me where the shepherd or his wife was to be found?

She looked somewhat puzzled, and then really surprised me by saying, " But I am the shepherd's wife ! "

" I beg your pardon ! " I said, " I am really very sorry ! But I thought it was the shepherd's wife who looked after us all so well on the day of the valuation ! "

" Well," said she, " and so it was ! "

" But no ! no ! " I protested, " I mean the big stout woman who was in charge."

" Well," she insisted, " the big stout woman was me ! "

" But bless me ! " I bleated, fair puzzled, " I just do not understand. I . . . ? "

" Oh ! I see ! " she said with a grin. " But if you go to the kitchen till I finish this cow, and see that the baby in the cradle is all right, perhaps you will begin to understand."

I went to the kitchen. There in the cradle I found an exceptionally healthy specimen of a baby boy. He had been born on the morning of the day after the valuation; he was not two days old and his mother was in the byre blithely milking the cow.

But the high-water mark in hospitality at a sheep-stock valuation in my experience was reached that time we sat down to a lunch that started at 1 P.M. and didn't really finish till 4 A.M. next day. True, many of the original starters didn't stay the course: there were several casualties and departures in the late afternoon and there were somewhat hazy intervals here and there when it could not be claimed that all the survivors were *eating* at the tables. But always, up till 10 P.M., a dozen or two could be relied on to carry on with the knives and forks while the others kept 'up the general hilarity to the best of their ability; which latter was of no mean order.

There followed a pretty tough session till midnight, by which time all but twenty of the original starters weren't there. At 3.30 A.M. the remaining eight of us found ourselves seated at one table feeling quite peckish and putting in a hearty finish to the long lunch. Included in the party were A and B who, though bosom friends of many years, had recently fallen out over something and hadn't spoken to each other for months. Not even the extreme cordiality which characterised the day's proceedings had broken down the barriers—a state of affairs which became all the more delicate in so small a company. Tension was relieved, though, when we observed that A, with head sunk on chest, had presumably fallen sound asleep.

At this stage B got to his feet and begged to announce to the assembled company that before parting on this so auspicious occasion he felt it incumbent on himself to propose a toast: the toast of "The Arbiter." The proposal met with a hearty approval that gave no hint of the fact that the arbiter had already in the course of the evening been toasted at least a dozen times. We hear—heared! with virginal zest.

In a model of a speech of some six minutes duration, B extolled the virtues of the arbiter's parents, his boyhood, youth and manhood, and touched on his crowning glory as an arbiter.

All bar A, who was apparently still sound asleep, did full justice to the occasion and in chorus shouted "Arbiter!

Arbiter ! Arbiter ! " and resumed our seats. That is, all but B, who remained upright and, as soon appeared, was of the opinion he had got up to say something. Then it came to him. He begged to announce to the assembled company that, before parting on this so auspicious occasion, he felt it incumbent on himself to propose a toast: the toast of " The Arbiter " ! And word for word like a gramophone record he reproduced the model speech.

Though some of us were somewhat surprised we all got up as best we could and again gave cordial reception to the toast. A was still asleep.

Still B remained on his feet, deep in mental struggle, and—to the surprise of all of us this time—again submitted the toast of " The Arbiter."

And again we responded.

But when B for the fourth time began to beg to announce to the assembled company, etc. . . . the spell under which we had laboured for nearly twenty minutes was suddenly broken. The sleeping A, with the aid of a firm grip on the underpart of the table, managed to raise his bottom about six inches from the chair. Through half-closed eyes he peered round the table.

" Gentlemen," he said, " as shelf appoined shairman of shis meeting I beg ta nounsh to shembled cupney that speshes be of shree minitsh shurashion—AN NO REPETI-SHUNS ! "

During this surprising announcement B stood gazing malevolently at the interrupter. Now in concentrated anger he addresses the enemy.

" Sir, do you mean to insinuate that I am *boring* the company? "

A again raised his bottom off the chair, glowered vaguely in the direction of B, said, " I jew," sat down and went off to sleep.

The electrical atmosphere could be cleared only by a diversion; so we all struggled to our feet and in honour of the arbiter, sang " He's a jolly good fellow " about ten times over; followed up with Auld Lang Syne, and beat a hurried retreat while the going was still good.

CHAPTER XVII

Shetland—Self-help—Seafaring Breed

THE official name now is Zetland, but like most people I feel more at home with Shetland. Here is a county of more than a hundred islands, of which over twenty are inhabited. Foula, the island of film fame, stands sentinel some thirty miles out to the west of the mainland; and Fair Isle, some twenty-five miles south-west of Sumburgh Head, is a sort of half-way house to Orkney.

From Sumburgh Head in the south, to Muckle Flugga in the north—the most northerly land (or rather rock) in Britain—is some seventy miles.

A visit to the Muckle Flugga is something to be remembered. The day we went the weather was so fine that our boatman decided to take us through a tunnel opening in a cliff. At high tide or in a heavy swell it is impossible to get a boat through this hole in the wall of rock. Even on that good day there was a dreadful moment when it seemed that the gentle swell would result in our being crushed like an egg-shell against the roof of the tunnel. We were heartily glad to get safely through; but when we got to the base of the Muckle Flugga at the landing place from which an incredible number of steps cut in the rock-face lead to the lighthouse at the top, it was only fear of losing face that goaded us into making that fearsome ascent. The indescribably impressive view from the top temporarily dispelled even our dread of the down-coming; and of course we got from the lighthouse-keeper the sort of welcome which only lighthouse-keepers can give.

Shetland is so deeply indented by " voes " (firths) that any figure of breadth from east to west would have little meaning; enough to say that although at its widest it is 22 miles broad, you cannot stand on a spot in Shetland that is three miles from the sea.

Roughly up the middle of the long streak which forms the mainland there is a back-bone of hills rising from 500 to 900 feet and culminating in Ronas Hill, which is nearly 1,500 feet and the highest point in the county.

The total land area is 352,000 acres; but of this only 14,000 acres or so is cropping land. The great bulk of the remainder is common pasture—or " scattald " to give it its local name. A feature which at once attracts the notice of a stranger is the comparatively large area of cabbages. The Shetlander sets great value on his cabbages as a winter feed for stock. The favourite variety is of a purplish colour and peculiar to these islands. Cabbage seed is preserved each year and sown for safety in " plantiecruives." The plantiecruive is a small nursery out on the scattald, with high walls to protect the young plants from the devastating winds, and from the depredation of even the most enterprising of sheep—which is saying a good deal in Shetland !—until transplanted in garden land and well-enclosed paddocks near the house. Despite disadvantages of soil and climate the standard of agriculture has been markedly raised in recent years.

Shetland is a county of small-holdings. Out of a total of nearly 4,000 agricultural subjects over 3,000 are under the 50-acre standard (disregarding share in scattald), and of these 3,000 more than half do not exceed five acres. The rights of participation in the scattald grazing is a subject so complicated as to be almost incomprehensible to an outsider, but to the participants themselves it seems simple enough. That is not to say they are always of one mind about it—as the Scottish Land Court, whose unenviable duty sometimes is to settle local differences of opinion on the matter, very well know !

Everybody knows that Shetland has a pony of its own;

also that it has its own miniature collie dog. But not so many know that Shetland has also got its own breed of cattle and sheep.

The Shetland pony is too well known to require description: it should be emphasised, though, that the sleek, well-groomed, well-mannered specimens familiar at Lowland shows bear but little resemblance to the shaggy, wild-eyed creatures which roam in droves over their native scattald.

Ponies used to be exported in considerable numbers. They made ideal pets for children of the well-to-do, but the main demand for them was as pit-ponies for hauling coal from the working face to the elevators at the pit shaft. Soon after the Great War, following the installation of electric power in the pits, the demand for them became so poor that few were exported. The result was an embarrassing increase in their numbers at home. They ate up the sheep's pasture to such an alarming and lossful extent that scores of them had to be shot and buried. In one case I had to do with, where over fifty ponies had to be cleared off the ground, as an alternative to shooting (which I couldn't bring myself to do) I had them sent for sale at Aberdeen; but to meet all charges for freight, keep and commission I had to pay £15 in excess of the total sum realised from the sale! In recent years the demand for Shetland ponies has revived, and at the moment they are fetching good prices.

The Shetland cow is a sort of Shorthorn in miniature, very hardy, a good milker and said to be free of tuberculosis. With this reputation she is in considerable demand as a " family " cow both in and outwith Shetland.

In recent years there has been a good deal of crossing of the native sheep with the Cheviot, Black-face and other heavier breeds, but the real Shetland sheep is a dainty creature not so very much larger than an outsize Mid-lothian brown hare. The infallible mark of the breed is a short, *bare* tail. Colours are white, black, black and white, and a warm brown or "moorit." The wool, which is very fine, is not shorn but *plucked* off the body ("rooing"). This is the wool which is the basis of the world-famous Shetland hosiery industry.

The artistic skill and speed displayed by the women in designing and knitting have got to be seen to be believed. Shawls and garments of intricate design and of beautifully blended colours are made "straight out of their heads." Nor does the adage about the wisdom of doing only one thing at a time hold much meaning for these wonderful women of Shetland, who can simultaneously carry a creel of peats, drive a cow, enjoy an animated conversation with a neighbour similarly employed and knit one of these garments, all with amazing proficiency.

Minerals. Cromate and copper ore are known to exist in various places, particularly in the island of Unst, and to a limited extent the mines have been worked at different times in the past. In any national scheme of rural regeneration it is conceivable that these deposits may assume local importance.

Herring Fishing. After agriculture—and some might dispute the "after"—herring fishing is the great industry in Shetland. With the advent of the steam drifter in place of the old sailing boat the fishing industry has, during the past thirty years, centred mainly in Lerwick, to which English and West Coast boats and "crews" of lassies repair annually at the opening of the "season" in that spirit of high hope and adventure so characteristic of all engaged in this tantalising but occasionally very remunerative calling.

To the extent that the general circumstances of their lives are similar, the Shetlander and the man of the

Western Isles are very much alike. Insularity makes of each a good boatman and skilful fisherman; and he is weather-wise and independent in outlook. But certain characteristics attributable to racial differences are noticeable. When the Celt is impulsive and maybe dangerously imaginative, the Scandinavian is a philosopher in close touch with realities. Seldom does a Celt in search of a small-holding bother to reconcile his demand with his capital resources. With not a penny to bless him he will airily inscribe the figure 50 in the blank on the official form when he is invited to state the acreage of the holding he is applying for. That it takes around £500 to fully stock and equip a fifty-acre holding daunts your penniless Highlander not a whit, and he is indignant when a friendly but unfortunate official points out the snags. In marked contrast the Shetlander carefully counts the cost and inserts an acreage figure in strict accordance with his financial capacity; and if he is offered land in excess of that acreage he politely but firmly refuses to accept.

I shall probably get into hot water over this next bit, for, as a Celt, I can think of no epithet more likely to arouse hot resentment, when applied to my kinsmen, than that of " beggar." Yet the fact is that, in the course of the past fifty years, in his relationship with government departments and local authorities the Celt has acquired a skill in alms-collecting that amounts to genius. Singly and collectively, by political pressure, by telling the tale of woe with a skill worthy of the *seanachaidh*, the Highlander has contrived to ensure a considerable flow in his direction of the fluid that comes from such old milk-cows. Time and again he has successfully persisted in his claim to have a new road or path or pier. Seasons of potato-blight or bad harvests skilfully publicised have resulted in supplies of seed-potatoes and oats the following spring. He is still at it and likely to continue. Nor do I suggest that he has got anything in excess of his value to the nation in peace and war. I am merely concerned to show an interesting difference between Highlander and Shetlander.

The Shetlander suffers adverse circumstances in silence. Seldom does he make public moan. I well remember a case where the crofters in a Shetland township applied to the Department of Agriculture for enlargement of holdings. On local investigation I found that the land applied for was on the far side of a heather-clad moor and nearly a mile distant from the existing crofts; and there was no road across the moor. I had to point out to the applicants that, even if they got the land and grew crops on it they would not be able to get the crops home for want of a road—and that it was doubtful if the Department would regard the cost of a road as justifiable in this particular case. The applicants appreciated the point and said they would write me when they had further considered their problem. Six months later I had a letter from their secretary. Could I come to see them soon? *They had constructed a road across the moor and would be glad if the scheme for enlarging their crofts could now be proceeded with!* Of course I went—and found a well-constructed road from the crofts to the land they wanted. It transpired that, following on my previous visit, they resolved to overcome the obstacle by making a road for themselves; so they appointed as foreman one of themselves who had some skill in road work. Each of the others contributed a share of the labour necessary to complete the road—and there it was! Only in Shetland did I ever meet so amazing a capacity for self-help.

During the war a Secretary of State for Scotland paid a visit to Shetland. One of the things he particularly wished to see was one of those primitive little meal-mills, whose circular grinding-stone is made to revolve by the flow of water from a burn being directed towards its flanged spindle. The Agricultural College representative took us to see one. It was in excellent condition and hard at work grinding bere into meal. The Secretary of State was much impressed by the ingenuity and efficiency of the mill, and astonished to learn˙ that its every part had been made and put together by the crofter to whom it belonged and his father.

The crofter offered to show us the kiln where he dried the grain before milling. To get to the kiln we had to go through an exceptionally well-constructed barn. The Secretary supposed that this was the work of a professional builder?

" Weel, as a matter of fact, no: it was himself who had built the barn too " ! was the modest claim.

I noticed in the barn a neatly finished fanner—but not of any " make " known to me.

" Did you make this too? " I inquired.

" Oh weel, yes : he had made that too—in his spare time one winter."

The kiln was of the " bellied-cone " type, built of stone, about ten feet high at the apex and perfect in its proportions and symmetry. Even I did not think any amateur could have built so perfect a structure—and said as much. But he had !

" But how on earth did you get the outbulges and the inward curves so faultless? " I wondered.

" Oh weel, I hed to think oot that one weel before I started. First I cleared the foundation. Then I fixed a peg in the centre and with a piece of string attached to it I drew a circle of the size I wanted. Then I took oot the peg and put a ten-foot pole standing on the same spot, and plumbed it there with light wood-stays. Then I drew on a piece of paper (to scale) a plan of the kiln I wanted, with its sides bulging out from the centre and then curving in to converge truly at the apex. Then I

cut a number of strings of the different lengths required
to give me my right radius from the centre pole at every
half foot of height—and man! it cam oot fine! "

After this it came as no surprise that the very substantial
and well finished dwelling-house, from foundation to roof-
ridging, had been planned and executed by this master
craftsman, who had never learned any trade but coopering.
But indeed the Secretary was moved to genuine admiration,
and in the course of conversation was distressed to learn
that our host was beginning to feel the work of the place
too much for one of his years.   Worse still, of his two
sons, the one who used to help him was already in the
navy and the other one who was in a bank and helped
him at week-ends was due to join the army next week.
It was certainly a hard case and the Secretary, who was
very human and kind of heart, had a whispered conversation with the senior departmental official who was present.
The senior official, while equally sympathetic, very rightly
pointed out the danger of making any promises which
might not be fulfillable.   So the Secretary was very
guarded in expressing to the old man the hope that
something might be done; he would see; he would do
his best; but he could not promise. . . .

Not till then did our host suspect what had been the
subject of the whispered conversation.

" Are you telling me, sir, that you may be able to do
something to keep my boy at home? " he asked.

Well, the Secretary would like to—he would try; but
of course he couldn't promise.

The old man was wistfully silent for a minute, then:
" Well, sir, that is very kind of you, and I expect it would
take a load off his mother's heart—although I'm not sure
that she would like it either.   But you see, sir, the last
time he was with us we could see he was unhappy at not
being away at the war with the rest of them.   And we

don't want him to be unhappy—and I hope you will not misunderstand or think me ungrateful, but we would raither you did not do anything about it but just let things be. But thank you very much for your kindness."

Seafaring is in the Shetlander's blood. The proportion of men from these islands who earn their livelihood by going down to the sea in ships (in ways more peaceful than those of their viking forebears!) is very great. In Shetland you can meet hundreds of men who are as familiar with Sydney harbour and Magellan's Strait as they are with Lerwick and Scalloway; quiet, keen-eyed, clear-headed, decent men worthily upholding in every quarter of the globe the best traditions of their breed. But their roots are deep in Shetland whither they repair between voyages to recuperate on the land; and later to seek refuge and peace in the evening of life.

CHAPTER XVIII

Usgar* : Being Red-letter Days in the Life of a Highland Cow

(This chapter is for bairns only—of all ages)

SHE was born out on the machair of a township in the Hebrides. It was a bonnie April morning that set the larks acarolling in the sun despite a remnant of winter's chill in the air.

She wasn't quite yellow, nor yet quite brown, but yon in-between colour which denotes a hardy constitution. And she was as curly as a toy teddy bear; indeed, that was what she looked like lying in the shelter of the tuft of sea-bent.

Her mother (Annag), not content with the thorough cleansing she had already given her baby daughter, was still giving a lick here and there, and softly moaning an invitation to be up and doing at a first meal from an udder that ached with its amplitude of rich warm milk. Suddenly mother sensed approaching danger and whipped round on the defensive! . . . But it was only her mistress, Kirsty, coming to see if the expected calf had yet arrived. A glance at the little stranger and Kirsty knew that her wish of many years was at last satisfied.

" *M'usgair bheag!* " (" My precious little jewel! ") cried Kirsty, and her gently caressing the curly coat while Annag looked on with a fondly-fatuous expression of eye that was comical in the extreme. Now the reason for Kirsty's great joy was this:

Annag's great-great-great-grandmother Morag had come to the croft as a wedding gift to Kirsty's husband's father from *his* father. That was a long time ago, but always since then there had been on the place a descendant of

* Sound the u *not* as in *but* but as in *puss* ; and the word as a whole sounds *usscar.*

136

the wedding-gift cow. But it had looked as if Annag would be the last of her line. For years Kirsty had hoped that Annag would produce a daughter. But no! year after year it was a great big son she presented to Kirsty; and now, after so many disappointments, there was Annag's little daughter that would one day take up the succession as the favourite cow on the croft. No wonder that Kirsty called this calf her precious little jewel! That evening, her tummy well filled with milk, wee Usgar lay beside her mother on the machair looking far out to sea, where a great golden ball was sinking slowly out of sight and sending up into the sky a succession of resplendent yellows and pinks and reds and purples that together on this first day of her life evoked in Usgar a vague bovine bliss.

. . . .

In describing the first day of Usgar's life I purposely made no mention of the less pleasant subject of death; but the fact is that Kirsty's man Donald had died some years before Usgar was born. He, too, had been hoping that Annag would some day have a heifer calf; and that was another reason for Kirsty's joy at sight of Usgar. Meantime her son Donald had joined the Cameron Highlanders and was away at the war, while the widow was doing her best to carry on the croft with the help of neighbours.

There came a day in late autumn that brought to little Usgar the first great unhappiness of her life. The previous day there had been a blood-red sky as the sun went down. Angus, the herd "Aonghas a' bhuachaille" prophesied to Kirsty that this foretold an early frost. Sure enough that very night there was a sharp frost and a million stars in a steel-blue sky. The ground hardened. Ice came on the pools. The calves' skins felt creepy with the cold. By morning they were feeling pretty miserable. But far, far worse was yet to come! When Aonghas came along that morning Kirsty came too, and Hector and Calum Saighdear and three or four dogs. Why all this? But when the people and the dogs tried to separate them from their mothers the youngsters sensed that something unusual and unpleasant was afoot.

Truth to tell, for some time past they had not been keeping so very close to their mothers because, with the browning grass, milk was getting scarce; and they took a mischievous pride in keeping far away from the cows, who would get alarmed and start calling at them to come back. But there was a mighty difference between calves voluntarily separating themselves from their mothers and being forcibly driven from them! For a while they defied every effort in that direction, but in the end, with the help of hard sticks and biting dogs, the people managed to turn back the calves while their mothers were driven through a gate and far away out of sight.

Little did the youngsters think that never again would they taste a drop of their mother's milk. Surely before long they would be allowed to join their mothers again! But hour after hour passed and they got really alarmed. Not till then did they realise how much their mothers meant to them. They started a chorus of heart-broken bellowing that their mothers could have heard in St Kilda. Anyhow, they heard it where they were, for they set up a bellowing too; and so it continued through that awful day of black misery and thirst. At last thirst compelled them to sip the ice-cold water, which gave them a toothache and pains in the tummy. By night they were too tired and miserable even to bellow. For them the end of the world had come as they lay on the cold frosty ground to pass the most wretched night of their lives.

But after a few miserable days they were still alive— and began to take an interest in life again. So much so, that when one morning Aonghas opened the gate and drove them over to where their mothers were they seemed somewhat ashamed of all the noise they had made about the separation. They merely sniffed their mothers when they met—all but Calum Beag who was calf enough to try for a sip at the old source—and got kicked in the face for his impudence! Calum was deeply offended, but the rest of them with tails in air danced for joy at his discomfiture, and felt quite grown-up and self-reliant.

.   .   .   .

By the time she was eighteen months old, Usgar had grown into a fine stirk and was already showing a pair of horns of great promise. Soon she had learned that if Kirsty had a kind heart she had also a quick temper and a hazel switch with which to beat one sorely!

But how can a young creature full of life always be minding p's and q's even if forgetting them may bring a spot of trouble? Anyway, Usgar and her friends got themselves into a whole peck of troubles this day. They had been grazing slowly over the machair from one side to another, with Aonghas a' Bhuachaille keeping an eye to see that they didn't get into mischief. But old Aonghas loved an afternoon nap, and that sometimes gave them the chance of a stolen bite. This day, as they were nearing the dyke that separated the machair from the arable land and feeding on the now rather tasteless autumn grass, the band of youngsters suddenly ceased grazing and stuck their noses in the air to sniff the breeze that came from the crofts. Never had so delectable a smell entered their noses! What it came from they could not guess, but that it was from something that would be good to eat there was no doubt at all. It brought slobbering slavers to their mouths!

Soon all the noses were pointing straight at a dark green patch in Kirsty's croft. Well they knew from painful experience that the crofts were forbidden ground. But their buachaille was sound asleep! And there were gaps on the dyke where they could easily get over! With one accord they jumped the dyke and raced for the green patch.

As that was the first time they had seen turnips they did not know how good the bulbs were to eat. But that didn't bother them : the green shaws had a flavour that stirred their hearts to a frenzy of joy. So for a few happy minutes they just pulled up turnip after turnip and chewed off the green tops.

While they were still hard at their feast there came a shriek from Kirsty and her calling loudly for the dog. Roy came racing at them in a most unfriendly way, barking like mad and snapping at their heels. The noise wakened up old Aonghas, who now ran over with *his* dog and belaboured them on the ribs with his big stick. By this time, too, Kirsty herself had arrived to help with her hazel switch, and with some dreadful names she called them in the Gaelic. Usgar, in her terror, turned on the yapping Roy and with her horns tossed him clean over the dyke, so that he began howling too! Kirsty and Aonghas and the dogs and themselves bawling and bellowing and howling together! Never was such a hullabaloo about a few turnips!

Thinking it all over as they lay on the machair that night with sore heels and ribs, Usgar came to the conclusion that if they wanted to escape trouble in future they had better leave turnips alone—and yet! they smelled so good and tasted so divinely! Perhaps it was meant that way? that for things worth having it is worth risking a spot of trouble? Anyhow, they had those glorious few minutes, even if it did upset the old lady and Aonghas and the dogs—*Nyum Nyum!*

,   ,   ,   .   .   ,   ,   ,   ,   ,

Young Donald was now home from the war. Through the lovely green-grass days of spring and summer Usgar saw him and his neighbours hard at work on the land, sowing and planting, and carting the seaware and peats. Why on earth human beings should always be work-work-working away must be difficult for a cow to understand; but surely it must give them no little satisfaction to see men and women spend most of their days in preparing food for them, so that they may lie in the sun blissfully chewing the cud!

Late in July there came into Usgar's life another of those days which she would long remember. It was the day of the agricultural show. Nearly all the people on the island came to it. That morning Donald had tied a rope round Usgar's horns, brushed her long silken coat with a brush in a way that she half liked and half didn't, then he led her off to the show-ground about five miles away. There they found gathered together the pick of the island's cattle. Usgar was led into the ring by Donald when it came to the time for heifers of her age to be judged—and Donald became the envy of the island that day! For Usgar, now over three years of age, had developed into a beauty that even in that select company was outstanding. While still retaining the sprightliness and glorious bloom of youth she had acquired some of that stateliness of carriage, that majesty of mien, that was to distinguish her for the rest of her days. Not one moment did the judges hesitate. The first prize red ticket was tied round Usgar's horns; and before the show was over there was an assortment of championship tickets with it, dangling over her nose. Both for Kirsty and Donald this was indeed a memorable day.

Then a thing so dreadful happened that it hurts to tell of it. Ever since he returned from the war Donald had been moody and nervous and not like his old self at all; more than once he had taken more drink than was good for him. This hurt Kirsty to the heart, but she rightly put it down to the upset of the war, and hoped and prayed that some day her son would grow into his old reliable self again. Unfortunately, though, he had not yet regained his serenity and stability; and his outstanding success at the show was too much for him: along with several friends he had made a merry night of it. He was never quite sure of what had happened, but was horrified next morning when a drover came to take Usgar away with some other beasts he had bought! So *that* explained the large sum of money Donald had found in his purse! He had sold Usgar! Usgar that was the pride of his mother's heart—and indeed of his own!

So their day of triumph was followed by a day of grief too deep even to be spoken about. Usgar and the others were driven off to the pier, and that same evening hoisted in a sling to a most alarming height and then dumped down in the bowels of a ship to be carried far away, and finally forced into the sea to swim to the rough, rocky, uninhabited island which was to be Usgar's home for seven years.

 . . . .

After swimming to land on their new island home, Usgar and her friends walked across the little sandy bay and scrambled up a dangerous path through rocks in search of something to eat. The people who used to live on this island had left some years before Usgar landed there. Only cattle and sheep lived there now, and it might be months before a man came to see how they were doing or to shear the sheep or take away some of them to the sales.

While the newcomers were doing their best to satisfy their hunger by eating the short but sweet grass they found above the rocks, what should move into sight, not a hundred yards away, but a number of Highland cows that had been there for years? These old-timers grew quite excited on seeing the strangers. Soon they decided that the strangers had no right to be on their grazing. Two or three of the biggest and wildest looking, with noses to the ground and up-staring eyes, moved towards the newcomers bellowing an awesome challenge. No wonder if most of the tired and still hungry youngsters were terrified and made off for the hills. But not Usgar. For in cattle, as in people, blood tells, and in Usgar's veins ran the blood of that famous sire of old, Tormaid Buidhe of Baile Raonuill. She was young and would probably get hurt by this infuriated and full-grown cow, but she could not run away like one base-born. So she lowered her head to the challenge.

Surprised and further angered by such presumption the big cow, who was clearly the Queen of the Fold, rushed forward to heave Usgar over the almost precipitous face of the rock. But Usgar, well knowing she would have no chance in a head-on charge with a cow nearly twice her weight, flashed round to the side so that in her mad rush the big cow charged straight on—at nothing! Usgar saw her chance—and took it. Before the old cow managed to pull up near the top of the cliff Usgar charged; and what she lacked in weight she made good in youthful agility. Over the rock went her huge adversary, emitting a terrified bellow as she fell.

The old cow was not killed—as she might well have been; nor did she break a leg. But she was badly bruised and slightly lame for the rest of her life. And from that day on Usgar reigned the undisputed Queen of the Island.

.   .   .   .

Every year to the Scottish Highlands from April till October there is a constant stream of visitors to enjoy the peace and grandeur of our scenery. They come from all over the world, and many of them come year after year. The majority of them keep to the main routes, but always there are some who go searching into all sorts of odd and out-of-the-way places. It was one of this kind who one day landed on the island to which Usgar swam ashore some seven years earlier. He was a wealthy gentleman farmer from England and had with him his fifteen-year-old daughter who was greatly enjoying her first visit to the Hebrides. It was the girl who first caught sight of a number of animals, the like of which she had never seen before—and which indeed gave her quite a fright with their great long horns and shaggy coats. But her father assured her they were just Highland cows and very quiet and docile. The cattle had been longing to see a human being and readily made friends with the strangers. One of the friendliest was a magnificent animal with long silky hair and great level horns that spread wider than the length of the girl's body. This beautiful cow came right up and licked the lassie's hand with a rough but kindly tongue, and the father thought the two of them made a rare picture. In a jiffy he had taken a snapshot of them. As father and daughter were about to set off again in their boat, a man came over the hill and gave them a friendly hail. He turned out to be the owner of the cattle and was paying one of his periodic visits to see how they were doing. Mr Osborne made a complimentary remark about the cattle they had seen, and made special mention of the beautiful big cow that was so friendly.

Mr Stewart agreed they were a fine lot and regretted he must soon sell the big cow, because, although she was by far the best, she had disappointed him in that she had never produced a heifer calf: seven bull calves in a row!

Now Mr Osborne had often thought of starting a

small fold of Highland cattle at his place in England. Here might be his chance—and it was almost certain that a cow which had so many sons would soon have a daughter!

In a few minutes a bargain was struck. Usgar—for Usgar it was—would be shipped next week to Kyle and railed to the south of England. And the clattering and rattling of the train and the awful hunger of that long journey remained in her memory for many a day.

. . . .

Other seven years passed. Donald had long ago settled down into a steady-going man with wife and family. Kirsty was now an old woman, but still hale and hearty. Never one word of reproach had she spoken to Donald about the selling of Usgar. But well he knew how it had hurt her, and many had been his own remorseful moments about that unhappy affair.

Donald had flourished exceedingly on the croft, and when they got news that a favourite niece was to be married in London before leaving for Canada, nothing would do but Donald must go and give away the bride.

At the wedding he met a far-out cousin of whom he had little previous knowledge. But, of course, cousins are cousins. This one was manager on a farm a few hours by train west of London. Donald must go to see him before starting for home.

The cousin never said a word about having Highland cattle on the farm; he wanted to give Donald a real surprise. And he did! There were over a dozen very fine cows and a few younger beasts. As the two men stood in the park to have a right look at the animals, there happened to be grazing quite close to them a cow of magnificent proportions, but obviously well up in years. Moving slowly along as she grazed, this cow got right into Donald's " wind " just at the moment when

Donald expressed his admiration for so grand a cow:
" *'ille! nach eile i sin math ged a the i aosda?* " Suddenly
the old cow ceased grazing, raised her head and sniffed
into the breeze. Then she came slowly towards the men,
with her nose still in the wind. They watched her with
curiosity. She came right up and sniffed Donald's Harris
tweed plus-fours !—and then looked up straight at him.

" Strange ! I never saw her do the like of that before,"
said the cousin in the Gaelic.

" Aye," said Donald, also in the old language, and
him fair trembling with excitement and looking closely
for certain colourings on the cow's sides till he found
what he was looking for. " Aye ! it's her right enough !
It must be—it is our *Usgar!* " And, as if in confirmation,
the old cow was now licking his one hand while he rubbed
behind her ears with the other.

Briefly Donald told the story of Usgar to the cousin.
He knew she had been taken to the island, but there
had lost all trace of her. The cousin told of how she
came from the island seven years ago, that she had a
heifer calf in her first year on the farm but all bull calves
since. She was now in calf again; he was selling her
soon but he would try to buy her calf back if it should
be a heifer.

" You are selling her this very day," said Donald,
" and that to me. And you will never get her calf whatever it is ! " And that was how it was settled between
them without further ado.

.   .   .   .

So it was that Usgar once again found herself in a
railway truck on a long, long journey. But she was
neither lonely nor hungry this time, for Donald travelled
by the same train and had a word with her whenever
there was anything of a wait at a station. He also saw
to it that she had plenty to eat and drink till they reached

Oban. And when it came to getting her aboard the steamer for the Outer Isles there was no need for twisting tail or slashing stick. The old cow walked down the tilted gangway in the manner of one knowing where she was going.

Out in the Minch, while the Islands were not yet in sight, Usgar was seen to be strangely excited and kept turning her head towards the side of the ship where a modicum of daylight showed. At the pier she walked briskly ashore. From then on it was Usgar that led the way—and at such a pace that Donald was hard put to it to keep up with her. Before they reached home it was dark. She made straight for the gateway that gave entrance to the machair. Donald let down the rails. Usgar walked in and made for where other cows had gone to rest for the night. Soon she lay beside them, tired indeed, for she had travelled far and was heavy with calf, but so much—so very much—*at home.*

Donald walked over in the darkness to the house. He regaled the household with tales of London and the wedding; but of the extraordinary story of Usgar he did not breathe a word.

. . . .

Next morning Donald was up early. There was promise of a good day: already the sun was breaking through the vapoury mist of an April morning.

" Mother," said Donald to Kirsty, " I would like you to come with me to the machair to see one of the cows."

Kirsty wondered why; but Donald made subtle flattery of her greater wisdom and experience in bovine troubles: he would like her advice. So the two set off.

Kirsty could not help thinking how like this lovely morning was to that morning of long ago when . . . But no: she must not allow her thoughts to dwell on that old sore.

The usual cattle were there and Kirsty wondered which it was that Donald wanted her advice about; they all looked in the best of health.

But Donald led on round the bent-covered sand-dune to the very spot where Usgar had seen the light of day for the first time. And there was a great old cow licking her new-born heifer calf.

And in a jiffy, there was Kirsty with the tears running down the runnels in her wrinkled cheeks, once again fondling a curly coat and saying over and over again " *M' Usgar bheag!* " just as she said it that morning seventeen years ago.

CHAPTER XIX

Lord Leverhulme in Harris

In my book *Highland Journey* where I try to tell something of the local reaction to the late Lord Leverhulme's well-meant effort to introduce an industrial régime in the island of Lewis, I deliberately kept to the main feature of the story for fear of wearying readers with non-essential details. Yet some of the side-happenings were not without humour in themselves, and highly interesting as emphasising the wide and fundamental difference in outlook between the great industrial magnate and the native crofting people.

It might have been assumed that so shrewd a man as Lord Leverhulme, after listening to the amazingly eloquent exposition of the local point of view by a crofter-fisherman, would have sensed the deep-rooted cause of the local opposition to his schemes and made some changes in his plans and policy calculated to get round the difficulty. Certainly, at the time, he seemed thoroughly to appreciate the importance of what had been said. But it soon became apparent that to a man of his experience, a philosophy of life and living so simple as that of the crofters was just incomprehensible: to such a man, the acquisition of money must surely be the dominant motive in all men's lives! True, he did make one astute effort. The idea originated on the night of the dinner at the Castle. In our after-dinner private conclave despite my candidly expressed conviction that, by fighting the people on the question of granting them crofts under the Act he could never hope to get their support to his schemes, he continued to press hard for my support and assistance. Was there any way I could suggest that might help? Anything he could do?

I doubted if there was; but in any case there were in every district natural leaders without whose good-will nothing could be done. At the meeting at the farm that morning he had told them of the grand houses and prosperous circumstances of his employees in Port Sunlight. But in such matters seeing was believing. Perhaps if some of the local leaders could see with their own eyes . . . ?

There was no need to say more. Like shot he was on to the idea.

Who were the leaders? How many of them? Ten? Twenty? Fifty? A hundred? He would have the matter arranged first thing in the morning. . . . This was Tuesday. . . . They would leave by special ship on Thursday morning. . . . They would have several hours in Port Sunlight seeing factories, houses, people, and would be home by Saturday night! His enthusiasm was devastating, and I was sort of sorry to have to point out that he would have to ca' canny: this was the week of the Uig "sacraments." Next week they would be in another parish and would continue in succession round all parishes in the Island. It would be most unwise to attempt to promote a visit to England regardless of the respect accorded to Comanachadh in Lewis, and, anyway, no person of influence in the community would absent himself on such occasions. So his Lordship had to curb his ardour until the circuit of holy ordinances had been duly solemnised. Then he did actually organise a visit to Port Sunlight by a large company of prominent men selected from the various townships: a luxurious holiday which they greatly enjoyed. At Port Sunlight, too, they were impressed by much of what they saw and heard; so much so, indeed, that some of them admitted to me later that they were nearly dazzled into siding with Lord Leverhulme. But as they "contemplated" on the voyage northwards and drew nearer to the little *dachaidh* (home) on the Island, somehow the Port Sunlight impression got blurred. By the time they landed at Stornoway it had vanished completely; and the sentiment of the deputies in the whole matter was succinctly expressed by Ruairidh Chaluim:

"*Ach an deigh na h-uile car, cha' neil càl an sud ach an tràilleachd!*" ("But after all, there is nothing yonder but slavery!")

It may seem strange that so able a man should be so pathetically incapable of understanding the native mentality and point of view. Hence the absurd assumption by Lord Leverhulme of the title "Lord of the Western Isles." And he would live up to that dignity, too: he would have a piper to play appropriate tunes while he dined. When not engaged in playing the bagpipes the man was expected to work in the gardens; in itself a solecism of which his Lordship was innocent of all knowledge—but an indignity which, it must be admitted, caused no undue concern to this modern MacCrimmon!

On a spring evening, after contributing the measure of music deemed necessary for the creation of proper atmosphere and flow of digestive juices, Donald wished respectfully to have a word with his Lordship.

"Well, what is it, my man?"

"Well, my Lord. I was just wanting to tell you that in a fortnight it will be time to be planting the potatoes, and I will have to be going home then to put them down, but if the weather is right I will finish the job in a week and will be ready to come back then."

"But you are now in regular employment! I pay you a good wage! I provide you with good food. You are not hard worked. You now earn as much money in a week as will buy sufficient potatoes for you and your family for a year. I require you here. *I cannot agree to let you off for a week to plant potatoes.*"

" But, Lord Leverhulme, the potatoes must be planted ! I will need to go home and plant them at the right time ! "

" Listen to what I say, my man. I am giving you good advice. You had better take it. If you do not—if you go without my consent—you should clearly understand that by so doing you will lose your job: I shall have no further need of your services."

It was with no small degree of self-satisfaction his Lordship told me next day the story of how he had made the foolish fellow see sense. For, to the ultimate threat of dismissal, Donald had merely given a " Very good, my Lord," and continued in the dual capacity of piper and gardener. But when his Lordship sat down to dine a fortnight later there was no music to stimulate the juices. Donald was late ! His Lordship was annoyed. He gave instructions that Donald should immediately play the pipes. But back from the kitchen came astounding information: *Donald had left word that he had gone home to plant the potatoes—and would not be coming back!*

. . . .

The full story of the influences and undercurrents of local diplomacy which ultimately succeeded in transferring Lord Leverhulme's affections and creative urge from Lewis to Harris would make interesting telling, but as many of the people concerned are still very much alive I will refrain from mentioning names. Not that there is anything discreditable to anyone in what was done; rather the other way about. But even then I feel sure that the principal actors would prefer to remain in modest obscurity. And in any case my purpose in attempting a brief résumé of an interesting episode in Hebridean history is not so much to show up faults or virtues on either side as to bring into relief the fundamental differences in their respective philosophies and ideologies.

For more than a year it had been obvious to some men in Harris that things were not going well with Lord Leverhulme's schemes on the sister isle: that indeed, because of his lordship's refusal to establish any further crofts in Lewis, his schemes were meeting such strong opposition that he must be feeling sore about the whole business and probably looking for a way of escape that would not involve loss of face. So, over a dram, two or three of the worthies put their heads together and concocted a letter purporting to be written on behalf of the people of Harris. (It is more than doubtful if the latter knew anything about the letter, but that is by the way.)

The people of Harris had watched with great interest his Lordship's efforts on behalf of Lewis; and how deeply they deplored the failure of the people of Lewis to appreciate and grasp their opportunity! If only his Lordship would consider coming to *Harris*—where, they ventured to suggest, the natural scope for development was even greater than in Lewis, what a different reception he would receive from the people there!

The letter couldn't have arrived at a better time. It came as solace to a vexed soul. Had he not often heard it said that the people of Harris were quite different from the people of Lewis! True, so far as his own observations had gone, the two peoples were quite indistinguishable. But here was the proof of the difference! Obviously the people of Harris were kindly, appreciative, shrewd. *They* knew which side of their bread had the butter!

This was a matter for further investigation. He would like to meet these people. He did: a huge gathering of them who came in response to the fiery-cross summons initiated by the " delegates " immediately on receipt of

the letter from Lord Leverhulme requesting the favour
of a meeting. Just what the purpose of the meeting was,
was not at all clear to the great majority before starting
out for the rendezvous. But when his Lordship at the
outset thanked the people of Harris for their so very
kind letter (by the way, this was the first time they had
heard of it!) it did not take the astute Hearachs long to
grasp that something big might be afoot, and they played
up nobly. It was a great meeting—utterly free of the
bickerings and disputations so characteristic of meetings
with the people of Lewis. Nor was it without its emotional
moments, which were as a balm to his Lordship's smarting
wounds.

But in business, emotion was a treacherous guide.
They must be practical. What were the facts?—distances
from fishing grounds, etc.? Ample information on such
points was immediately forthcoming.

A safe and suitable harbour?—After all, Stornoway in
Lewis was a good harbour!

They agreed: Stornoway was indeed a good centre.
Yes—but what about Obbe` in Harris? Wasn't it even
more central to the fishing grounds than Stornoway?
True, Obbe had a disadvantage in the dozens of tidally
submerged rocks outside its harbour in the Sound of Harris.
Yes, but surely a few rocks like that would not stand for
long in the way of a man of Lord Leverhulme's forceful
genius!

This was stimulating talk indeed. Nor was his Lordship
dismayed by those rocks. Not a bit—they might have
been deposited there by the Creator just to give the
opportunity one day of showing the greatness of His
creature. Pouff! What was dynamite or gelignite for
if not for blowing obstacles out of the way of reformers?

Clearly here was a way out of the Lewis impasse. Here
was a people who appreciated him; who would appreciate

schemes he might set a-going for the betterment of themselves and their island. He would come again with his experts to examine the problems and practicable possibilities on the spot. And so it came to pass. He was like a small boy with plenty of money in his pocket looking at a fascinating toy in a shop window. Soon his mind was made up: he must have that toy. So he bought the whole of South and East Harris, extending to many thousands of acres of which an incredible portion is bare rock and bleak mountain on which even heather cannot grow—although, surprisingly, in between the rocky ledges there is indeed a growth of short, sweet, fine fescue grass beloved by Black-face sheep, which yield the finest-quality mutton in the world.

But it was the harvest of the sea that was the great attraction; and the vision of his great fishing fleets bringing in their silvery cargoes for the plenishing of the breakfast tables of the world was the genesis and inspiration of all his schemes in the Hebrides.

.   .   .   .

Exasperated, frustrated and finally sickened by the stubborn refusal of the people of Lewis to give adequate support to his schemes because of an incomprehensible regard for their wretched little crofts, the opportunity now opened to him in Harris rekindled in Lord Leverhulme the blaze of enthusiasm for adventure and "progress." That the people of Harris might be equally foolishly attached to their even more wretched little crofts was to his Lordship unthinkable; and the people of Harris were much too astute to bring so delicate a subject into the discussion: if a good milk-cow came offering its services to the island their concern should be, not to frighten it away, but to milk it; and to that task they heartily applied themselves.

There followed such a stir of activity as Harris had never known—nor is likely to see again. The harbour had to be enlarged, involving the blasting away of those rocks. A new pier of a size adequate to cope with the future large volume of shipping must be built. A modern town would be established on the bare slopes surrounding the harbour—a town in which the streets must not be straight and in which no two houses must be identical in plan. A cinema, clubroom, offices, shops . . . Roads converging on the new metropolis must be improved, and new roads made. Then there was the cannery that had recently been erected near Stornoway—that would be taken down stone by stone and beam by beam, transported to Obbe and re-erected there.

Some of the local officials who had previously gone about their business at the leisurely, decorous pace characteristic of the Hebrides, suddenly found themselves caught up in an incredible whirl of activity. The local road surveyor—a man who had never before found full scope for his really great ability—as consulting architect for the new proprietor was one of these. Plans and estimates, and still more plans and estimates to satisfy the voracious appetite of the inspired reformer, were constantly being called for. Soon a juvenile staff of assistants had to be recruited and special furniture bought for holding the ever-growing pile of plans and estimates.

One of the troubles of the architect (or *was* it really a trouble?) was that Lord Leverhulme was by way of being an authority on art and architecture himself, and therefore prone to argument and change of mind in such matters. A plan of a building or a street or whatever it was would be agreed on one day. But in the small hours of next morning the alert mind of his Lordship might detect in it a flaw or two. Ah! that must be studied again on the spot. So to the architect would go the urgent message,

" Meet me on ground ten to-day with Plan 5007." And off the architect, with Plan 5007 and note-book, would rush to reach the rendezvous in time.

Hm—yes: it's obvious now that you see it; that window is too high and too near the door—must be altered accordingly.

Certainly: appropriate alterations sketched on plan and noted in book.

Then this bend in the road?—too sharp—widen it—*so*.

Quite, but that will seriously encroach on site of proposed house !

Well, that cannot be helped ; must have adequate curve on road—erase house.

House erased from town plan.

And so on for two hectic hours resulting in urgent necessity for several more plans and estimates. A heart-breaking man to work for ! But of course there was the brighter side to such exasperations—and the surveyor carried on with a cheerful heart.

Hundreds in Harris joined the pick-and-shovel brigade, mending and constructing roads, digging foundations; tradesmen, too (pucka and pseudo) were busy building bridges, piers and houses. There was a well-paid and not over-strenuous job for every able-bodied man on the island.

But to the Highlander at home continuous application to manual labour soon becomes monotonous: after all, if the labourer is worthy of his hire is he not also worthy of reasonable leisure for contemplation? Absenteeism was creeping in.

This would never do ! It might jeopardise his schemes ! The danger must be effectively countered. It was—very astutely. To everyone who would give satisfactory service up to a specified standard and for a stated period there would be presented a paid-up life insurance policy of amounts ranging from £100 to £500. That was a real incentive that worked like magic. Would present-day Minister of Labour please note?

Soon, though, the anxiety was on the other side: the man was getting old—more whimsical and unpredictable every day. *What if he suddenly lost interest in the Harris schemes!* Not but some of the schemes might be daft enough; but that wasn't the point. The really important thing was that easily earned weekly pay-packet. Something must be done to safeguard that . . .

The " delegates," under inspiration of another dram or two, concocted another letter. This one said the people of Harris desired to put before him a proposal of a purely personal nature which they ventured to believe might be of interest to his Lordship.

Again the fiery cross went round; again the people of Harris responded in force—and again they were curious to know what it was they wished to see his Lordship about.

The first few words uttered by his Lordship shed a bright light on the mystery, and they loudly cheered! He referred to their desire, as expressed in their wonderfully kind letter: their desire to show to him and to posterity their profound appreciation of what he had done for them and their island. He could scarcely find words to express his appreciation of their appreciation! He was moved—deeply moved—by so wonderful a gesture (actually with a handkerchief he had to wipe away the tears). The suggestion that their purpose might be most appropriately achieved by naming the main centre of his activities (which was Obbe) after him was particularly attractive, and he would of course be delighted to defer to their wish. But—if he might?—he would like to make just one suggestion. He observed that the suggestion in the letter was that the new name should be " Levertown." Now (as somewhat of a connoisseur in such matters) he must be frank with his friends by admitting to them that "Levertown" rather jarred his musical ear; there was a plebeian note in it! But "Leverburgh," now? That to him sounded just right; and if they did not mind . . . ?

No! Not at all! They were grateful for the suggestion! *Of course* "Leverburgh" was the right name! Hear, hear! Loud cheers.

And so it was that the old hamlet of Obbe died and the new town of Leverburgh was born.

The new pier was completed. To it came ships carrying bricks, timber, ironmongery, steel girders, lime, cement and the thousand other things requisite for the creation of the new régime. Leverburgh was fast becoming a town in embryo, and generally the transformation of Harris went on with undiminished speed. But his interests were many and far-spread. A visit to West Africa became an urgent necessity. Full directions for the prosecution of the works in Harris during his absence were duly given. Reluctantly he proceeded to that far-off land of palm nut oil; but he would return to his beloved Harris at the earliest possible moment.

Then one day to Harris there came a telegram with the shocking intimation that Lord Leverhulme had died, and that all activities on the island were to cease forthwith!

Nor were they ever resumed. From the day of his death it was a process of disintegration and shutting down and finishing up of everything that Lord Leverhulme had done and planned for Harris.

It took many months for the people to adapt themselves to the sudden vacuum which succeeded the stir. Nor was the loss of the pay-packet now the only regret. For, towards this strange little man of dynamic personality and unbounded courage and resource there had grown up among the islanders a degree of respect that was almost affection. He might be tyrannical—oh, yes! But he could also be kind, in his own way ; and he was terribly clever.

Leverburgh never attained the stature of a town: just a score or so of houses and some scars on the moor (now healed by kindly time and vegetation) where streets and buildings were meant to be.

And the pier—that imposing structure of piles and planks that seemed to cover acres. Three years ago, when I landed there off a motor-boat from Berneray the piles were rotting and the planks sagging to such an extent that we were glad to get off them on to firm land. The last I have heard of it—quite recently—is that about a year ago the Local Authority, to whom its dangerous condition was an embarrassment, sold it to a company of Harris crofters, who have sawn it into boards and battens and fencing stobs and firewood for sale in the neighbourhood; and rumour has it that the crofters made a modicum of profit on the deal.

True Celtic philosophers that they are, in due course the people of Harris settled down to their wonted pace and way of life. So far as they and their island are concerned, by and large, Lord Leverhulme might not have been. And is it not something to be profoundly thankful for that, despite repeated attempts to convert a free and forthright people to the status of city serfs, they are still essentially free to maintain and develop that God-given individuality in human life and outlook which elsewhere is being so ruthlessly smothered?—that in respect of our Highlands and Highland people we can still rejoice that no tyrant sound of factory horn offends their tranquil air?